A LITTLE HISTORY OF PSYCHOLOGY

'Will make you writhe, ripple
and froth with pleasure.'
Stephen Fry

'Brilliant, irresistible: a
wonderful surprise.'
Philip Pullman

Explore the LITTLE HISTORIES

Illuminating, energetic and readable, the Little Histories are books
that explore timeless questions and take readers young and old on an
enlightening journey through knowledge. Following in the footsteps of
E. H. Gombrich's tour de force *A Little History of the World*, the family
of Little Histories, sumptuously designed with unique illustrations, is an
essential library of human endeavour.

Which Little History will you read next?

A Little History of the World by E. H. Gombrich

A Little Book of Language by David Crystal

A Little History of Philosophy by Nigel Warburton

A Little History of Science by William Bynum

A Little History of Literature by John Sutherland

A Little History of the United States by James West Davidson

A Little History of Religion by Richard Holloway

A Little History of Economics by Niall Kishtainy

A Little History of Archaeology by Brian Fagan

A Little History of Poetry by John Carey

A Little History of Art by Charlotte Mullins

A Little History of Music by Robert Philip

New titles coming soon!

Visit our websites:

US – yalebooks.com

UK/Europe/ROW – yalebooks.co.uk

Find us @:

twitter.com/littlehistoryof

facebook.com/littlehistory

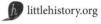 littlehistory.org

NICKY HAYES

A LITTLE
HISTORY
of
PSYCHOLOGY

YALE UNIVERSITY PRESS
NEW HAVEN AND LONDON

Illustrations by Karin Rytter

For information about this and other Yale University Press publications, please contact:
U.S. Office: sales.press@yale.edu   yalebooks.com
Europe Office: sales@yaleup.co.uk   yalebooks.co.uk

Set in Minion Pro by IDSUK (DataConnection) Ltd
Printed in Great Britain by TJ Books Limited, Padstow, Cornwall

Library of Congress Control Number: 2023952215

ISBN 978-0-300-26994-9

A catalogue record for this book is available from the British Library.

10 9 8 7 6 5 4 3 2 1

MIX
Paper from
responsible sources
FSC
www.fsc.org   FSC® C013056

Contents

CHAPTER 1

In the Beginning

THE GREEKS, GALEN AND THE INFLUENCE OF THE EAST

Psychology is fascinating and, in many ways, it is at the heart of being human. After all, understanding – or trying to understand – other people's minds and behaviour is something all of us do every day. It's how we get along in families, social groups and societies.

And, quite often, we get it wrong. We might think we know what other people are like, and then we're astounded when they don't seem to see things as we do, or they behave in a strange (to us) way. We form ideas about human nature around what we have read or watched, which can be misleading. We often fail to appreciate that our understanding of people is rooted in our particular time, place and culture, and might not apply to others. Or we take for granted beliefs that people have held for millennia, without questioning where they came from.

The common accounts of human nature that float around in society are generally a mixture of assumption, anecdote and sometimes plain silliness. Psychology is different. Psychology is the branch of science that is devoted to understanding people: how and why we act as we do; why we see things as we do; and how we interact with one another. The key word here is 'science'. Psychologists don't depend on opinions and hearsay, or the generally accepted views of society at the time, or even the considered opinions of deep thinkers. Instead, we look for evidence, to make sure that psychological ideas are firmly based, and not just derived from generally held beliefs or conjecture. As different as human beings are, there are processes and principles that we all have in common, and there are processes and principles that produce our wonderful cultural and social differences. These are what modern psychology is all about.

Psychology is as multifaceted as the people it studies. There's no single one-size-fits-all psychology, partly because as individuals we are all so complex, partly because people become themselves in so many different cultures, and partly because psychology has many different roots, coming from many different perspectives. And there is also no single type of psychologist. Although many psychologists are academics, by no means all of them are. Since its beginning, psychology has been applied in the real world, and in many areas. For instance, there are clinical psychologists, who work with people who have mental health problems or difficulties in living; there are organisational psychologists, who can advise management as to the best ways of dealing with their workforce; there are forensic psychologists, who assist criminal investigations; and there are educational psychologists, who work with schools to provide appropriate education for children who have many different needs. From coaching and health advice to aviation training and AI, psychologists today apply their psychological understanding to help people in an extraordinary variety of ways.

So where did it all begin?

For many centuries, writers from the ancient Greek and Roman eras had a major influence on European thought. Right up until the Renaissance, these 'ancients' were considered to encompass the full range of scientific knowledge, and their ideas were incorporated in religious orthodoxy – so much so, in fact, that, when some early scientists like Galileo challenged their ideas, they were viciously persecuted as heretics. Some people see the origins of psychology as being in the writings of ancient Greek philosophers like Plato and Aristotle, or later thinkers like the physician Galen, who was Greek but lived and worked in Rome during the time of the Roman Empire. They had their own ideas about what people were like, and those ideas continued to influence Western thinking even after the Renaissance.

The Greek philosophers were revered as deep thinkers who developed ideas about the natural world, about the cosmos, and about human nature. But they were not scientists. And some of their ideas were distinctly simplistic. In his book *The Republic*, for example, Plato described three different types of people in society: bronze, silver and gold. The bronze people were workers, not particularly bright or literate, but doing the basic manual work that society needed. The silvers were managers, administrators and scribes, who dealt with the detail that allowed a complex society to function. And the golds were the leaders, their intellects and abilities making them natural governors for his ideal society. He assumed that these three types would always breed true: the idea that a child with 'silver' abilities might be born into a 'bronze' family wasn't considered in his account.

Plato was describing an ideal society (at least, ideal in his terms), but his ideas left their mark. For many centuries, Europe was dominated by feudalism, with its aristocracy in charge, its artisans making a living from their crafts, and the peasantry living in poverty and owning very little, if anything. Sound familiar? Plato's ideas portrayed a rigid social structure that was fundamental to the ideology and beliefs underlying feudal society: that people were born into their fixed level in society. Even after feudalism had been gradually abandoned, people were generally expected to occupy the social positions they were born into. The industrial revolution produced some challenges to this, as self-taught entrepreneurs challenged the status quo and educational opportunities for ordinary people began to arise. But, as we will see in Chapter 6, Western society as a whole clung firmly to the belief that abilities and intelligence were inherited. And that was a belief that had far-reaching, and often tragic, consequences.

It isn't just Plato's ideas that have shaped our thinking. Aristotle, for example, stated that human beings have just five senses: sight, hearing, touch, taste and smell. This idea has been widely accepted ever since: children are still taught it in primary school today. But Aristotle was wrong. His account completely ignored all our internal senses and some of our more subtle external ones as well. For example, we have kinaesthesia, which tells us about our movements; proprioception, which tells us how our limbs are positioned; thermoreception, which tells us about heat and temperature; and many other senses. At my last count, neurologists had identified over forty different ways that we receive information – that is, through different senses – from both our bodies and our external environments.

Does this matter? Well, yes, it does. Ignoring these senses leads us to the idea that we are separate from the rest of the world: receiving information from it, but being essentially independent of it, and unaffected by it. But even the most basic knowledge of psychology shows us that this is far from the case: we don't perceive what is happening objectively; we actively select our perceptions and notice only what is relevant to us. Our memories are not factual recordings of what has happened; they are shaped by our own knowledge, expectations and experience of subsequent events. And our judgements are not logical appraisals of facts; they are shaped by our culture, our social groups and our personal experiences. We're not separate from our worlds: we participate actively in them.

The Greeks also prized logic as being the ultimate advancement in human thinking. Thanks to Aristotle, Plato and others, the assumption has always been that logic is superior, and that people were making 'errors' by not thinking objectively or using dispassionate reasoning. In fact, we don't make logical decisions, we make human ones; and we don't have objective memories or perception, we interpret and recall experiences in terms of their human meanings. It has taken a long time for psychologists to realise that these are not errors – they are part of being human, and sometimes, in the real world, they actually work better than formal logic. It's taking even longer for our social institutions to realise it.

Another early idea that has continued to influence thinking right up to modern times comes from the Greek physician Galen, who refined an idea about physical illness which seems to have originated from Hippocrates. Hippocrates believed that diseases arose from an imbalance in the four 'humours' of the body: phlegm, blood, yellow bile and black bile. An excess of various types of bodily fluid produced the illness, and treatments aimed to restore that balance. The medical practice of bloodletting, for example, was a standard response to fever for centuries, as the flushed face and heat were thought to have been caused by excess blood in the body.

Galen's contribution was to argue that these humours also affected personality. He believed that there were four distinct personality types, and that these came from the balance of these humours in the person's body. People with an excess of phlegm, he argued, were calm, and dependable; those with blood dominant were cheerful, extraverted and social; people with an excess of yellow bile (choler) were energetic and passionate, and also short-tempered at times; and those with an excess of black bile (melancholer) were considerate and kind, but also easily depressed and inclined to be gloomy.

We can still see Galen's influence in our language. Consider these four sentences, for example, each of which reflects one personality type from Galen's model.

'She's a fairly sanguine type. I don't think she'll object.'
'Hamlet is a classic melancholic.'
'His choleric disposition meant that his staff were always wary if there was bad news.'
'She accepted the news phlegmatically, just leaning back in her chair.'

It's not just in our language. Even now, there are educational and psychological theories that adopt these personality 'types' as their basic approach. A well-known psychometric theory of personality developed by H.J. Eysenck in the 1950s directly reflected Galen's four basic humours, and those ideas still appear in some popular books. I recently saw a 2023 version of the same theory in a new book on an airport bookstall. And, of course, we still use the word 'humour' to describe the mood someone is in.

We have many other words that have their origins in earlier times and have changed their meanings to describe what we now see as psychological processes. The word 'attitude', for example, began as a description of the body postures actors used to indicate emotions or states of mind in Greek theatre. We automatically ascribe meanings to people's postures – we'd see someone who is hunched over and looking downwards and interpret their mental state as being preoccupied and possibly distressed, while someone standing tall with outstretched arms would be communicating a very different mental state to us. So 'attitude' nowadays is usually taken to reflect a state of mind or set of opinions rather than as a physical description of posture.

Although European culture is often seen as a straight-line development from the ancient Greeks and Romans, there were other, more subtle, influences from other parts of the world. It's easy for us to take a simplistic view of the ancient and medieval worlds because they didn't have the same level of technology as we do. That only meant, though, that ideas took longer to spread. But spread they did. Arab culture, for example, had a well-developed body of scientific knowledge, including mathematical theories and complex ideas about human nature, revealed in its poetry and art. So did many other ancient cultures. These became known in the West, as they were transmitted by trade and travellers. As early as the thirteenth century, for example, Marco Polo described the highly developed Chinese culture: its social organisation as well as its luxury goods, which came into Europe along the silk roads to Venice.

European awareness of Eastern cultures had influence, not just on art and ceramics, but also on social practices. It has been argued, for example, that psychological testing really began with the Chinese, who used tests and interviews to select for a meritocratic civil service during the Han dynasty, from 206 BCE to 220 CE.

Their ideas spread to the West during the explorations and expansions of the nineteenth century, when Europe became fascinated by 'Oriental' ideas, art and culture. The East India Company adopted the Chinese system for testing prospective employees in 1832, and their lucrative success meant that the same idea spread to other Western organisations. As psychology developed, psychological measurement for selection became a major area of interest and is now a significant industry in itself.

So people have been interested in human nature for millennia. But are those ideas psychology? No, they aren't. They are certainly about people, but, really, they are ideas and impressions. Psychology is a science, and the study of people only becomes psychology when it is fully backed up by research evidence. Early ideas have influenced psychology, it's true, but if we really want to understand people, we need to go about it scientifically. It was the emergence of science and scientific methods that allowed psychology as we know it to develop.

CHAPTER 2

Evolving Science
IDEAS ABOUT THE MIND FROM DESCARTES TO DARWIN

Europe was in upheaval. A succession of disasters, including famines, plague and extreme climate change, in the fourteenth and fifteenth centuries had essentially halved its population and brought about a number of dramatic changes in society. People began to think differently and to challenge existing authorities – both in terms of revolts and uprisings, and by questioning established knowledge. Artists began to represent people in their everyday lives, rather than religious images or classical mythology; writers developed new forms of literature; and philosophers began to challenge conventional assumptions. It became known as the Renaissance – the rebirth – as these new ideas spread across the Western world. Those changes were important precursors to the eventual birth of modern psychology.

René Descartes was a key thinker in the new movement. A French philosopher born in 1596, he challenged established philosophical ideas by arguing that reason is the chief test of knowledge. This contradicted the existing assumption that all knowledge is innate – that is, the result of information coming through our senses – rather than arising from reflection and thought. While Descartes accepted that some knowledge is innate, he believed truth can only be realised through intellectual deduction. Descartes' ideas expressed the movement that came to be known as rationalism: a mode of thought that rapidly became popular throughout Europe.

However, Descartes went further than this. He was a mathematician and one of the early scientists, as we know science today, and he wrote extensively about human nature. He believed, for example, that the mind and the body were entirely separate – that the body is effectively a machine, governed by the laws of physics and physiology, while the mind is entirely different. This idea has become known as 'Cartesian dualism', and it had a major influence on European science and medicine. It was not until the second half of the twentieth century, largely through the work of neuropsychologists and previous psychological research, that medicine really began to acknowledge how the mind and body interact with one another, each influencing the other.

His machine model also attempted to explain the difference between people and animals. For Descartes, animals didn't have either reason or intelligence, only sensations. Effectively, they were just complex physiological machines. This was another influential idea, which became widely accepted. It was used to justify cruelty to animals in social life, farming and science. Even now, the idea hasn't died out completely, although it is gradually disappearing, and few modern scientists would see it as valid. But what really distinguished people from animals and made us special, according to Descartes, was that people have minds and are able to use them. The mind isn't physical – it's the ghost in the machine, as it was later described – and it gives us the ability to think and reason, which, in Descartes' view, makes us human. 'I think, therefore I am' is the famous translation of Descartes' remark 'Je pense, donc je suis.'

Like Plato, Descartes has a lot to answer for. His idea of animals as simply machines dominated our understanding for centuries, until it was challenged by Darwin's theory of evolution; and his mind–body dualism distorted, and in some cases continues to distort, the development of medical knowledge. But he left a positive legacy too. Descartes conducted a number of systematic scientific investigations. He showed that studying the workings of the body's processes as if it is a complex machine actually has value in itself. He produced a major work on optics, for example, showing how light is processed by the eyes. Essentially, Descartes helped to establish the whole idea of acquiring knowledge through experimentation and thoughtful reflection, rather than by studying the writings of the ancients.

While rationalism prevailed in Europe, philosophers in Britain pursued different theories. The rationalists believed that some knowledge is innate, but that it is made meaningful through reasoning and reflection. But British philosophers like Thomas Hobbes challenged both aspects of this approach. Hobbes disagreed with Descartes' idea of the mind as separate and immaterial. Instead, he argued that human beings are part of the universe, and therefore entirely physical. Even the ways that our minds work, said Hobbes, is the result of physical laws. (We're still exploring that one.)

John Locke took up the challenge by arguing that there is no such thing as innate knowledge at all. When we are born, Locke insisted, our mind is a tabula rasa – a blank slate, ready for experience to inscribe knowledge on it. So our knowledge comes entirely from what we experience. Even reflecting on experiences is an experience in itself, according to Locke; we don't inherit any form of knowledge or awareness, but our minds are entirely shaped – possibly even programmed – by what we experience from birth onwards, and how we make sense of it.

Another British philosopher, David Hume, also believed that knowledge is acquired from experience. Reasoning alone can't explain the world, Hume argued, because we also have what he described as our 'animal passions'. These are basic emotions and instinctive drives like hunger and avoiding pain. These animal passions, he believed, also influence how we think. Our reasoning isn't 'pure' or abstract, but effectively a reflection of these other influences and experiences, as well as thought itself.

Together, Hobbes, Locke, Hume and other philosophers formed a school of thought that became known as British empiricism. Its central idea was that experience is the key to understanding knowledge, and that measuring experience is the way to develop understanding of how people think. Their ideas had a major influence on the development of psychology, particularly in America and Britain. They may also be at the heart of the profound differences that emerged between European and American psychology, which we will explore later in this book.

These philosophical arguments took place during the sixteenth to eighteenth centuries CE, but they were not the only upheavals that were taking place. At the end of the eighteenth century, the French revolution opened up many new ideas, not just in politics and social organisation but in other areas too. Among other things, it gave the physician Philippe Pinel the freedom to explore his ideas about how the mentally ill should be treated. He had been developing those ideas for some time, observing the inhumanity of the existing institutions for the mentally ill, and the inadequacy of the treatments that existed. With the advent of the new French Republic and its radical approach to society, he was able to put them into practice.

Pinel became famous for removing the iron shackles that were used to chain people considered to be mentally ill. Together with a colleague, Jean-Baptiste Pussin, he instituted an entirely new system. (It was actually Pussin who was the first to remove the shackles, but it was Pinel who was shown doing it in a famous painting, so he tends to get the credit for it. They both agreed that it was necessary, though.) Instead of using force and restraint, Pinel's staff adopted a firm-but-gentle approach, treating the patients as reasonable people who just needed extra consideration. He did away with uncomfortable and unpleasant treatments like purging and bleeding, and replaced them with close and regular discussions with the patients. Pinel also set up a system of careful observation and note-taking, which allowed regular reviewing of each patient's condition and showed explicitly the remarkable improvements that these treatments produced. He also kept an eye on other medical developments, and the first vaccinations in Paris were given in his hospital.

Pinel's approach became known as 'moral therapy', and his success rate (not surprisingly to modern minds) was extremely high. Many of his patients recovered completely, while others became much more manageable and co-operative. Pinel published his approach in a book, *Memoirs on Madness*, which is often referred to as one of the fundamental texts of modern psychiatry. More to the point in terms of our book, Pinel and his colleagues also generated an interest in psychotherapy and in alternative approaches to mental illness, and these ideas were significant forerunners of modern clinical psychology.

For many, though, the most significant of all the forerunners of psychology was Charles Darwin. In 1831, Darwin signed up to a round-the-world investigative expedition on HMS *Beagle*, as a 'gentleman's companion' for Captain Robert FitzRoy (later famous as the founder of modern weather forecasting). Although he wasn't the ship's official naturalist, the natural world was Darwin's main interest, and he made meticulous observations of wildlife during the voyage. He also collected a range of fossils and observed how different species had adapted to some very different environments. He returned home after five years, in 1836, and continued to develop his ideas, exploring various aspects of species differentiation and change.

After more than twenty years of publishing academic papers and establishing the details of the theory, Darwin's groundbreaking book *On the Origin of Species* was finally published in 1859. Its publication caused a storm in nineteenth-century Western society. Darwin had suspected it would, and in fact had delayed publication for exactly that reason. However, 'it steam-engines when it's steam-engine time' – in other words, ideas become popular when the time is right for them – and other naturalists gradually began to come to similar conclusions. When Darwin heard from Alfred Russel Wallace that he was about to deliver a paper outlining a very similar theory, Darwin finally put his book into print. Then he kept his head low, and left it to his friend and supporter Thomas Henry

Huxley to deal with the fall-out. It was Huxley who published popular descriptions of the theory, argued publicly with older, doubting scientists, and in 1860 even took on the established church in a public debate with the Bishop of Oxford, Samuel Wilberforce. Huxley, a well-known and respected scientist in his own right, was largely responsible for ensuring that Darwin's theory became as well known as it did. He is often remembered as 'Darwin's bulldog' for that reason.

Evolutionary theory directly challenged the empiricist idea of the mind as a pure tabula rasa at birth. Darwin had shown how species didn't inherit just physical characteristics but also behavioural ones, and that those were shaped by the environment in which the species had developed. His famous observations of the Galapagos finches, for example, showed how they had adapted to the different food sources on the different islands by adapting their behaviour as well as their physical characteristics. Some would seek out insects by poking into crevices, for example, and had developed long narrow beaks for the purpose, while others sought out hard seeds and had developed thick strong beaks for crushing them. Evidently, they all began as the same species, but their different environments had caused their behaviour as well as their beaks to change.

So far so good; but that was about animals, and, as we have seen, accepted philosophy viewed human beings as entirely different. But Darwin's theory also showed how human beings had evolved, highlighting the idea of a common ape-like ancestor (which generated much ridicule in popular papers of the day) and also discussing how human beings had characteristics in common with other species. His paper, 'The Expression of the Emotions in Man and Animals', discussed similarities in facial expressions across mammals, comparing, for example, dogs and humans. Even though other people might disagree with them, pet owners know that their dogs have different facial expressions and can tell when they are smiling – well, never mind the scoffers, Darwin knew it too, and wrote about it in 1872.

Darwin's meticulous work, then, presented a serious challenge to the idea that humans and animals were qualitatively different and proposed that there were mental similarities as well as physiological ones. In that, it offered scientists a new way of thinking about both people and animals, opening up possibilities of investigation that became fundamental to the later emergence of the science of psychology. Those possibilities were supported by some key developments in neuroscience, which we'll explore in the next chapter.

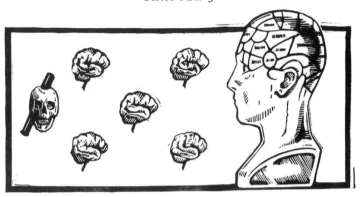

CHAPTER 3

The Legend of Phineas Gage
THE BEGINNINGS OF NEUROPSYCHOLOGY

Towards teatime on 13 September 1848, Phineas Gage, a foreman on the Hudson River railroad construction gang, was setting an explosive when one of the men behind him attracted his attention. As he turned round to speak, the explosives went off, driving his tamping iron into his skull. It entered just above the lower jaw and went right through the left frontal lobe of his brain before coming out again at the top of his skull. His co-workers found it about 25 metres away, covered in Gage's blood and greasy from brain tissue. Gage was thrown on his back but was soon able to get up. He walked to an oxcart and sat upright while he was driven to his lodgings in the nearby town. There he sat on the porch and chatted with passers-by while he waited for the doctor to come. 'Doctor, here is business enough for you,' he said when that man actually arrived – possibly one of the greatest understatements in neurosurgery!

That doctor did little more than poke bits of brain back into his skull and ask Gage a lot of questions, not really believing what had happened. But at 6pm another doctor, John Harlow, arrived.

Although an ordinary country physician, Harlow was an intelligent man who had, fortunately for Gage, learned from accounts of other cases. He got Gage upstairs to his bed and began cleaning the wound, reaching right through it from both ends to take out bits of bone. The bleeding stopped not long before midnight, and Harlow closed the wound, although he left part of it open for drainage. He replaced the dressings regularly, and for the next few days Gage appeared to be recovering, able to talk with his mother and uncle. Soon, though, he developed an infection, and his brain swelled. He would have died from the pressure on his brain from the swelling, but Harlow performed an emergency drainage operation. Although things were touch and go for a while, and he lost the sight of one eye, Gage eventually recovered.

Gage had been lucky. His work involved packing explosives down into holes specially drilled for the purpose, and to that end he had designed his own tamping iron to do it with. Unlike the standard ones, his tamping iron was straight, tapering to a point at the top end. The usual irons had a kind of claw at the end, and the difference probably saved Gage's life. It allowed the iron to pass straight through, relatively cleanly, so, although it made quite a large hole, it didn't drag extra brain tissue out with it.

But what really interested brain scientists, of course, was the psychological consequences of his massive brain injury. Gage's story became a legend and, like many legends, it changed in the telling. Versions of the story accused him of having become violent, impulsive and irrational, and of having all sorts of other character changes. Some of these accusations were true for a few days in the immediate aftermath of the injury and as he suffered from brain infection, but they all disappeared once he had recovered. A list in Wikipedia itemises fourteen different false accounts of his changed temperament, including that he mistreated his wife and children (he didn't actually have either), and that he showed a lack of forethought or concern for the future, when actually his main concern was whether he could return to work.

Why so much mythology? Mainly, it was what people wanted to believe. There have been so many different ideas about the brain and how it works, and particularly about the importance of the frontal lobes as the heart of thinking and decision-making, that people have been reluctant to believe that there were no extremely dramatic consequences.

Some accounts even claim that he died from his injury within a year or so, but again the reality was very different. Ten weeks after his accident, Phineas Gage had recovered enough to return to his parents' home in New Hampshire and was able to do light work around the farm. He applied for his old job on the railroad but was turned down. For a while he worked as a kind of human exhibit at Barnum's American Museum (not the circus) in New York and made occasional appearances at shows in Vermont and New Hampshire – according to contemporary accounts, he would pass his tamping iron through his head! For the most part, though, he continued to look for steady work. He worked for a stabling and coach service in New Hampshire for eighteen months, before accepting a job in Chile as a long-distance stagecoach driver. That was a skilled job, involving tact and diplomacy with passengers over many days, and considerable driving skill and animal care in managing a six-horse team. If he had really shown the impulsivity and aggression described in some later accounts, he would never have been able to manage that work, but he did it very successfully for the next seven years.

His health wasn't all that great, though, and eventually he returned home, where his mother and sister looked after him. He took a job with a local farmer, but in 1860 began to experience epileptic seizures, eventually dying from a prolonged convulsion. When Dr Harlow heard about Gage's death, he approached the family and was allowed to take his skull, and his tamping iron (which Gage had liked to keep by him). Harlow's meticulous diaries and accounts of Gage's treatment secured Gage's place in neurological history, and his skull and tamping iron are in the Warren Anatomical Museum at Harvard, occasionally being allowed out for special exhibitions. I have seen them; they're a remarkable exhibit if you know the history.

The case of Phineas Gage became legendary in the study of how the brain works. From then on, brain functions and the consequences of accidents became a fundamental part of brain science and, later, the new discipline of psychology. What is perhaps unfortunate, though, is how that influence came mainly from the mythology emerging around his accident's psychological consequences, rather than from the truth of what really happened. Nonetheless, the scene was set.

Gage's case continued to attract attention partly because it challenged a popular idea that was just beginning to die out. This was 'faculty psychology', also known as phrenology. In the first half of the nineteenth century, there was a popular belief that mental 'faculties' like conscience, benevolence, conscientiousness and so on were located at specific places on the surface of the brain, being enlarged if they were well developed, and smaller if they were underdeveloped. Their size could be detected by the shape of the skull at the relevant area: a well-developed faculty would be revealed by a raised area of the skull, and professional phrenologists would map those bumps in the skull to provide readings of the person's character.

The theory was developed by Franz Gall, a German physiologist, and published in 1798. It attracted massive popular interest. It was such a common belief that phrenological evidence was even accepted in the law courts, and it is often referred to in the literature of the time. For example, in an early scene in their relationship, Jane Eyre's employer, Rochester, indicates his forehead and invites her to judge whether he is intelligent; she acquiesces but, noticing the absence of the 'bump' of benevolence, challenges him as to whether he is a philanthropist. He admits he is not but points to other 'prominences' which indicate that he does have a conscience. Many ceramic models of heads still exist from this time, which illustrate the various faculties and the areas of the skull that were supposed to reveal them.

Phrenology became thoroughly discredited as scientists learned more about the brain. In the early nineteenth century, anatomist Marie-Jean-Pierre Flourens conducted a series of studies removing parts of the brains in animals and birds. Flourens identified a number of basic functions in parts of the brain, which didn't connect with phrenological ideas at all. Phineas Gage had also challenged them in the way that his injury hadn't produced the changes in character that phrenologists would have predicted. But the main challenge for brain scientists came from the work of the surgeon Paul Broca, in his study of the location of language ability in the brain.

This came about because two of Broca's patients had significant problems forming words for speech, but neither had any difficulty understanding it. Broca was struck by the similarity and, when those patients died, he performed post-mortems on their brains. In both cases he found damage in a small area at the bottom of the left frontal lobe, but no damage anywhere else in the brain. This area became known as Broca's area, and was one of the first indications that, yes, there might be specific areas of the brain that performed particular roles; but, no, they weren't anything to do with bumps on the skull or faculty psychology in general.

Broca reported on his autopsies in 1861, and his findings were followed in the next decade by a similar report from Carl Wernicke, who discovered another area involved in language. Some of Wernicke's patients had no difficulty speaking, but they had difficulty in understanding what people said to them. Post-mortem examination of the brains of these people again showed localised damage, but this time towards the back and at the top of the temporal lobe. This rapidly became known as Wernicke's area. Together, then, the implication was that not only was language understanding located in a different area of the brain from the part producing language, but also that neither were associated with the linguistic 'faculty' described by Gall.

By the end of the nineteenth century, phrenology had been thoroughly discredited, and neurologists were beginning to identify other areas, like the angular gyrus in the parietal lobe, which in literate adults is concerned with reading, and in people who don't read is an area for face recognition. It seems that understanding expressions is the basic function, and part of it adapts as we learn to read. The general picture that emerged was that some functions were localised in particular places, but that there were also general areas of the brain's surface – the cortex – which didn't seem to have any specific functions.

This idea was strengthened even further by the work of Gordon Holmes, an Anglo-Irish neurologist, who studied servicemen who had acquired injuries to the brain during the shelling in the First World War. Those with injuries at the rear and underneath the brain – that is, in the cerebellum – showed difficulties with movement and balance, while, when the injury was to the cortex at the very back of the brain, they experienced visual disturbances and even blindness, depending on the amount of damage. Holmes' book *Studies in Neurology* outlined these major findings and other aspects of localised functions, and his emphasis on neurological precision set the groundwork for later research, as clinical psychologists began to explore the psychological consequences of injuries and brain tumours.

At the beginning of the twentieth century, too, there was a growing interest in electricity. Physiologists discovered that animal brains emit bursts of electricity, and medical practitioners were using electrical stimulation to treat various physical disorders. The first studies of animal brain activity, as electroencephalograms, or EEGs, were around 1912, and in 1924 Hans Berger published the first record of a human EEG. This showed how electrical brain activity could be linked with, for example, epileptic seizures, and also became a significant step in the development of clinical psychology.

The developing knowledge of how the brain works was one of several strands of research that led to the emergence of psychology as a formal discipline. Towards the end of the nineteenth century other researchers were also taking an interest in how the mind works, and their explicitly experimental approach shaped psychology's future development.

CHAPTER 4

Psychophysics and Early Psychology
MEASURING MENTAL ABILITIES

Do we have to learn how to see? I don't suppose any of us can remember being infants, but new babies do seem to take a few days before they can focus properly on what's around them. Maybe they are learning, or maybe it's just happening automatically – a kind of innate process that just happens as the baby grows.

Does it matter? Maybe not to you and me, but in the nineteenth century that sort of question was a hot topic. It comes down to the 'mind problem' in the end. Descartes, as we saw in Chapter 2, believed firmly that the body was a machine, but that the mind (and soul) were immaterial and didn't have a physical presence, which meant that you couldn't study them. You could study the workings of the machine, as Descartes had shown with his work on optics. But what the mind actually did with the information – well, that was metaphysical, and not something you could study.

Or so people assumed. But by the second half of the nineteenth century, science was taking hold, and scientists were not happy with the idea that they couldn't study everything. It was within this new culture that Herman von Helmholtz, engineer, physiologist and scientific polymath, began to think about how perception works. Helmholtz had a chequered career: he had an abiding interest in practical engineering and held various professorships in surgery, anatomy, physics and physiology. He invented several different types of scientific equipment, including the myograph, the ophthalmoscope, the galvanometer and even the electromagnetic motor. His inventions opened up a number of new findings. For example, he changed ideas about how the nervous system worked as a result of his experiments with the galvanometer, because it allowed scientists to measure the speed of the nerve impulse accurately for the first time.

Helmholtz didn't accept the idea of perception as a mystical innate quality. But he didn't think it was entirely a mechanical process either. Instead, he took a middle ground: he accepted that perception was based on messages from the senses, but his studies showed him that these were incomplete, and possibly distorted. So he thought that the mind was actively interpreting the sensory data it was receiving. But Helmholtz was primarily an empiricist, and he wanted to explore scientifically how that perception worked.

For Helmholtz, perceptions were learned. He argued, for example, that we learn to interpret distances unconsciously, through the different ways that our eye muscles work when we are looking at near or far objects. He developed a theory of colour vision that argued that the cells in the retina were of three different types, responding to three primary colours, which work together so we perceive different colours – an idea that was widely accepted and became known as the Young–Helmholtz theory of colour vision when it was slightly modified by Thomas Young. He developed a similar model for hearing, arguing that different places on the organ of Corti in the inner ear respond to different wavelengths of sound.

Although not a psychologist himself (the discipline didn't really exist at the time), Helmholtz made a number of discoveries that were fundamental to the eventual emergence of psychology. These discoveries came partly from his ideas about perception, and partly from his invention of instruments that allowed scientists to measure subtle physiological processes. He was a powerful influence in the development of psychology as an empirical science, working with many others who became founders of the discipline, including Gustav Fechner and Wilhelm Wundt.

Another experimental pioneer of the time was Ernst Weber, who also studied perception and the nervous system. Weber and Helmholtz were both interested in electricity and how it works in the nervous system, but they disagreed on several issues – so much so, that Helmholtz strongly opposed the proposal that the basic unit of electrical current should be called a 'weber', backing the term 'ampere' instead. But Weber also made significant contributions to the developing understanding of perception.

One aspect of this was about how we perceive differences. Weber pointed out that what we perceive isn't the actual quantity of anything. Instead, it's all about proportion. We can easily feel the difference between a one-kilo and a two-kilo bag of sugar. But it would be much harder to tell the difference between a suitcase weighing twenty kilos and one weighing twenty-one. This observation led Weber to the idea of the 'just-noticeable difference', usually referred to as the 'jnd'. The jnd is the amount of change we need in order to perceive a difference. It depends on the quantity that we're comparing it with, whether we are talking about loudness of sound, shades of light, weight, or any other type of sensory information. It's not an absolute measure, but a proportional one.

Gustav Fechner worked with both Weber and Helmholtz, adding to Weber's theory by identifying the mathematical relationship between the changes in jnds, and working with Helmholtz on other aspects of perception. He published a book, *Elemente der Psychophysik*, in 1860, which made an immediate impact, mainly because it challenged the argument about innateness by showing how perceptions can be measured after all. Fechner is often described as the founder of psychophysics because of his work linking sensory experience with the physical measurement of the brain and the senses. Psychophysics provided a strong basis for the developing science of experimental psychology.

Wilhelm Wundt, like Fechner, had worked with both Weber and Helmholtz. He went on to establish the first psychological laboratory, in Leipzig, in 1879. His laboratory attracted many eminent scientists who were interested in the new area of psychology, and he had many students, supervising over 150 doctoral dissertations in psychology. Most of the famous names associated with psychology at this time studied at or visited Wundt's laboratory, including the Russian physiologist Ivan Pavlov. In the late nineteenth century, psychology was only just beginning to become differentiated from philosophy, and Wundt wrote a number of significant books in both areas. His influential *Principles of Physiological Psychology*, published in 1873, set out a basic framework for what we now see as experimental psychology. After his death, his entire library was sold to Tohoku University in Japan, which outbid both Harvard and Yale, paying the modern equivalent of about $1 million for the collection.

While he was recognised as a founder of experimental psychology, Wundt's work became gradually distorted in successive textbooks, partly because he advocated introspection as a valid method of scientific enquiry, which was taken as lacking scientific objectivity. But that was a misrepresentation of his approach. Wundt's introspection involved rigorous training and systematic investigation. He demanded that everyone in his laboratory was explicitly trained in it, to a high standard, and insisted that their introspective analysis followed specific rules. For instance, the researcher should only include immediate experiences and should maintain their full focus on the experience itself. He also emphasised the importance of replication and of varying the conditions of the study so that results could be generalised across a wide range of situations.

Wundt also produced a major ten-volume text on social psychology, his *Völkerpsychologie*. Although this was largely ignored in British and American psychology, it set a firm foundation for social psychology in Europe, influencing the later social perspectives of the Gestalt psychologists. Although his overall contribution to psychology was profound, Wundt's work was often misrepresented in American psychology – partly because of some fundamental disagreements with the influential American psychologist, William James. Wundt believed in an experimental approach and argued that experience can and should be broken down into its component parts. But he also insisted that these experimental methods were not suitable for higher mental processes. James, however, ignored that caveat, representing Wundt's approach as reductionist and not appropriate for the study of real human beings.

It was William James who became the hero of American psychology. While Germany was leading the field in developing new methods of investigation, not everyone was able to travel to Germany or read the German language, and it took some time for books in German to be translated into English. William James had spent some time in Germany and was interested in many of the new ideas about psychology. But he also dismissed many of them; for example, he saw the quantitative approach of psychophysics as being effectively meaningless for psychology, and also (quite wrongly, in my view) he described Wundt's introspectionism as lacking scientific rigour. He did, however, open up several new areas of enquiry, and his hugely influential book, *Principles of Psychology*, published in 1890, is still cited today by many psychologists.

James was as much a philosopher as a psychologist: he developed a version of radical empiricism, arguing that experimentation at the physical level isn't enough, and that investigation needs to be able to explain the relationship between physical processes and other levels of experience, like meaning, values and intentionality. But his contribution to the development of American psychology was considerable, and he is still regarded as its founding father. He was responsible for the first psychology department in the US, at Harvard University, and taught what is generally described as the first course in psychology. Ironically, however, and despite his founding-father image, James himself was unconvinced that psychology should be a distinct discipline. Apart from his textbook, his main academic writings were in philosophy rather than in psychology itself.

What James is most famous for in modern psychology, however, is his theory of emotion, which took a radical approach, arguing that our emotional feeling comes about because of our perception of physiological changes in the body. James saw emotion in terms of a succession of events, beginning with an arousing stimulus, such as tripping on the stairs or being faced by someone who is very angry. This generates a physical reaction, which the mind then interprets as an emotional reaction to the situation. His most famous remark is often paraphrased as 'We do not weep because we feel sorrow; we feel sorrow because we weep.' We will come back to this idea in Chapter 21, when we look at emotion in more detail.

James was not the only critic of the new experimental psychology. In 1893, Wilhelm Dilthey published an open critique, arguing that descriptive psychology was more significant than experimentation because the mind was too complex and could only really be studied by introspection. He was immediately challenged by Hermann Ebbinghaus, who responded with a long and scathing article arguing that Dilthey was out of date and not taking into account the experimental methods that he, Ebbinghaus, had been promoting.

Ebbinghaus, following the experimental tradition, had conducted a lengthy series of experiments on memory. These culminated in his book *Uber das Gedächtnis* (*On Memory*), which was published in 1885. His aim was to study 'pure' memory, uncontaminated by associations and personal experience, so his research consisted of memorising lists of three-letter nonsense syllables. It allowed him to identify features of memory such as primacy and recency effects – the way that the first and last items on a list are more easily remembered – and to formulate the characteristic learning curve, which shows how long we take to memorise information, and the forgetting curve, which shows how memory fades.

Ebbinghaus also identified four distinct ways of remembering: recall, or being able to remember without prompting; recognition, or remembering something when seeing it again; re-learning savings, which is the way that we take less time to learn a list we've learned before; and redintegration, which is being able to organise listed items in their original order, even if the list can't be recalled, because it 'feels right'.

By the end of the nineteenth century, then, a distinction had emerged between those psychologists who were interested in how the mind was organised, known as the structuralists, and those who were interested in what mental processes were used for, known as the functionalists. They formed opposing and hotly debated schools of thought, although to modern eyes the division is more extreme than it needs to be. But that was only in academic psychology; in the applied field, and particularly when dealing with people who had psychological problems, psychologists continued to develop and promote their own theories regardless of those academic debates.

CHAPTER 5

The Unconscious Mind
FREUD AND PSYCHOANALYSIS

'No, no,' cried little Hans. 'I don't want to go out.'

'Come now, little Hans. You know it's time for your walk,' cajoled his nurse.

'But I don't want to go out,' sobbed Hans. 'I'm frightened of the horses.'

'There's nothing to be frightened of,' his nurse replied. 'You see horses every day.'

'But they make a big noise with their feet,' the little boy cried. 'I don't want to go.'

'What's going on?' asked little Hans' father, hearing the argument and coming into the room.

'It's been like this for a week, sir,' the nurse answered. 'Ever since he saw that horse collapse. It was pulling a big bus, alone, and its feet clattered as it fell. Shouldn't be allowed, if you ask me.'

'It made a big noise with his feet,' repeated little Hans tearfully. 'It was loud.'

'He hasn't wanted to go out for his walk ever since, sir.'

'Now, young man, pull yourself together. Go on out with nurse. There's nothing to be frightened of.'

Four-year-old Hans gulped and obeyed his father. His father, though, remained concerned. What could be causing the boy's fear? He decided to write to his friend and colleague, Sigmund Freud, to discuss the issue. In their correspondence, Freud diagnosed Little Hans' trouble as being a phobia resulting from his Oedipal conflict. The Greek hero Oedipus unwittingly killed his own father and married his mother, which was the origin of the name of the conflict. Freud believed that each male child saw himself as being in competition with his father for his mother's love, but had an unconscious fear that his father, being bigger and more powerful, might castrate him as a result. In Hans' case, according to Freud, the horse, being large and powerful, represented Hans' father and the loud noise represented the threat of castration. Freud didn't actually meet Little Hans. His diagnosis was entirely through his correspondence with the boy's father. But that didn't stop the case from going into psychoanalytic history as evidence for his idea of the Oedipus conflict. By that time, Freud had become famous as the originator of psychoanalysis, and his theory had become well known to professionals across the Western world.

Essentially, Freud argued that we are driven by an unconscious energy – the life-force known as the libido. It produces powerful impulses, which are largely sexual in nature. These are socially unacceptable, especially in the strictly regulated society of the nineteenth century, so the conscious mind represses them. They remain, however, in the form of unconscious motives and drives.

The idea of an unconscious mind is familiar to us nowadays, but Freud was working at a time when it was assumed that the mind was conscious and essentially rational. His interest had been stimulated by the work of Franz Mesmer, a German physician who demonstrated what we now call hypnotism but was then referred to as 'mesmerism'. Freud became even more interested through his mentor, Joseph Breuer, who developed the 'talking cure' – a method of treating patients who had what was then described as hysteria: physical problems with no known organic origin, which were commonly diagnosed in women at the time. (We might observe that, given the extremely repressed lives of middle-class women in that society, this condition wasn't totally incomprehensible, but back then it was considered an intractable medical problem.)

Breuer's most famous case was Anna O (real name Bertha Pappenheim), who suffered from paralysis, speech disturbance and visual problems. Breuer observed that each of these symptoms became much reduced after she had discussed them with him, and that she was particularly helped by reliving emotional experiences from her childhood. As the treatment continued, Anna O's symptoms eventually disappeared. Freud was very interested in this case, and Breuer encouraged him to try the same approach with other hysterical patients. Their book *Studies in Hysteria*, published in 1895, became the foundation for the eventual practice and theory of psychoanalysis. Sadly, though, the close friendship between the two colleagues became increasingly strained, as Freud insisted that sexual issues were at the root of all hysterical problems, while Breuer argued that other factors were involved. This disagreement was later mirrored in Freud's separation from Jung (see Chapter 12) and several other colleagues.

Freud's insistence on sexual energies was at the heart of his theory. His therapy with hysterical female patients had revealed memories of sexual abuse as children in almost all cases. At first, he believed these accounts, but he eventually became persuaded, both by his (male) contemporaries and by the remarkable frequency of these memories, that they must be untrue. Therefore, he concluded, they must represent unconscious wishes or desires on the part of the patient. Knowing what we do nowadays about the prevalence of child sexual abuse, and about the way that it was regarded as unremarkable in the eighteenth century (one member of the UK parliament objected to a proposed law against it on the grounds that sex with young serving girls was every gentleman's 'right'), we might wonder whether, in fact, Freud had tapped into a real issue.

Nevertheless, having concluded that these memories were unconscious fantasy, and being convinced that repressed sexuality was the source of most of the psychological problems he encountered, Freud developed his model of the unconscious mind. He proposed that the mind has three parts: the id, which is the primitive, impulsive part; the ego, which is the practical part that deals with the real world; and the superego, which is the internalised 'strict parent', which expresses rules, obligations and conscience. The id and superego, he proposed, are constantly pulling in opposing directions. The id acts according to the pleasure principle, careless of consequences, while the superego demands rigid adherence to social and internalised rules. It's the ego's job to keep the balance between them, bending sometimes one way and sometimes another, depending on what the real-world situation allows.

Freud was convinced that medical science would eventually discover these parts of the mind, or at least their physiological equivalents, and would also find that they were entirely energised by the libido, which was sexual in nature. As the twentieth century moved into the First World War, he began to believe that there was also a dark energy in the human mind, which his followers named 'thanatos': essentially a self-destructive death instinct. But most of his theory was concerned with libido as a constant source of energy that must be expressed in some way. For Freud, libido energised both behaviour and mental concerns, and would become particularly demanding when sexuality was repressed. Freud argued that small children are inevitably concerned with exploring erotic sensations: at first through the mouth, tasting and sucking objects – the oral stage; then in the anal stage as the child becomes toilet-trained and begins to derive erotic pleasure from defecation; and finally in the phallic stage at the age of five or so, where erotic pleasure comes from handling the genitals. After this, the child enters a latency stage until puberty, when sexual satisfaction is again derived from the genitals.

As Freud's popularity grew, this aspect of his theory was converted into significant advice to mothers. He argued that inappropriate child-rearing could produce negative consequences in adulthood. Oral fixation could happen either through weaning too early or too late and would produce an adult with an excessive interest in oral stimulation, resulting in over-eating, nail-biting or chewing things. Mishandling potty training could produce an adult who was anal-retentive – that is, mean and selfish, or anal-expulsive and overly generous. And the phallic stage, according to Freud, was all important in resolving sexual identity, as the male child (Freud's theory was almost entirely about male development) had to resolve his Oedipal conflict. The child would resolve his fear of castration by stressing his similarity to his father and so reduce the likelihood that his father would see him as a rival.

Freud's theory made a significant impact on the society of the time. It proposed the existence of an unconscious mind, with needs, desires and images that were entirely different from the person's consciousness. It outlined a clear structure for the development and nature of that mind, and it also asserted that the unconscious mind could be detected through dream symbolism, free association and occasional speech errors that seem to imply a different meaning from that intended, and which we now call 'Freudian slips'. Through discussion groups and correspondence, Freud gathered a number of others who were interested in his theory and explored its further development through discussion and the sharing of ideas. They became known as the 'Vienna Circle'.

Although Freud established psychoanalysis as a recognised school of thought, his was not the only theory. Many members of his circle developed their own approaches to psychoanalysis, including Erich Fromm, Alfred Adler and, the most influential of all, Carl Jung. Like the others, Jung was initially a colleague of Freud – indeed, Freud saw him as his potential 'heir' – but after a few years they had a bitter falling-out, as Freud refused to consider Jung's view that perhaps sexuality was not the only energising source for human behaviour. Jung developed his ideas into the approach known as analytical psychology, which we will look at in Chapter 12.

Despite the inherent sexism of Freud's theory, he also welcomed a number of women into his inner circle. Sabina Spielrein, a Russian psychiatrist, became a famous psychoanalyst in her own right but was murdered in the Holocaust. Freud's daughter Anna and another colleague, Melanie Klein, became well known for applying psychoanalysis to children, although they argued over the most appropriate way of doing it. Anna Freud favoured her father's approach, using traditional psychoanalytic methods to focus on ego development and defence mechanisms, while Melanie Klein emphasised early relationships rather than ego development, and saw free play as an alternative to formal psychoanalysis when working with children.

Freud's theory had emphasised how adult neurosis derived from complexes acquired in childhood, and both Anna Freud and Melanie Klein saw their work as aiming to balance the child's emotional development, to avoid adult neuroses in later life. Anna Freud became particularly well known for her work with the 'Bulldogs Bank' children – six children under four who had survived the Theresienstadt concentration camp for over two years. Their parents had been killed soon after entering the camp, and they had lived by scavenging and sharing food and avoiding the guards.

When found, they could hardly speak and reacted with extreme distress to any threat of separation. They were flown to a rehabilitation camp in Windermere, and gradually learned to interact with other people. A condition of their fostering was that they should keep in touch with one another, and their bond continued throughout their lives. Anna Freud and Sophie Dann used their experiences to show how even children without adults could make strong attachments to others; that even very small children could develop a sense of fairness; and how children could recover even from severe deprivation in a loving and stimulating environment. Extremely disturbed behaviour, they showed, doesn't always come from suppressed conflicts, as Freud believed. It could sometimes just be a natural response to a disturbed environment.

Melanie Klein's focus was on a different aspect of childhood: the two-way attachment between infant and mother. She developed what became known as 'object relations theory', with 'object' as the opposite of 'subject' – in other words, awareness of the other person. Her work set the scene for many post-war developments in child psychology, and particularly for the use of play therapy, which has become a useful tool for identifying children's conflicts and problems, as a kind of indirect form of psychoanalysis.

Although psychoanalytic theory was known in America, it was mostly influential in Europe. In America, as we shall see in the next chapter, the concerns were with a rather different aspect of child development.

CHAPTER 6

Nativist Beliefs
EARLY IQ TESTING AND THE EMERGENCE OF EUGENICS

In 1897, a little girl was admitted to the Vineland Training School in New Jersey. Emma Wolverton was eight years old, handy at everyday tasks, able to sew and physically normal. Her mother had passed through a succession of relationships, and her latest husband refused to take in someone else's child, so Emma was sent to the school. She had little formal education and was unable to read and write, so her admission notes observed that she might possibly be 'feeble-minded'. Those two words were to condemn her to a life in institutions, without parole, for the next eighty-one years.

America at this time was going through great social change: urban populations were growing, and extreme poverty and crime were rife. For some, and in particular for Henry Goddard, the head of the Vineland Training School, the underlying reason for this was feeble-mindedness. People who were feeble-minded, he believed, would end up almost inevitably in a life of criminal degeneracy and prostitution, partly because that was their natural inclination, but also because their mental weakness meant that they were easily tempted into crime and easily manipulated by others.

What was worse was that feeble-mindedness was believed to be inherited, so it would be passed on to these people's children and grandchildren. This idea had been growing for some time – in fact, ever since Charles Darwin had shown how evolution happens through inherited characteristics. A growing body of writers and intellectuals had applied the theory to human beings, and several family studies had already been published suggesting that mental weakness or lack of intelligence could be passed on through the generations. Henry Goddard took that idea and ran with it.

Goddard published a book that described several generations of one family, whom he renamed the Kallikaks (from the Greek words *Kallos*: beauty and *Kakos*: bad). The family, he said, had two very different branches. One branch consisted of upright, worthy citizens, while the other branch consisted mainly of thieves, prostitutes and other moral degenerates. The respectable branch had descended from Martin Kallikak's marriage to a respectable Quaker woman. But the criminal branch resulted from his 'dalliance' with a feeble-minded barmaid when he was younger. It was the perfect natural experiment.

The book, by Goddard's own admission, was a morality tale, and rapidly became a bestseller. It claimed to be a scientific family study, describing how Goddard and his assistants had traced back the generations of this particular family. Many later researchers have found that it was largely a work of fiction. But it was massively influential at the time, attracting huge attention both in the US and elsewhere in the world. It gave convincing 'evidence' for the evils of 'bad' heredity and encouraged the belief that society would benefit if such people were prevented from passing on their genes to future generations. Goddard himself believed that it would more or less eradicate crime and poverty in society.

Emma Wolverton (renamed Deborah Kallikak) was the central character in Goddard's book. She became the poster girl for his campaign, showing how living a protected life without having to face up to the evils and temptations of society at large could produce a healthy, capable person who was a benefit rather than a scourge on society. The book was illustrated with photographs – pictures of Deborah looking calm and serene in her institution, contrasted with (crudely retouched) pictures of the other members of her side of the family, looking villainous and/or poverty-stricken. Without the protection of the institution, Goddard asserted, Deborah would have inevitably fallen prey to evil people in society and ended up like the rest of her side of the Kallikak family.

Emma herself, though, was very different from the way Goddard portrayed her as 'Deborah' in his book. She grew up to be a capable needlewoman and carpenter and worked as a teacher's assistant and also as a nursing assistant at a time of illness in the institution. Despite Goddard's insistence that Deborah remained illiterate, Emma was able to read and write, although she still preferred practical work. She even wrote letters, keeping up a steady correspondence with several friends. She died, still living in the institution, at the age of eighty-nine. But society at large was unaware of Emma Wolverton: it was Deborah Kallikak who was held up as showing the need for, and value of, institutional care for those who were less intellectually capable.

Emma's relatives, too, turn out to have been quite different from Goddard's portrayals of the 'bad' Kallikaks. Many were respectable farmers and traders, even bankers. For the most part, their only crime was that some of them were quite poor. None of them, apart from Emma, had actually been assessed for intelligence or feeble-mindedness: Goddard and his assistants gathered their evidence from anecdotes and accounts, and deliberately exaggerated any bad qualities they could detect. It all made for a better story. Belief in the 'menace of the feeble-minded' became so strong that laws were passed in many US states promoting compulsory sterilisation of anyone assessed in that way.

Meanwhile, on the other side of the Atlantic, Alfred Binet was wrestling with a rather different problem. The French government had set up special residential schools for 'subnormal' children, who were unlikely to benefit from standard education. Binet's challenge was not parents avoiding the stigma of their child being classified as subnormal; rather, it was parents coaching their 'normal' children to act as subnormal so they could get into these schools, to benefit from the free board and lodging they offered. How to tell the difference?

Intelligence, Binet reasoned, is something that develops as a child gets older. Children manage different tasks at different ages – for example, naming the days of the week, counting up to ten or recognising the letters of the alphabet. So Binet and his colleague Theodore Simon put together a series of tasks that children would normally be expected to do at different ages. They tested them on a number of children, developed standard versions of each task and combined them into a test that could estimate a child's mental age – the age at which most children would be able to achieve the same result. They had developed the very first intelligence test. This measure, Binet said, would help teachers to guide the child's education. It would also, of course, allow them to distinguish between 'normal' children and those who needed special schooling.

Following Binet's work, William Stern, a German psychologist, proposed dividing mental age by chronological age to obtain a single number – the Intelligence Quotient, or IQ. His formula was: mental age / chronological age x 100, meaning that 100 would be the 'standard' score of an average child; a child with a mental age lower than their real age would score below 100, while a more advanced child, by comparison with others of its age, would score over 100. For Binet, his measure of intelligence simply described the developmental stage the child had reached. But when Binet's test was translated into English along with Stern's measure of IQ, it was quickly seized on by Goddard and his colleague Lewis Terman. In their hands, IQ changed from being a diagnostic indicator to being seen as a fixed measure of intelligence. Binet objected strongly to those ideas, describing them as a 'brutal pessimism', which should be challenged whenever it was encountered. But his view was largely ignored. Here, finally, was the ideal way to distinguish the feeble-minded from the rest of the population.

In the UK, nativist beliefs about intelligence – that is, the idea that intelligence was inherited – were also popular. Their main spokesperson was Francis Galton, who in 1869 had published a book, *Hereditary Genius*. In this book, he argued that high ability ran in families and was clearly inherited (he was very proud of being a cousin of Charles Darwin). In 1884 Galton set up his 'Anthropometric Centre' at the International Health Exhibition in London. Visitors could pay 3d to do various activities and received a souvenir card that listed their physical measurements – arm, hand and leg strength, lung capacity, keenness of eyesight, and so on. In total, Galton collected data from 9,337 participants. The exhibit proved so popular that he relocated it to the South Kensington Museum when the exhibition closed.

When the data for each physical measurement was plotted on a graph, it almost inevitably formed a bell-shaped pattern, known as a 'Gaussian curve'. This pattern shows only a few measurements at the extremes, with increasing numbers of the scores clustering around a central point. As Galton's studies showed, it was so common in human physical measurement that it became known as the 'normal distribution'. But Galton also insisted that it would be bound to apply to mental characteristics such as intelligence, as well as physical ones.

That idea was also an instant hit in the US. American psychologists Lewis Terman and Robert Yerkes developed a test combining Binet's ideas with Galton's normal distribution principle. The result was the Stanford–Binet test, a version of which is still in use today. Galton had coined the term 'eugenics' for the idea that society would benefit if people of below-average intelligence were prevented from breeding, and the new tests were an absolute gift for the eugenicists. They argued that IQ, being normally distributed, gave society a precise way of detecting those with 'inferior' genes.

For Terman, Yerkes and others, IQ tests could even identify those 'high-grade defectives' who were living unremarkable lives but might pass on their inferior genes to future generations. There were, they asserted, tens of thousands of such people in society. They believed that using IQ tests to detect them, and then sterilising them, could result in eliminating crime and pauperism in society – a claim that was made openly in the introduction to the first edition of the Stanford–Binet intelligence test.

Henry Goddard was equally active in promoting the idea. In 1913 he carried out widespread IQ testing of would-be immigrants to the United States, which resulted in large numbers of Jews, Hungarians, Italians and Russians being identified as incurably 'feeble-minded' and refused entry – even though the translators administering the IQ tests protested that they wouldn't have been able to do them either, when they first arrived in the country. That data, alongside results from US Army tests showing that soldiers from central and southern Europe scored lower in IQ tests than soldiers from northern Europe, provided the 'scientific' evidence for laws heavily restricting immigration from those countries.

It wasn't just in America: the Kallikaks had made a worldwide impact, and eugenic beliefs were widely held across Europe in the first part of the twentieth century. Adolf Hitler was a great admirer of the way that the United States was dealing with this 'problem', and he enforced compulsory sterilisation on people who were disabled or 'feeble-minded' in the early years of his chancellorship. As he became more powerful, their 'treatment' became euthanasia. Some 80,000 disabled Germans were murdered.

The eugenic idea of improving society through euthanasia became linked with a spurious evolutionary theory which held that Jews, 'Gypsies' (or Romani people) and others came from more 'primitive' genetic stock, so their interbreeding with people from the more 'advanced' Aryan race was a backward step in human evolution. Although that theory was scientific nonsense, its combination with eugenics provided an ideological excuse for the Nazi Holocaust – arguing that eliminating 'inferior' races as well as 'inferior' people would create a superior version of the human race. And the strict immigration laws resulting from Goddard's IQ tests meant that, for many of those at risk, fleeing to the US for asylum was no longer an option.

The eugenic movement suffered a major blow when the concentration camps were liberated, and people saw what eugenics really meant in practice – that is, systematic murder and genocide, as

6 million Jews and thousands of Romani and others of 'inferior' stock were murdered. Sadly, those ideas have not yet died out completely. Less extreme genetic beliefs remained commonplace, in psychology and in society at large, fuelling many 'nature/nurture' debates. IQ testing continued to develop, making a major contribution to professional psychology, and new versions were developed to challenge bias. As Chapter 36 shows, though, even now they are still controversial.

CHAPTER 7

The Behaviourist Challenge
STIMULUS-RESPONSE LEARNING AND THE
CHALLENGE TO NATIVISM

The little cat miaowed unhappily, pacing around the small cage, pawing at the floor, the roof, and trying to reach through the bars. It was hungry, and it could see food outside, well out of reach, which only increased its agitation. Suddenly, the door opened, and the cat ran out, making straight for its food dish.

The next day, it happened again. As the cat struggled to escape from the cage, the door suddenly opened. It happened again on the third day, and again, day after day. Each time, the cat escaped just a little bit more quickly. Eventually the cat was no sooner placed in the box than it would escape again. It had triggered the door opening by stepping on a weight that was attached to a string, which pulled the latch to open the door.

Did the cat know what it was doing? Almost certainly not, according to E.L. Thorndike, the researcher who was carefully timing the cat's escapes. The accepted psychological view at the time was that the cat would have learned how to open the door by 'insight' – that is, by suddenly perceiving the solution to its problem. But Thorndike's results challenged that. If the cat had an insight, there should have been a sudden drop in its escape time. Thorndike's chart, though, showed a gradual curve: the cat escaped just a little more quickly each time. The cat was definitely learning, but it was changing its behaviour gradually rather than having a sudden cognitive insight.

So how was that happening? According to Thorndike, it was because doing the action produced a positive effect. The cat's learning happened gradually through trial and error but was strengthened if an action produced what Thorndike called a 'satisfier' for the animal. This observation formed the first of three 'laws of learning' that Thorndike proposed – the 'Law of Effect'.

The second law that Thorndike derived from his observations was the 'Law of Exercise'. In essence, this was the idea that the more often a connection between a stimulus and a response is made, the more likely it is to happen again. This law was welcomed by educationalists, as it seemed to justify the use of repetition and practice in teaching and learning. But Thorndike regarded it as a weak law, which only applied sometimes, not always. It was a factor in learning, but not generally regarded as being as important as the Law of Effect, so it was eventually dropped, or at least generally disregarded.

Sometimes, however, it was apparent to Thorndike that these two factors alone didn't always explain what was going on. If the cat wasn't hungry, for example, it might curl up and go to sleep instead of trying to escape. He introduced a third law of learning, the 'Law of Readiness', but it didn't really catch on. This may have been because of the way he phrased it, saying that the animal must attend to 'specific stimuli of consequence' in its situation. The problem then was producing a purely behavioural definition of how an animal could identify which stimuli mattered and which didn't. Eventually that law, too, was quietly dropped.

So Thorndike is remembered nowadays for the Law of Effect. But his research in establishing a behavioural account of learning had profound consequences, not just for the study of animal psychology, but also as part of the theoretical background for a much more dramatic change in psychology as a whole.

The winds of change were blowing across Europe. Advances in science and technology meant that the beginning of the twentieth century was totally different from the beginning of the nineteenth – socially, physically and politically. Society had become urban-ised, as people moved from agricultural work to factory employ-ment in cities; advances in medicine and health meant that diseases like smallpox and cholera were no longer the constant threat they had been, and everywhere republican rumblings were challenging the old royal houses and inherited privilege.

For the visionaries, it was the start of a new era – of modern times, when old traditions had outlived their usefulness and could be discarded in favour of new, innovative ways of doing things. This was the modernist movement, and it extended right across society – in art, architecture, fashion, music and even in experiments in social organisation. It all aimed to build a better society through progress and applying modern knowledge. Not all of this was positive – the eugenic movement, of course, was a prime example of that, as we saw in the last chapter. And not everyone agreed with the changes. But most people not only accepted the idea of progress, but welcomed it. Society was evidently changing: the aim was to make it better than it had been. And science, for many, was the key.

Psychology too had been affected by these winds of change. Wundt, Titchener and the others had established the idea that psychology should be a scientific discipline. For them, being scien-tific meant studying human experience systematically, through introspection and experiments, or by collecting other people's memories and reports. But modernists like Thorndike rejected these Victorian methods. They avoided ideas like thinking and insight, concentrating instead on measurable changes in behaviour – that is, in what people, or animals, actually did. And as these ideas developed, a division gradually emerged within psychology. It was brought to a head by John Broadus Watson, who changed the direction of psychology for over half a century.

For Watson, that old-style psychology, which explored experi-ence and mental activity, was a dead end. Modern science, he believed, should deal with empirical, observable facts about the real world. He thought that, since the workings of people's minds can't be directly observed, they couldn't be a 'real' scientific subject of study. For the modern scientist, Watson believed, what actually matters is behaviour that can be observed directly. And nothing else.

Watson had studied experimental psychology and was familiar with its ideas, but he was always more interested in psychologists who focused entirely on behaviour, like Thorndike and Pavlov. He was familiar with Thorndike's work and readily joined the growing opposition to theories of consciousness and the mind. His doctoral thesis was about how the behaviour of young laboratory rats correlated with their brain development, and he shared with Thorndike a growing conviction that learning was at the heart of psychology.

Watson had also been inspired by the work of Ivan Pavlov, the Russian physiologist, and his now-famous experiments on conditioned reflexes. The special thing about Pavlov's work was that he had shown how even physiological processes, always assumed to be entirely automatic, could be learned. Pavlov's major insight came while he was studying digestion in dogs and measuring how much they salivated while they were eating. Pavlov observed that the dogs would begin to salivate even before they received their food – in fact, at the sight of the assistant bringing in the dishes. What puzzled Pavlov was that salivation is a reflex – it doesn't involve thinking at all, but it's the body's automatic response to eating food. So it shouldn't have been set off by the sight of the lab assistant. He then conducted a number of highly successful experiments, like sounding a buzzer before the food was brought in. Sure enough, the dogs would eventually begin to salivate when they heard the buzzer. For Pavlov, this indicated that learning is an essential part of the living organism: that it doesn't require consciousness and can apply even to the most basic functions.

Thorndike had shown how learning can happen by trial and error and not by insight, and Pavlov had shown that any type of behaviour, even reflexes, can be learned. For Watson, this was real objective science and the key to scientific progress. In 1913 he published a paper, 'Psychology as the Behaviorist Views It', which outlined his beliefs in behaviour as the only appropriate subject of study for psychologists.

This happened in an era when 'progress' was the watchword and meant developing a healthier, wealthier and altogether better society. And, as we've seen, science was expected to contribute to how progress was made. But what defined science? Over the past century or so, all the physical sciences had been transformed through the identification of their fundamental 'building blocks'. In physics, this was the discovery of atoms, as the basis for all matter. In chemistry, it was Mendeleev's creation of the periodic table, which showed how elements relate to one another. In biology, it was the discovery that all living things are made up of cells; and in the newly emerging branch of biology, called genetics, it was the way that units of heredity called genes determine what kinds of cells a living organism will develop.

Each of these discoveries had expanded understanding in their disciplines and opened up entirely new possibilities. Science only became really useful, Watson believed, when it had identified its basic units. So that was what a truly scientific psychology also needed to do. It needed to identify the basic building blocks under-pinning human and animal behaviour: the psychological equivalent of atoms, elements, cells or genes.

What would be the building blocks for a truly scientific psychology? For Watson, as we've seen, learning was at the heart of everything psychological. He argued that it is the learned connection, the link between a stimulus and a response, which is formed through experience, that is psychology's core unit, like the atom for physicists and the cell for biologists. Understanding how that happened would create a psychology that was truly scientific and could explain everything.

Unlike Thorndike, Watson believed that it was the Law of Exercise that was the most important factor in learning. The more often a connection between a stimulus and a response is made, the stronger the learning will become. He adopted Pavlov's model of learning, which described how learning can happen by repeatedly associating a neutral stimulus with one already known to produce a response. An unconditioned reflex can become a conditioned, or learned, reflex in this way. (Strictly speaking, the name should be 'conditional', but the term 'conditioned' became firmly established as a result of a minor error in the translation of Pavlov's book.)

Watson's 1913 manifesto, understandably, created a furore in the psychological world. He was directly challenging the psychological establishment of the time and generated virulent criticism from almost all camps – the hereditarians, the psychoanalysts and the traditional researchers. But Watson wasn't one to give up easily. He followed his paper up with more publications in the same vein, developing his ideas and repeatedly insisting that learning is at the core of all psychology. Despite his academic credentials, Watson's uncompromising stance on these matters made him a controversial figure, which wasn't helped by the discovery that he was having an affair with his assistant, Rosalie Rayner, while his divorce was going through (they married after it was finalised). The press seized on it as a major scandal, and he was forced to retire from his position at Johns Hopkins University.

Following this, Watson took up a job in advertising, and we'll look at how he went about that in the next chapter. In later life. he focused on child-rearing – although the fact that three of his four children attempted suicide, one of them successfully, doesn't exactly fill one with confidence regarding his methods. He argued strongly against the eugenic movement, and in fact one of his most famous quotations was the 'twelve infants' statement, in which he claimed that with a dozen healthy infants and his own specified world to bring them up in, he could produce any type of specialist, from doctor or lawyer to beggarman or thief, regardless of heredity.

Watson's influence on psychology was profound. Although it began initially as a minority movement, behaviourist principles gradually gained acceptance, until by the 1970s behaviourism had become the dominant approach in psychology, particularly in America but also in Britain.

CHAPTER 8

Psychology at Work
EARLY APPLIED PSYCHOLOGY, THE HAWTHORNE STUDIES AND THE HUMAN RELATIONS MODEL

Repetition, repetition, repetition!

How often have you heard the same slogan or advertising jingle? It's all based on Watson's Law of Exercise. (Actually, as we saw in the last chapter, that was originally Thorndike's law, but it was Watson who seized on it and promoted it as a fundamental principle of learning, so it's now usually attributed to him.) Watson took up a career in advertising following his departure from Johns Hopkins University in 1920 and was extremely successful, working up from door-to-door sales to vice-president of the company in only two years.

One reason behind that success was, of course, his application of the principles of 'scientific behaviourism' to advertising, and particularly Pavlov's ideas about conditioned emotional responses. He recommended deliberately stirring up emotions, using material that would generate responses of fear, anger or affection in the consumer. He applied other learning principles, too, such as associating a well-known person with a particular product. It had been done before, but Watson's use of the behaviourist rationale helped to establish it as a popular advertising technique. He became particularly well known for a series of adverts for Ponds cold cream, which combined emotionally sensitive messages about ageing with testimonials and explicit illustrations of how to use the cream. The campaign was massively successful, as were his toothpaste adverts, which were all about making the user more attractive to the opposite sex. Inevitably, much of his advice emphasised the importance of repeating the name of the product, linking the product name with the act of purchasing. In psychology, Watson is known as the father of behaviourism; but in the consumer industry he is known as one of the founders of modern marketing.

Watson, though, wasn't the only psychologist working in industry. From the beginning of the twentieth century, psychology was put to work. F.W. Taylor, in 1911, was probably the first Western psychologist to introduce a way of looking at work that emphasised what people were actually doing, and tried to make it happen more efficiently, although psychological ideas had been adopted in both Japan and China by that time. His first experiment was with labourers loading pig-iron into railway trucks. On average, each man loaded about 12.5 tons of pig-iron a day. Taylor approached one man and got him to agree to work exactly as he was told – lifting when he was told to lift, resting when he was told to rest – and promised that he would earn more that way. By the end of the day, the man had loaded 47.5 tons of pig-iron. This, Taylor argued, was scientific management: identifying the most efficient way of working and ensuring that workers kept to that efficient practice.

Taylor became known as the father of the 'time and motion study' – an approach that analysed each task in terms of the actions required and the time needed to do it. With the increase in outputs, this was understandably popular with employers, although it left a lasting legacy of suspicion among factory workers. Treating people as machines generates resentment and a sense of alienation from work, and this in turn encouraged radical movements like unionisation and the growing interest in socialist and communist ideas.

At first it was assumed that progressive and enlightened management could counter these movements. But this didn't seem to be the case. The management of the Hawthorne works of the Western Electric Company in Chicago, for example, were puzzled by the high level of dissatisfaction among the workforce. They had provided recreation facilities, pension and sickness schemes, and other welfare benefits for their employees. So why were they still discontented?

Evidently it was time to call in the psychologists. Henry Roethlisberger and William Dickson began their investigations by looking into lighting levels in a workshop, as this was suggested as a possible cause of the problem. They selected a part of the workshop and divided its employees into two groups. One group received improved lighting conditions while the other was a control group whose working conditions didn't change. The first group's output went up, apparently supporting the idea that it was lighting that was hindering the efficiency of the workers on that floor. But, completely unexpectedly, the output of the control group went up, too. Strange. The experimenters then tried lowering the lighting levels, eventually reaching a level equivalent to bright moonlight. Still output went up. Finally, they reset the lighting levels to what they had been originally, and that workshop's output was higher than it had ever been.

Obviously, whatever was happening didn't have anything to do with lighting levels. They tried another experiment with a group of women who assembled small, complicated parts for telephone relays. First of all, they put the women on piece work so they were paid according to how many units they assembled. Output increased. Then they introduced five-minute tea-breaks, morning and afternoon. Output increased again. The tea-breaks were extended to ten minutes; again output increased. They tried dismissing the women half an hour early, and again output went up. It seemed that, no matter what they did, it improved their productivity – except in one trial, when they gave them six five-minute tea-breaks during the day, and the women complained that they were being distracted by constantly having to break off what they were doing. At the beginning of the experiment, each woman was producing, on average, 2,400 relays a week. By the end, they were each producing about 3,000 relays a week.

So what was this mysterious factor? It obviously wasn't to do with the physical environment, or the working shifts. Rather, the psychologists found, it had everything to do with appreciation. During all these experiments someone sat with the women as they worked, keeping them informed about what was going on, and listening to the suggestions they made. Because of this, the women felt that (a) someone was interested in them, and thought that their job was worth studying, (b) that they were being listened to, and (c), most important of all, that they were being treated as responsible adults who could be given considerable freedom of movement and trusted not to abuse that freedom. As a result, the women became more responsible and trustworthy. And again, when they reverted to the original conditions of work, their output was the highest it had ever been.

Roethlisberger and Dickson set up a programme in which every employee was interviewed and encouraged to talk about their work and the factory. One worker spent all the time complaining about the factory canteen. He came along to the researchers a week later and thanked them for achieving such an improvement in the canteen's food. But the researchers hadn't done anything at all about the complaint. Just being listened to was enough to make that worker feel more at ease, and so his dissatisfaction disappeared. The general morale of the factory improved, and – importantly for management – so did their workers' output.

Except in one department. When Roethlisberger and Dickson investigated the bank-wiring room, they found that their interventions made no difference. The work in that room was to attach wires to pieces of apparatus. Of the fourteen men employed there, nine attached the wires, three soldered them and two were inspectors. The group of men working there kept up a steady working output that didn't vary, regardless of the actions of the researchers.

The department was noted for having a strong group feeling, and the psychologists found a definite 'code' of behaviour among its members. The code consisted of (a) each man keeping up his share of the work and not slacking; but also (b) not working too hard and 'rate-busting', because that pressurised others; (c) not telling a supervisor anything that might reflect badly on a work-mate; and (d) not acting officiously if you were put in a position of responsibility. These were strong group norms, which they all adhered to, and which made them resistant to change from outside.

The Hawthorne studies are famous in psychology and became widely known as a result of a book written by Elton Mayo, who had teamed up with Roethlisberger and Dickson in 1928. *The Human Problems of an Industrial Civilization* presented a very different model of management from Taylor's rather brutal modernist approach. Rather than seeing the worker only in terms of physical efficiency, and not as a human being, Mayo's book showed how the social side of work was an essential factor in worker motivation.

Another factor emerged when the same researchers were asked to investigate job satisfaction in aircraft factories in southern California. These factories had very high staff turnover, mainly in people leaving the army and going into industry. Typically, they would come and work for a short while, and then leave. But one particular workshop had a very low labour turnover and also a very high production record. The psychologists decided to investigate the social relations in this workshop, to see what it was that made it so distinctive.

They found that the group had its own natural leader, who handled any problems with employees as they came up or referred them to a higher authority if he couldn't solve them himself. The official foreman of the department, knowing that this group could be relied on, rarely came to visit it, and the floor supervisor, for the same reason, only popped in once or twice a day. Because the group leader didn't have any official position in the factory, he was able to concentrate on the group and its problems, while the actual foreman was too busy to be able to spare the time. Largely because of this unofficial leader, the group worked well and was trusted by the supervisors, and that in turn encouraged the workers to be trustworthy.

Mayo and his colleagues also found that the leader had a definite procedure for introducing new people to the work. First, they were introduced to the others working in that section and set to work with someone they seemed likely to get on with. Once they had become used to their own section's work, they were taken along to the end of the assembly line, to see how the part made in their workshop fitted into the finished aircraft. So new people were given a sense of belonging to the group as quickly as possible, and also allowed to see their work in context, so it didn't seem to be just a meaningless, repetitive activity.

Many work groups have an informal leader who might not have an official position but is, nonetheless, accepted as the best person to ask questions of or bring troubles to. These leaders emerge informally from the everyday interactions with their workmates, which means that someone who couldn't live up to the position wouldn't get into it in the first place. That's not the case, though, with people who have been appointed to formal leadership positions. So Mayo's observations also generated interest in what makes a leader effective.

Typically, the psychologists found that the supervisors with the most productive departments were more concerned with their employees than with production outcomes. They were also more confident in their own position as supervisors. Those who took the view that production was all-important were less effective than those who concentrated on keeping human relations smooth. After all, nobody works well if they have a supervisor breathing down their neck and pushing them to work harder.

All this led to what became known as the 'human relations' model of management. Psychologists had shown how human factors like attention and camaraderie are more powerful motivators than physical conditions or monetary gain. They showed how group norms and cohesiveness matter in working teams, and the importance of feeling part of the whole enterprise. It reflected a growing interest in the social side of psychology at work, which has continued to be a concern of social and organisational psychologists ever since.

CHAPTER 9

Testing Times
THE START OF THE PSYCHOMETRIC INDUSTRY AND APPROACHES TO PERSONALITY TESTING

Mud, cold, corpses and life-threatening explosions: the First World War was a traumatic experience for frontline troops, and 'shell shock' was rife. Soldiers became anxious and uncoordinated, behaved strangely and even had hallucinations and nightmares. Nowadays we understand this to be PTSD (post-traumatic stress disorder), but in those days, it wasn't really understood at all. Nonetheless, shell shock was common enough that by 1917 mental health among the troops was recognised as a serious problem.

So in 1917, as the United States was about to enter the war, the US military command gave psychologist Professor Robert Woodworth two weeks to find a way of identifying recruits who might become emotionally disturbed. Woodworth quickly compiled a set of questions, such as 'Do high places make you feel like jumping off?' or 'Have you ever walked in your sleep?' Not particularly subtle, this was probably the first personality test.

Even though Woodworth's 'personal data sheet' only dealt with neurotic symptoms, it established a way of measuring personality characteristics by asking people questions about themselves. Other psychologists continued to develop personality assessments that adopted the same pattern as Woodworth's test. People were asked direct questions that seemed intuitively to be relevant to their problems. Unlike in psychoanalytic tests, their answers were taken at face value – to be a true report of how they felt.

The problem, of course, is that what people say doesn't always match what they actually do. Several studies have shown this, but one of the most influential at this time was a widely publicised study by Hartshorne and May, in 1928, who compared children's stated attitudes towards stealing and honesty with how the same children behaved in a situation that allowed them to behave dishonestly without (they thought) anyone knowing. Their results showed inconsistency throughout: there was no connection between what the children said and what they did, and no consistency between one situation and another. The researchers, in accordance with the behaviourist perspective of the time, broadcast their conclusion that personality traits don't exist. Instead, they argued that people behave entirely according to the situation they are in, and this behaviour has nothing to do with any stable internal disposition.

Not so, thought Gordon Allport. People really are consistently different from one another, there really are personality traits, and, what's more, we can develop ways of identifying them. Together with his older brother Floyd, he began a series of studies in what became the dominant focus of his life's work. The brothers began by trying to develop a somewhat more objective test than the early questionnaires had been. Rather than asking people directly about their personalities, they asked how they would behave in particular situations. Their early paper identified a number of personality traits, such as extraversion/introversion, ascendance/submission and susceptibility to social stimuli, and assessed them using a variety of indirect methods. One question used to assess ascendance/submission, for example, was to ask how the individual (all males in their study) would respond to a patronising older person. Another test, used for evaluating susceptibility to social stimuli was to ask the person to identify the emotion in the facial expression of an actor. The brothers acknowledged that their measures were fairly basic, but their main interest was in exploring, firstly, the consistency of the various traits and, secondly, how they fitted together to make an image, or profile, of someone's personality.

At the same time, another type of personality test was being developed, this time from a psychoanalytical perspective. Like other European psychologists of the time, the psychoanalysts worked with ex-service people suffering from shell shock. Freud had two clinics, one in Berlin and later one in Vienna, which specialised in providing help for these people, and supporters of his theory developed a number of tests based on psychoanalytic approaches.

As we've seen, Freud's theory of human personality saw the human mind as being like an iceberg, most of it below the surface, unconscious, while still being the main influence on why people act as they do. Because the unconscious mind is, by definition, unconscious, people are not directly aware of it. It is only revealed indirectly, through symbols in dreams, slips of the tongue, or by the unconscious mind projecting its concerns or obsessions onto ambiguous or neutral stimuli.

Interpreting a stimulus like an ambiguous picture, it was argued, would allow the analyst to uncover the hidden parts of the mind. This was the idea behind the famous Rorschach test, in which the person is invited to interpret various inkblots. Hermann Rorschach published the first version of his test in 1921, drawing on a technique that was already in common use, and using inkblots he had selected – or possibly designed – himself, because they offered plenty of possibilities for interpretation. Based on psychoanalytic theory, the person's answers are taken as revealing their own underlying concerns and conflicts.

Another successful projective test, which, like the Rorschach, is still in occasional use today, was developed during the 1930s. This is the *Thematic Apperception Test*, which uses a series of pictures that are open to different interpretations. An image of a group of men lying beneath a tree, for example, might be interpreted in many ways, such as that the men were sleeping, drunk, resting, dead and so on. The person taking the test would be asked to describe what was happening in the picture, and their answers would be taken as indicative of their underlying conflicts or motivations.

While Allport was directly challenging the extreme behaviourists by insisting that personality is consistent and can be measured, he wasn't interested in digging deeply into the psyche in the way the psychoanalysts did either. As a young man, while visiting Europe he had sought a meeting with Freud in Vienna. During his visit, Allport, just twenty-two years old, was star struck and tongue tied, unable to find words to talk to the great man. Freud sat in absolute silence. Finally, Allport, casting desperately around for a way of making conversation, came out with an anecdote about a mother and young boy he had seen on the way there. Freud simply asked him, 'And was that young boy you?' – a response that confirmed Allport's growing belief that sometimes you need to look rather less deeply into motives, and simply take account of what is actually happening at the time: in this case, a social situation needing a conversation.

Gordon Allport's major concern was how personality traits affect the way that people act in particular situations. As he continued his research, he developed different methods for exploring personality traits. At one point, he and a colleague counted all the words in the dictionary (about 18,000) that described mental or psychological characteristics, and grouped them into four categories: traits, temporary states, metaphors and reactions to other people. When these last three categories were excluded, Allport was left with roughly forty-one different sets of words representing personality traits. There were more than 4,000 words making up those sets.

How to make sense of it all? He concluded that traits are organised hierarchically: there are higher-order or cardinal traits that represent the overarching characteristics of someone's personality, like ambition or honesty. But people would also have maybe five to ten central traits, which are more ordinary but could nonetheless be regarded as typical of that person, and a larger number of secondary traits, which depend on the situation they are in. This model, Allport believed, could explain why the actions of the children in the Hartshorne and May study were so different from their words: their actions arose from secondary traits, while their words described central traits.

Using his range of measures, Allport was able to develop personality profiles – diagrams that indicated how people scored on a series of comparable traits. But these were still largely descriptive. It took the work of another psychologist, Raymond Cattell, to establish personality testing as a truly 'scientific' endeavour.

In Chapter 6, we saw how intelligence testing began and became established, firstly through a wish to help those in need of special education, but later because of the firm beliefs in inherited intelligence and the eugenicist idea that stopping those who had inferior genes from breeding would directly benefit society. The combination of intelligence testing and the development of personality testing marked the beginning of what has become the massive psychometric industry: the development of instruments to measure psychological characteristics.

At the heart of that industry are two fundamental concepts. The first is the idea of the normal distribution – the bell-shaped curve that was almost inevitably produced no matter which physical characteristic Galton measured in his anthropometric laboratory back in 1883. Galton's assumption that normal distribution would apply to psychological characteristics as well as physical ones became accepted as dogma. Ever since, psychologists have designed psychometric tests of all kinds with the assumption that the particular mental characteristic under investigation will be normally distributed. Any new test which didn't produce that result would automatically be regarded as invalid.

The second concept arose from the development of the statistical technique known as 'factor analysis'. This explores correlations between different measures and how much they have in common. If two or more personality traits fit together well, the idea is that there is probably some underlying factor – in this case a higher-order trait – influencing both of them. Factor analysis was first developed in 1904 by Charles Spearman, who was mainly concerned with measuring intelligence, but it rapidly became applied to other mental characteristics.

Raymond Cattell was the prime mover in this. He began developing his model of personality by obtaining data from life records (like school grades or work absences), self-ratings and objective tests. From these, he developed a large range of questions and tested them on a large number of people. Factor analysis showed that the answers to these questions tended to cluster together, forming sixteen major groups. Each of these, Cattell believed, was a separate personality trait, and the result was Cattell's 'sixteen-factor theory of personality'.

Cattell's theory was the basis for a widely marketed test, the 16PF, and his sixteen factors also formed the basis of the later MMPI, or 'Minnesota Multiphasic Personality Inventory'. These tests were widely used by clinical, occupational and educational psychologists for many decades. They were only superseded towards the end of the twentieth century, when a more sophisticated factor analysis of the test elements in frequent use at the time indicated a different model of personality structure. That was the 'five-factor theory', by Costa and MacRae, which proposed that there are five underlying personality factors: extraversion, agreeableness, neuroticism, conscientiousness and openness to experience.

Cattell's wasn't the only personality model of the time which was based on factor analysis. During the 1940s, a British psychologist, Hans Eysenck, also used the factor analysis technique to explore how people acted in different situations – or at least, how they responded in questionnaires about their behaviour. Eysenck concluded that there were two main dimensions of personality: introversion/extraversion and stability/neuroticism, which were independent of one another. Interestingly, but not really coincidentally, these fitted with Galen's four 'humours', which we explored in Chapter 1. In Eysenck's model, a stable introvert would be phlegmatic, a neurotic introvert melancholic, a stable extravert sanguine while an unstable extravert would be choleric.

Eysenck's tests also included a 'lie scale', with questions like 'Have you ever been late for anything?' or 'Have you ever told a lie?' The questions were so extreme that they were taken to indicate that the person must be lying if they answered 'No', on the grounds that nobody is really that perfect. Later, he introduced a third personality dimension, normality/psychoticism, which he believed indicated how strongly people respond to conditioning, and how conscientious they are in following society's rules.

Factor analysis, then, made all the difference to personality testing, changing it from a collection of intuitive judgements to a more objective system dealing with both behaviour and self-reports. It became standard in psychological testing, showing how a series of tasks or questions could give a numerical score that indicated the strength of underlying factors. These tests fitted well with the quest for scientific objectivity, which dominated psychology at that time. They also allowed measures of personality to be integrated with other experiments, such as in the behavioural studies of social psychology, which we will look at later in this book.

CHAPTER 10

Understanding Social Life
ALLPORT AND WUNDT, THE FATHERS OF
SOCIAL PSYCHOLOGY

It's 1897, and two children are sitting at a strange apparatus. Stretching in front of each of them is a silk cord with a small flag attached to it. The cord loops around a wheel about two metres away and returns to the frame immediately in front of the child, where it loops around a fishing reel. By turning the reel's handle, the children can make the flag travel up to the far wheel, around it, and back again to complete the circuit.

At the signal, each child starts turning the handle to make the flag move as fast as they can. The experimenter carefully measures the time it takes for each child's flag to complete four circuits. Sometimes, there is just one child at the apparatus; sometimes, as now, there are two. On looking at the results, it seems to the experimenter that the children work harder when there are two of them than when they are on their own. He concludes that the presence of the other child facilitates the children's performance.

This study, reported by Norman Triplett in 1898, has been widely cited as the first social psychology experiment – although, in fact, there had been several studies of social processes carried out before this, mainly in Europe. We'll come back to that idea later in this book. Twenty-six years later, Floyd Allport, brother of Gordon, published a textbook called *Social Psychology*, which brought together the relevant psychological knowledge of the time. Floyd himself conducted research into many different aspects of social psychology, including social influence, conformity and attitude measurement, as well as the work on personality that he had carried out with his brother. And it was Floyd who claimed that Triplett's study was the first social psychology experiment – a claim that has been replicated in social psychology textbooks ever since.

Social Psychology was distinctive mainly because of the way that it brought social psychology into line with other areas of experimental psychology. In the book, Allport claimed that social psychology should not deal with concepts that were 'woolly' and insubstantial, like culture or society. Rather, he argued, social psychology could and should be part of the objective and increasingly behavioural science of psychology.

Allport's book was to have a profound and lasting impact on American psychology. As well as describing existing social psychological studies, he applied his individualistic perspective across psychology, interpreting needs, emotions, attitudes and even culture in terms of the psychology of the individual. He also argued strongly that psychoanalysis could be entirely explained in terms of individual behaviour and learning, and that it had nothing to do with any 'unconscious' mental processes. In a later book, Allport applied the same views to explain institutions like organised religion, politics and institutions. His emphasis on psychology as being purely concerned with the individual's behaviour ruled out broader forms of analysis and introduced a growing rift between psychologists, sociologists and anthropologists.

His dismissal of psychoanalytic concepts was also a major factor in a developing rift between the psychoanalytic school and mainstream psychology. What was becoming apparent was that there were fundamental differences in what counted as acceptable data. For the psychoanalysts, accounts from patients and indirect inferences from dream symbolism, errors of speech, and even avoidance of particular topics, all counted as evidence for the unconscious mind. But in the increasingly materialistic mainstream of experimental psychology, that was anecdotal and unscientific. While not everyone working in experimental psychology would describe themselves as a behaviourist, the influence of the behaviourist quest for objectivity was beginning to permeate American experimentalism.

Throughout his books, Allport called for stricter research designs and clearer definitions of what was actually being investigated. His integration of accepted psychological knowledge and ongoing research led him to propose a set of concepts for research into social psychology, showing how things like attitudes, the presence of others, habits and reflexes, and even social conformity could all lend themselves to objective or behavioural experimentation. His book *Social Psychology* was so influential that he came to be known known as the father of experimental social psychology, and it became the blueprint for social psychology, at least in America, for the next sixty years.

Allport's form of social psychology was distinctively American, in that it focused entirely on the individual and interpreted the wider influences of communities and societies as just the result of individual psychological processes. For Allport, higher-order concepts such as culture, society or religion were only suitable for the discipline of psychology if they were explained in individual terms, as he had done in his book about institutional behaviour. Otherwise, psychologists shouldn't be studying them because that research wasn't 'scientific' enough.

A very different tradition had emerged in Europe. Psychoanalytic psychology was European in its genesis, and European psychology remained largely untouched by American behaviourism. Psychoanalysis remained an influential part of psychology at this time, for European psychologists who were continuing to interpret social interactions and understandings in terms of the influence exerted by the unconscious mind. Even in Europe, though, psychoanalysis didn't go unchallenged: another form of social psychology was also central to European psychology at this time, largely through the influence of Wilhelm Wundt.

As we saw in Chapter 4, Wundt is commonly acknowledged as one of the founding fathers of experimental psychology, but his contribution to social psychology was largely ignored in both the US and the UK. His laboratory in Leipzig had established experimental standards and procedures that were hugely influential in psychology's development, even in America. But as we have seen, he also devoted much of his time to the study of social psychology, and his substantive *Völkerpsychologie* explored the psychological processes underpinning everyday social interaction.

Although Wundt had a firm belief in the value of experimental psychology, he also believed that it could never be sufficient on its own. It could only deal with some aspects of the human mind and would always have to be supplemented by other psychological studies, which could investigate the social aspects of human mental processes. To do that, social psychologists would need to deal with wider aspects of social living. Wundt, unlike Allport, firmly believed that social psychology couldn't be explained fully by how individual people interact. He argued that a realistic study of psychology would have to include how people are also shaped by wider aspects of everyday life, like customs and culture, language, mythology and art, and religion. But he insisted that these aspects of psychology must be explored with the same scientific rigour that was devoted to laboratory-based experimental work.

Wundt's *Völkerpsychologie* was published in ten volumes between 1900 and 1920, with its fourth edition being published in 1926. It dealt with language, art, myths and religion, society, law, culture and history. He didn't just cover these topics themselves, explaining their relevance in social psychology, but he discussed in detail how researchers should go about studying them. In some areas of social psychology, experimentation was possible, while in others it wasn't, but Wundt insisted that rigorous qualitative approaches could supply the objective data that a science of psychology would also need.

Völkerpsychologie had a profound influence across the social sciences, being widely accepted in Europe as a fundamental publication for sociology and anthropology, as well as social psychology. Wundt encouraged a number of his students and followers to take up social psychology in their research, and was a significant influence on Émile Durkheim, the founding father of sociology. But in America the work didn't take hold at all. One reason was that only two of the ten volumes were translated into English, so the whole theory didn't become widely known. Another was the way that Wundt himself was so prolific and covered so much scope in his psychological research that his students, who often became eminent psychologists themselves, tended only to discuss those aspects of his research that they felt were congruent with their own perspectives.

One of his students was Edward Titchener. Titchener went on to set up a department of psychology at Cornell. He helped to establish the scientific status of psychology in America, being firmly committed to the importance of experimentation in the analysis of the human mind. He was a major proponent of Wundt's ideas in the US, although he was rather dismissive of *Völkerpsychologie* because, unlike Wundt, he didn't see rigorous analytic introspection as an appropriate research method.

Titchener's main interest was in analysing the components and structure of mental experience. Again, his ideas differed from those of Wundt, who had argued that mental activity tends to be goal-directed and purposeful, so it is necessary to understand people's goals in order to understand their mental activity. Titchener, though, believed that understanding the structural components of the mind would be enough for a complete explanation. This structuralist view would eventually lead to a head-on confrontation with the functionalist perspective being proposed by William James at the same time, and, as the structuralist perspective lost influence, many of Wundt's ideas died out too.

Wundt always saw his *Völkerpsychologie* as working alongside and in conjunction with experimental psychology. But a series of misrepresentations and mistranslations of his work led to that relationship becoming distorted. One significant mistranslation, for example, led to the term '*Völkerpsychologie*' being rendered as 'cultural psychology' rather than as 'social psychology'. That attracted Floyd Allport's condemnation, as he argued that culture was more the province of anthropology or sociology and was not relevant to social psychology, which should always be the study of individual people.

Another of Allport's criticisms was that *Völkerpsychologie* was advocating a woolly and unscientific form of research. This too was a misrepresentation of what Wundt had actually said. Wundt had certainly argued that qualitative approaches were more appropriate for exploring the historical issues of social life, because sometimes looking for measurement wasn't relevant, and stories, histories and other meaningful accounts were more useful. But he was far from dismissing the experimental method in social psychology itself. What he argued was that experimentation in an artificial laboratory context was sometimes inappropriate, not the actual process of conducting experiments. And he always insisted that the same careful rigour should be applied to research into social processes as psychologists used in other types of psychological research.

In Europe, Wundt's influence never waned, giving rise to a range of perspectives in social psychology, including those of the Gestalt psychologists, which we will explore in the next chapter. But his support of German nationalism and the hostilities of the First World War meant that many in the US and UK came to regard his work with suspicion. This, together with the hostility of Allport, the misrepresentations of his work by Titchener, the problem of direct access to the work itself, and its incompatibility with behaviourism, meant that *Völkerpsychologie* was largely unknown in the English-speaking world. Wundt remained known as the father of experimental psychology, but his contribution to social psychology remained predominantly in Europe. That rift between European and American social psychology was underplayed, and many psychologists were entirely unaware of it, but it never really healed, as we will see later in this book.

CHAPTER 11

The Gestalt School
Seeing the Whole as Different from the Sum of its Parts

Sultan the chimpanzee sits morosely in his cage. Scattered here and there are various boxes, and above him hangs a banana, suspended from the wire ceiling. But Sultan can't reach the banana. He tries jumping up and down, but it's completely out of reach. He's tried dragging one of the boxes underneath it and standing on that, but even jumping from a box doesn't get him the banana. After several failures, he rages around his enclosure, jumping, screeching and throwing things about. Finally, he gives up and sits on a box, slumped over and looking depressed. Then, suddenly, he springs into action. He jumps up and begins to arrange the boxes one on top of another. He climbs on top of the pile and eureka! The banana is his.

Sultan's achievements, along with examples from several other apes, were published in *The Mentality of Apes*, written by Wolfgang Köhler in 1917. Köhler had taken the post of director of the Prussian Academy of Sciences Anthropoid Research Centre in the Canary Islands in 1913, and owing to the outbreak of war had to remain there for the next six years. He became particularly interested in how the apes used insight to solve problems, and he conducted a range of experiments to investigate it, giving them challenging tasks and observing them as they solved them.

In 1920, Köhler moved back to Germany, where he continued to work with two other colleagues, Max Wertheimer and Kurt Koffka. Together, the three formed a small group of highly influential psychologists whose ideas went on to dominate German psychology in the 1930s, and formed a powerful challenge to behaviourism. They became known as the founders of the Gestalt school of psychology.

The three psychologists had come together as a result of Wertheimer's interest in vision and movement. The story goes that in 1910 Wertheimer was on a train, watching the apparent movement of distant objects through the window, and thinking about other illusions of movement, like the zoetrope – a popular toy that gives the illusion of movement as images pass a series of viewing slits. Suddenly, he realised that perception isn't about the physical processing of the image in the retina, which was the dominant explanation of the time, but about how the mind interprets the information it is receiving. He was so excited by this insight that he abandoned his proposed holiday and got off the train at Frankfurt to consult with an eminent professor of psychology, Friedrich Schumann.

Schumann encouraged Wertheimer to follow up his ideas and assigned two research assistants, Koffka and Köhler, to help him. Through their experiments, the trio gradually formulated a theory of how the mind works that ran directly against the dominant beliefs of the time. Psychologists at the time tended to see mental experience as built up by combining small units of sensation: vision, sound and so on. The idea of the whole 'mind' had gone out of fashion, but Wertheimer, Koffka and Köhler challenged that. They argued that mental processes like cognition begin with a general idea, or 'Gestalt', and that it is the overall picture from this Gestalt that lets the brain make sense of sensory impressions.

Wertheimer's own studies were concerned with how we see movement. He described the 'phi phenomenon': the way that a sequence of lights flashing on and off can give the impression of movement. It's familiar to all of us nowadays as the basis of illuminated advertising signs and festive light displays. But Wertheimer's point was that the movement isn't actually there. It's added by the brain, creating an entirely new experience that is quite different from the physical information that is being received. In earlier times, Wertheimer had studied with the philosopher von Ehrenfels, who also believed that conscious experience is more than just combined sensory impressions. Ehrenfels would give the example of a musical tune. A tune can be entirely transposed into a different key, so every note is different, yet we still hear the same tune. Seeing experience as just a collection of responses to specific sensory stimuli can't explain that.

Wertheimer and Koffka went on to explore the many ways that the brain interprets sensory information. They identified a number of organising principles, which we now know as the Gestalt laws of perception, like the way we automatically see figures against backgrounds. If that background also represents a different figure, focusing on one makes the other one disappear; we can only see one at a time. M.C. Escher, the artist, was a close friend of the Gestalt psychologists and applied many of their ideas in his art: we can see the 'figure-ground principle' in his famous artwork 'Angels and Demons' as well as in several other pictures.

There are other Gestalt principles of perception, such as how we infer 'missing' figures from a suggested outline, or the way we automatically use proximity and similarity to group shapes or objects together. These discoveries received widespread publicity and are still taught in psychology courses today. At the time, they were particularly popular because they could satisfy society's ongoing curiosity about visual images. Many common nineteenth-century toys generated visual illusions, and 'moving pictures', or cinematography, had already become a major industry.

The influence of the Gestalt psychologists covered more than perception, though. For Köhler, their challenge to behaviourism was powerful and uncompromising. He was well aware of the idea that psychologists should only study behaviour, since only behaviour can be directly observed, and the behaviourists' insistence that behavioural change only happens through learned stimulus-response (S-R) connections. Köhler disagreed profoundly with both of those ideas. Neither human nor animal psychology, he argued, comes from a collection of elemental 'bits'. Psychology is about whole experiences, most of which just can't be explained as combinations of their constituent parts.

What the Gestalt psychologists were really objecting to was what we now call 'reductionism' – the idea that breaking experience down into its component parts will be enough to explain it. Not so, argued the Gestalt psychologists: there is much more to experience than this, and some things simply can't be reduced into sensations or S-R links. In any case, they argued, combining different elements often produces something entirely new. Essentially, what they were saying was that the whole is different from the sum of its parts – and the key words here are 'different from'. Misquoting the phrase as 'the whole is more than the sum of its parts' seriously annoyed Köhler because he felt that it completely missed the point. 'More than' gives the impression of a quantitative difference, about size or amount, whereas what they were saying was that it was entirely different. Combining the parts could produce something completely new, not just more or less of something else.

Köhler also challenged the behaviourists' strict focus on observable behaviour. Sultan's insights, and those of the other apes in the group, were very different from the pedestrian trial-and-error processes which were assumed by the behaviourists to produce all learning. Rather, the ape had given evidence of suddenly realising a solution to his banana problem, through unobservable mental activity. And it wasn't only Sultan. Köhler's extensive observations showed that insight was typical of how apes generally solved problems, not just the special achievement of one clever individual.

Other Gestalt psychologists had different areas of interest. Kurt Koffka, for instance, was particularly interested in developmental psychology, focusing on how the small child's mind develops. At the time, J.B. Watson was publicly insisting that children gradually build up their knowledge of the world through conditioning – that is, trial-and-error learning. Those on the nativist side, on the other hand, thought the mind emerged through genetic maturation and regardless of experience. Koffka challenged both these ideas, arguing that the child starts with an overall impression of its environment, and only gradually distinguishes its component elements. Moreover, unlike the behaviourists, Koffka saw imitation as essential in the child's cognitive development. His ideas helped to shape both psychoanalytic theory and the later work of Jean Piaget.

Together, these three German scientists brought together several different areas of psychological research. At the time, relationships across the developing world of psychology were close, particularly between Europe and America. Wertheimer was an ideas man. He was happy to talk about his theories and did several lecture tours; but he didn't like writing and, although he conducted extensive research, produced very few academic papers. But Koffka and Köhler made up for that. Through journals, lectures and later books, they developed and promoted their new Gestalt psychology. Köhler founded a new journal on psychological research and later produced an English-language textbook, *Gestalt Psychology*, in 1929, written particularly for the American market. Kurt Koffka had preceded this with their first English-language article, 'Perception: An Introduction to the Gestalt-Theorie', which was published in 1922, and all three lectured widely as their theory matured. As a result of their efforts, Gestalt psychology became highly influential, both in Germany and also in the English-speaking world.

In the early 1930s, the growing restrictions in German universities made academic life increasingly difficult, particularly for Jewish intellectuals. Wertheimer was Jewish, and Koffka half Jewish, and by the early 1930s it had become apparent that they would not be able to continue their academic work in Germany. Köhler wasn't Jewish, but he was an outspoken critic of the Nazi regime and openly refused to obey many of its edicts, like the instruction that every lecture must begin with the Hitler salute. Eventually, continued harassment by the authorities meant that he too was forced to leave Germany. Like the others, he moved to America for the duration of the war, but although he maintained his principal residence in the US, he kept up strong links with Germany, and frequently lectured at the Free University of Berlin after the war.

In America, their work continued. There is an impressive list of highly influential American psychologists, including Ulric Neisser, Solomon Asch and Leon Festinger, who studied with one or other of the Gestalt psychologists after the war. Although Gestalt psychology never became dominant, it was widely known and discussed, and its influence permeated psychological ideas for many decades. One of their students from Germany, Kurt Lewin, became known as a founder of social psychology. His interest was in social and organisational psychology, and in particular how people's experience takes place in a 'life space' that is unique to every individual.

Lewin had little time for the nature/nurture debate of the time, which argued that development must be either nature – that is, innate – or nurture – that is, learned. Instead, he anticipated modern thinking by seeing human development as the interaction between innate predispositions and life experiences. In common with the fashions of the day, he described this in a mathematical formula: $B = f(P,E)$ – that is, Behaviour (B) is a function of both Personality (P) and Environment (E). Lewin's field theory, as it was known, argued that we live our lives within a psychological field which develops and becomes more sophisticated as we age and gather more and wider experiences.

Although Lewin respected the need for experimental work, he also believed that studying human beings in the laboratory only produced artificial, limited results. Instead, he promoted action research, which offered the possibility of actually analysing human experiences in their own contexts – or life spaces. Action research, Lewin felt, worked in a repetitive cycle, beginning with a diagnostic stage when the psychologist examined and evaluated the situation, moving on to planning a change strategy, implementing those changes, and then re-evaluating the result to diagnose whether another set of changes would be appropriate. This idea, largely disregarded at the time, has now become widely used in modern organisational psychology. It is typical of the kind of subtle influence exerted by the Gestalt school on psychology's development. Developments like the humanist movement and the revolution in research methods towards the end of the twentieth century both had their origins in the ideas and research of the Gestalt psychologists.

CHAPTER 12

Two Post-Freudians

CARL JUNG AND THE COLLECTIVE UNCONSCIOUS AND ADLER'S INDIVIDUAL PSYCHOLOGY

The young man watched, entranced, as Daniel Dunglas Home rose from the ground, and hovered in the air. Home, the well-known medium, was famous for conducting seances in which tables were turned, mysterious tappings were felt and heard, and Home himself repeatedly demonstrated his power of levitation. For Carl Gustav Jung, this was definite evidence of the existence of the spirit world, confirming his belief in the paranormal.

That belief wasn't new: Jung's mother had been a medium, and his maternal grandfather had a firm belief in the spirit world. Jung himself had trained as a doctor, and had become interested in psychiatry, but he always retained an interest in those aspects of human experience that seemed inexplicable in material terms. His research was based on using word association with psychotic patients, and, from this, he became convinced that sometimes their delusions were not entirely fictional. Instead, they were tapping into a level of awareness that didn't exactly correspond with the material world. Their actions and responses seemed to reflect occult phenomena, and the data he gathered from this work served to strengthen his interest in parapsychology.

Jung is perhaps the most important of the post-Freudians. He first met Freud in 1907, having long been familiar with his work. The two got on like a house on fire, and for some time Freud regarded Jung as his heir-apparent – even nominating him to be lifetime president of the new International Psychoanalytical Association in 1910 (although the members only agreed to a two-year term). However, their friendship only lasted for a couple more years. By 1914, theoretical and personal disagreements had completely soured their interactions, and Jung and his followers finally made their formal separation from the Vienna school. Freud, a much older man, maintained a vitriolic hatred for Jung throughout the rest of his life and belittled his work at every opportunity. Jung was distressed by the break, and for three years suffered periods of depression, although later he described that period as having been one of the most creative times of his life in terms of developing his theory.

The core of the disagreement had to do with what Jung described as Freud's 'pansexualism' – the idea that everything, including dreams and behaviour, could be interpreted in sexual terms. Freud saw libido – the life-force that energises behaviour – as entirely sexual in origin, only becoming sublimated into other energies through life experience and often trauma. Jung disagreed: he saw the libido as a creative life-force that has other origins as well, including the spiritual and creative needs of the person. Although he agreed that sexual energies play a part, they are by no means the whole story. For Jung, dreams and unconscious actions can reflect spiritual and non-physical themes as well as sexual ones.

There were other sources of disagreement between them too. Freud was a committed materialist, who believed that his theory was firmly based in neurology. He warned Jung that his interest in the paranormal could ruin his reputation as a scientist. Jung responded that he was gathering important data about the human psyche, but that he was also maintaining a healthy scepticism while doing so. As it progressed, Jung's research led him to the belief that there is another layer to the unconscious mind – one that is shared by all human beings, and which he called the 'collective unconscious'. His model of the mind, therefore, was totally different from Freud's. Where Freud had made the tripartite distinction of the unconscious as id, ego and superego, Jung saw the ego as part of the conscious mind, underpinned by a layer of personal unconscious, based on the person's experience, but with a deeper layer of the collective unconscious underneath. Both models view each individual person's mind as being like an iceberg, but for Freud the conscious mind was above the surface while the id, ego and superego were below, like the four-fifths of the iceberg hidden under water, while in Jung's model, the conscious mind is the bit showing on the surface, while the personal unconscious is the part of the iceberg under water, but it is all floating in the sea of the collective unconscious shared by all human beings.

This collective unconscious, Jung believed, contains a number of powerful symbols, known as archetypes, which recur consistently in myths and legends. He believed that they represent universal patterns or images, which explains why they feel particularly meaningful to us when they appear in literature or art. Jung described many different archetypes: the earth mother, the all-powerful father, life and rebirth, the trickster, the creator, the wizard, and so on. The reason that these archetypes resonate so strongly with us when we encounter them, Jung argued, is because of what he called 'synchronicity' – that direct link with the collective unconscious. The psychological power of these archetypes, and their frequent recurrence in the folklore, myths and literature of different cultures (Jung believed that they occurred in all human cultures), was evidence for Jung that they were more than just the product of the individual's experience, as Freud would have argued.

One of the most important archetypes is the persona – the way that we present ourselves to others. Jung saw it as a kind of mask which manages the impressions we want to give and hides other aspects of ourselves. For example, Jung believed that male and female identity comes from socialisation. He argued that we all have both genders as aspects of our personality, but the persona masks the animus (masculine side) in women, and the anima (feminine side) in men.

The persona also has an opposite: the shadow, which can be either positive or negative. In someone with low self-belief, the shadow may be the confident self, buried in their psyche; in someone who maintains a persona of calm and balance, the shadow may be turbulent and angry. For Jung, everyone has a shadow, and the more it is suppressed and buried in the unconscious, the darker it will be. He argued that knowing and acknowledging your own shadow is an important factor in therapy and for the therapist too, as it helps them to understand other people. He saw knowing your own shadow, rather than suppressing or stifling it, as necessary for psychological growth.

Jung also developed the now-familiar concepts of introversion and extraversion. Like other aspects of personality in his model, he believed that we all have both: that those of us who are extraverts in terms of our outward persona also have an introvert self inside, while introverts have an extravert shadow self. The idea of introvert and extravert as styles of behaviour was taken up in personality measurement, although, for the most part, the idea of people having the balanced internal opposite remained confined to Jungian theory.

Jung's theory, while generally peripheral in mainstream psychology, nonetheless found a wide following. It was able to deal explicitly with the spiritual side of life, and as such it made a tremendous impact in the literary and artistic world. Because it encompassed religious belief and even made sense of some of the more unusual human experiences, like those studied nowadays by parapsychologists, it filled a knowledge gap in psychology. This was the same gap that Wundt had tried to fill with his *Völkerpsychologie*, but the nature of Jung's evidence was so different from mainstream psychology that his analytical psychology – sometimes referred to as a strand of 'depth psychology' – became a separate, although thriving, branch of psychoanalysis. But it was barely acknowledged by the mainstream psychological profession, partly because of the rejection of experimentalism.

Jung wasn't the only psychoanalyst to disagree with Freud, who was notoriously intolerant of those with different opinions. Alfred Adler was a colleague of Freud's rather than a pupil, and for a while the two were able to get along despite some open arguments. Adler was an experienced doctor, who was attracted by Freud's ideas and eventually became acknowledged as one of the co-founders of the Vienna school. But he disagreed openly with Freud on many counts. Initially, they argued about the nature of aggression, which Adler regarded as a separate drive from sexuality. Later arguments arose because Adler came to regard the external part of human experience – that is, the social realm – as being just as important in issues of mental health and wellbeing as the internal realm of conflicts and complexes. Freud, as we have seen, regarded the internal realm, and in particular the sexual dimension, as the source of all psychological problems.

By 1911, it had become evident that the two approaches were so very different that they could not be reconciled. Along with several supporters, Adler separated formally from Freud's Vienna school to found a new approach. He called it 'individual psychology' because he was concerned with the person as a whole, as being fully connected with the world around them, rather than just looking at the person in terms of a collection of unconscious conflicts and neuroses.

One of the central ideas in Adler's theory was compensation. As a small child he had suffered rickets, which caused him difficulty in walking, and as a clinician he had worked with circus performers, and particularly noticed how they adjusted to physical weaknesses. During his discussions with Freud and others in the psychoanalytic circle, Adler's interest in compensation for physical defects broadened to include how people compensate for psychological weaknesses too. This led him to the idea that the motivations underlying people's behaviour often serve to overcome or compensate for feelings of inferiority.

Adler is famous for the idea of the inferiority complex – that someone may have developed a sense of personal inferiority in their early years and be attempting to compensate for it effectively in other ways. He himself had experienced a fierce rivalry with his older brother, and analysis with his clients convinced him that such early interactions with family members often helped to shape a person's sense of inferiority or superiority in their future lives. Moreover, he believed, the position a child held within the family – whether they were firstborn, the second or the youngest child – generated very different experiences, and these could create different problems.

Oldest children, for example, tend to have a lot of attention from their parents right up until the second child is born, but at that point everything changes. This can generate feelings of what Adler called 'dethronement': from being the centre of everything, they now had to take second place. Moreover, they often then had to be responsible for their younger siblings, putting even more pressure on them. For Adler, this explained why oldest children were particularly vulnerable to neuroses or addiction in later life. The youngest child, by contrast, was often overindulged, which led to them failing to develop a full sense of empathy and social responsibility. Middle children, being neither dethroned nor overindulged, were more likely to develop their potential and be successful, but could also feel left out and become rebellious.

Adler believed that compensation was a natural and healthy response to feelings of inferiority. The role of the analyst was to help the client identify those feelings so they could develop positive compensatory strategies. He was the first of the analysts to abandon the couch and simply use two chairs for his consultations, as a symbolic statement of the equal relationship between therapist and client. That was part of his recognition of social contexts. Adler felt that understanding someone's social interactions, and whether they experience themselves as belonging to a community, was essential for effective therapy. In that sense, Adler has been called the first 'community psychologist', anticipating developments that would only become fully part of mainstream psychology in the following century.

Alfred Adler's impact on psychology has rarely been fully recognised. His work has influenced many different fields, ranging from classroom practices to parenting styles and leadership in organisations, and his theoretical approach had an enormous effect on the developing disciplines of counselling and psychotherapy. Two of the greatest names in those fields, Albert Ellis and Aaron Beck, both acknowledged him as having established the theoretical foundations leading to their own work in developing cognitive therapy and rational-emotive behaviour therapy; and his work was also a strong influence on Abraham Maslow, one of the founders of humanistic psychology. We will come back to these ideas later in this book. In the meantime, though, a very different type of psychology was gaining influence, particularly in America.

CHAPTER 13

Behaviourism Takes Hold
Little Albert, Operant Conditioning and
Skinner's Brave New World

Eleven-month-old little Albert sat peacefully on his mattress. He reached out to stroke the tame white rat he had played with before. Albert really liked the rat. But just as his hand touched it, a loud noise sounded out just behind him, as an iron bar was struck with a hammer. Albert jumped violently and fell forward. When he picked himself up and reached out to touch the rat again, the sound happened again. He fell over and began to whimper.

A week later, the white rat appeared again. Albert watched it steadily but didn't reach for it. It came closer and nosed at his hand, but Albert snatched it back. Then he tentatively reached his finger towards the rat. As he made contact the nasty sound came again, and Albert fell over. This happened several more times, until eventually when Albert saw the rat he began to cry and crawl away.

Albert (real name Douglas Merritte) had been a stolid, unemotional baby, not known to cry at anything, so the researchers congratulated themselves on having achieved this emotional reaction. It was, said J.B. Watson and Rosalie Rayner in their report, a completely conditioned fear response. Five days later, the response was still there, and Albert even generalised it to a white rabbit and a fur coat. Further experiments showed that he had become frightened of even more things, even including a Santa Claus mask with a beard. Albert had developed a phobia. They continued their experiments until he was one year and twenty-one days old, at which point his mother removed him from the hospital.

The researchers prided themselves on having shown not only that unpleasant experiences could induce fear in babies, but also that those fears could generalise into a full-blown phobia. Before the experiment, Albert had been a calm, phlegmatic child, almost never crying and rarely startled. Now, he was clearly phobic about white rats, and his fear generalised to anything he saw that was white and furry. Watson and Rayner were jubilant. It was one in the eye for the Freudians, they argued, who would probably want to attribute his phobia to some dream or unconscious conflict, when he was adult. History doesn't tell what Albert's mother thought, although it is suspected to have been unprintable.

Watson and Rayner's study was published in 1920, by which time the behaviourist ideas originally proposed by Watson in 1913 had become well known across psychology; although, of course, not everyone agreed with them. What this study did, though, was open up an area of psychology that had previously been confined to Freud and other psychoanalysts. Rather than explaining mental disturbance in terms of psychosocial conflicts, Watson showed that it could also come from stimulus-response (S-R) learning. It opened up a heated debate between the psychoanalysts and the behaviourists about the origin of neuroses and phobias, which raged throughout the 1930s and 1940s.

As behaviourists adopted the new approach, conditioning principles were applied to a number of different disorders. One of the first therapies to be established using conditioning principles was aversion therapy. The idea was that people could learn to avoid certain things or types of behaviour by pairing them with an unpleasant stimulus – like Albert and the rat – and this would help people with anti-social compulsions or undesirable behaviour traits to overcome them.

Aversion therapy was used in a range of contexts, including attempts to 'cure' homosexuality by giving gay men electric shocks if they showed the least arousal when they saw images of attractive men. There were also approaches to dealing with alcoholism through aversion therapy, such as using the drug Antabuse, which generates sickness and vomiting if someone taking it consumes any alcohol. The idea was that drinking alcohol would come to be associated with nausea through conditioning, dissuading the alcoholic from drinking. (It doesn't seem to work with teenagers, though!)

Another technique used learning principles to cure phobias rather than create them. Systematic desensitisation, for example, aimed to replace the behavioural response of fear with an incompatible reaction, like relaxation. Obviously, this couldn't happen instantly: it was a gradual process, in which the person was first exposed to the mildest possible version of the stimulus and learned to relax in its presence. If you had a fear of spiders, for example, it might just be a picture of a spider's web. Once that had been successfully learned, a slightly stronger version of the feared object or situation became the stimulus, and again the person would do relaxation exercises until they could relax in its presence. Step by step, the stimulus would become more like the real thing, until the person could face the object of their phobia and be able to relax and control their fear.

Other forms of behaviour therapy were developed and proved no less successful than the psychoanalytic methods. All approaches worked with some people, but none worked with everyone. Advocates of each method claimed their successes and argued their case: the psychoanalysts accused the behaviourists of only treating the surface symptoms and not the underlying causes, while the behaviourists said that the whole point was that it was only the surface symptoms that really mattered, and changing people's behaviour really was dealing with their problem. In the clinical world, however, behaviour therapy, being relatively quick, was demonstrably cheaper than psychoanalysis, which tended to take months, or even years. So, it became firmly entrenched as an alternative approach to dealing with some forms of mental disturbance.

In the wider world, too, behaviourism's influence was growing, largely due to the influence of B.F. Skinner, considered to be the third of its three founding fathers. Skinner clarified a number of the underlying principles of learning theory, bringing together Pavlov's work on conditioned reflexes and Thorndike's work on the Law of Effect. There were two kinds of behaviour, Skinner argued: respondents, which are reactions to stimuli like the reflexes Pavlov studied; and operants, which are actions that animals (or people) just do spontaneously, like the actions of the cats in Thorndike's puzzle boxes, described in Chapter 7. Respondents could be conditioned by repetition, but operants would be conditioned by rewards or consequences.

Skinner became the acknowledged authority on operant conditioning. He conducted exhaustive research into its various aspects, looking at how behaviour could be reinforced (strengthened) either positively, by giving a reward, or negatively, by allowing escape from an unpleasant situation, or avoidance of it. He spoke out strongly against punishment as a means of controlling behaviour, on the grounds that it could only suppress the wrong actions, but didn't encourage positive behaviour. There was nothing to stop the punished person doing something else equally wrong. Instead, Skinner argued, educationalists and correction officers should shape behaviour by judicious use of rewards and incentives.

In the classroom, he argued, pupils would learn more by getting things right than by getting them wrong, so learning experiences should be organised to maximise rewards and a sense of achievement. Since learning derives from S-R links, Skinner believed, teaching machines could be just as effective as human teachers, if they were carefully programmed to lead the student from simple facts to complex knowledge. These ideas also fitted with Allport's emphasis on the individual in social psychology and received widespread publicity. Several teaching experiments were tried along these lines, with varying degrees of success.

Skinner's main message was all about rewards. He showed how different schedules of reward could produce different effects, and how complex forms of behaviour could be learned a little bit at a time, through what he called 'behaviour shaping'. He would begin with operants that were vaguely similar to the eventual goal, and train those through reward until they appeared reliably. From there, he would only reward actions that were even closer, until eventually very complex behaviour had been trained. The story goes that, while giving a lecture, he would train a pair of pigeons to play a modified form of ping pong, on the desk in front of him, using those techniques to shape their behaviour.

Skinner, as you might guess, was a utopian: he firmly believed that society would be improved by social engineering through the application of conditioning principles. He wrote a novel, *Walden Two*, in which he portrayed a society run along those lines, and in 1972 he published *Beyond Freedom and Dignity*, in which he argued that both freedom and dignity are mythical concepts anyway, so society would be better off if it recognised that and got on with encouraging people to act as responsible citizens through the widespread use of benign conditioning techniques. Not surprisingly, this generated an even more heated debate than the psychoanalysis/behaviour therapy one.

The major spokesperson for the other side was the linguist Noam Chomsky. What had really riled Chomsky was the book Skinner published in 1957, *Verbal Behavior*. In this, he argued that the reason children acquire language is because it is carefully (though unconsciously) shaped by their interactions with other people. An infant babbles, making all sorts of sounds, and parents respond most positively when they make sounds that are like words in their particular language. This encourages the child to produce more of those sounds, which sometimes form actual words or noises that are close to them. The positive reactions from those around the infant reinforce that behaviour, encouraging the child to repeat it. So the child learns words, and gradually learns to use its words appropriately, according to the grammatical rules of its own culture.

Chomsky, the linguist, objected to this idea. Human beings, he argued, have an innate ability to acquire language. It's not just trial and error; they are born with an inbuilt 'language acquisition device', which renders them particularly able to pick up the relevant words for their culture. More, he argued that the language acquisition device sensitises them to the rules of grammar as well as to meaningful words. There are innate grammatical structures in every language: he called that the deep structure, exemplified by the simple grammar of the young child – 'Daddy ball' or 'Allgone milk'. This, for Chomsky, was universal and formed an inborn basis for the surface structure – the more complex grammatical rules of their particular language.

This debate between Chomsky and Skinner was one example of what became known as the nature/nurture debate. On the nature side were those who claimed that what people did and how they learned were governed by innate tendencies – in other words, that these tendencies were inherited, and that this was the most important aspect of human development. We came across the strong belief that intelligence is inherited in Chapter 6. But the debate didn't only apply in that area. It had, for example, been a dominant concept in child psychology, with famous psychologists such as Arnold Gesell advocating that mothers should give up any idea that they could influence their child's development; rather, their role was simply to provide a nurturing environment in which their child's innate abilities could develop. The idea that innate factors determined development remained popular and dominated some social policies right through to the 1960s.

On the nurture side of the debate were those who believed learning was more important than inherited abilities. J.B. Watson, of course, was one of them; but Skinner had taken up that torch and now ran with it, challenging the hereditarians on pretty well all counts. He openly and consistently argued that even complex and abstract behaviours could be explained using conditioning principles. For many who believed in progress through science, these ideas offered a degree of optimism. Perhaps human beings could change after all, and maybe wars were not inevitable.

Heated debates between the two sides continued for many decades. But there were always psychologists in between those extremes, calling for moderation in their own ways. We'll come back to this issue again in Chapter 36, when we look at how the nature/nurture debate on intelligence continued in the second half of the twentieth century.

CHAPTER 14

The Developing Mind
PIAGET, GESELL AND VYGOTSKY'S PERSPECTIVES
ON CHILD-REARING

'Your child's development depends on the training you provide.'
'Children develop as their nature determines; as a parent you cannot influence this.'
'It is important to adhere to a strict routine when it comes to infant feeding times.'
'Avoid distressing your baby at all costs; feed him when he lets you know he is hungry.'
'Be sensitive in matters of potty training; being either too strict or too lenient can produce anal fixations in adult life.'
'Strict potty training is essential and should begin early.'

Parents in the 1920s were faced with a bewildering set of choices: how to bring up their children? Many, of course, simply followed their own mothers' advice; but that was out of kilter with those modernist times, so others looked to science and experts for the 'best' way. But the experts, as we can see, were in clear disagreement.

Three major perspectives battled for psychological supremacy: the psychoanalyst view, that emotional balance in adults depended entirely on careful guidance through infancy and childhood; the nativist view, which argued that child development happened anyway, through genetic influences on maturation; and the behaviourist view, which was that child development happened entirely through conditioning.

In Chapter 5, we saw how psychoanalytic perspectives on child development emerged through the work of Anna Freud and Melanie Klein. They, along with other psychoanalysts, emphasised the importance of appropriate nurturing for healthy emotional development, and those ideas were in stark contrast to the view that heredity dominated development and parents had little influence on it. Arnold Gesell, the main advocate of that particular approach, had set up a successful clinic and institute for child research, and his advice to parents was widely followed. Parental responsibility, according to Gesell, was simply to provide an environment within which the child could mature; they should give up any notion that they could actually influence how their child would develop.

Gesell's view reflected the hereditarian assumptions that were both common and popular at the time. His institute produced a number of handbooks for new parents and others. But the growing school of behaviourism was promoting a different message. Its guru, J.B. Watson, also produced handbooks and guidance for parents on child development, and his message couldn't have been more different. Believing that conditioning was at the heart of all child development, Watson's famous assertion was that with a dozen healthy infants and his own world to bring them up in, he could produce any kind of person. Inborn abilities had nothing to do with it. It was all about learning.

For the behaviourists, the young infant was essentially the same as any other young animal – or 'organism', as they called them. They would learn by association, making links between stimuli and responses, and that learning would be reinforced by rewards or unpleasant consequences. They saw the infant mind as a tabula rasa – a blank slate, believing that what it did, what it remembered, and even language itself, was entirely learned.

Most psychologists were not so extreme. The usual assumption was that the mind developed as a child pieced together the small units of sensation and movement they experienced to recognise objects or people. Not everyone saw it this way, though; as we saw in Chapter 11, the Gestalt psychologist Koffka argued that the mind starts with general impressions, which gradually sort themselves into specific experiences. But, for the most part, psychologists regarded the developing mind as emerging from a combination of experience and a few innate tendencies, like that for language.

Enter an ardent biologist, with a passionate interest in molluscs and a firm belief in the relevance of evolution in explaining everything, including physiological and psychological abilities. Although not a psychologist himself, Jean Piaget was interested in psychology, and particularly in the higher mental functions such as formal logic and mathematics. How, he wondered, could these have evolved? As a biologist, Piaget believed that any theory of cognitive development must be based on evolution. But how could abstract analysis, problem-solving, and other complex forms of thinking shown by human beings, have evolved?

A popular idea of the time was known as 'recapitulation theory', drawn from observations of how the foetus develops in the womb. In the early weeks, a human foetus has gills for obtaining oxygen before lungs have developed; later they look the same as any other mammal; later still they become ape-like; and eventually they appear distinctively human. This, some argued, meant that the foetus was recapitulating, or rerunning, the stages of its species' evolution. Ontogeny (the development of the individual) recapitulated phylogeny (the development of the species).

That was the theory that inspired Piaget's research. If ontogeny recapitulated phylogeny in physical development, then surely that would apply to cognitive abilities as well? Which meant that studying children's thinking at different stages of their maturation would provide a key to understanding how the higher levels of human cognition evolved.

Piaget took Koffka's position as his starting point. When an infant is born, he believed, everything is just a mass of sensation. At that point, the infant is totally egocentric: their personal experience is their whole world. Slowly, though, they begin to realise that there is a difference between 'me' and 'not-me': that some aspects of their experience are different from the rest, and sometimes they are just not there. This, according to Piaget, is the start of cognition. From then on, he believed, cognitive development is an increasingly sophisticated reduction of egocentricity.

For Piaget, 'me' and 'not-me' are the very first mental schemas – that is, ways of describing and storing cognitive and personal experiences. He described how schemas become more sophisticated with experience: they are expanded to assimilate new information and adjusted, or even divided, to accommodate more complex knowledge. It's likely, for instance, that at first the infant's 'me' schema includes the mother (or caregiver); gradually the child realises that their caregiver is not always there, so the schema splits into 'not-me' as well as 'me', and 'not-me' gradually differentiates into other people, places or other types of experience. So, for example, a small child may call all furry animals 'doggy' before gradually learning to distinguish between dogs, cats, sheep and other animals.

Piaget saw all cognitive development as modifying existing schemas. But it only happens through experience, which Piaget believed could only be acquired by performing operations on the environment – that is, doing things that have an effect. Egocentricity reduces steadily as children become able to perform different types of operation. Infant operations tend to be simple and repetitive, like hitting a rattle to make a sound, or playing the throw-your-teddy-out-of-the-cot-so-daddy-picks-it-up game. As the child grows, schemas become more sophisticated. Young children can perform simple operations, but they are still egocentric, and generally unable to see things from another person's point of view. It's not uncommon, for example, for a very small child to put their hands over their eyes and assume that you can't see them, because they can't see you.

Modern developmental psychologists call this 'theory of mind', or 'TOM', and have found that it typically develops at around three and a half years of age, although Piaget's own studies implied that it was much later. For Piaget, young children are only focused on developing sensory and motor skills; older children go through a stage when they can deal with quite complex problems but only if they are rooted in the real world. As they mature, they can deal with complex abstract problems. For Piaget, this is the ultimate stage of cognition.

Piaget believed that these stages had a biological basis, and that certain operations wouldn't become possible until a certain level of biological maturity had been reached. Although this was a very minor part of his theory, it became over-emphasised by educationalists, possibly because it provided a convenient excuse for why some children didn't seem to learn well from their teachers. His theory dominated primary education in the West for several decades.

Piaget's theory reflected the individualism of Western thought. However, in the USSR, a very different approach was being promoted. The formation of the New Soviet Man (or Woman) was an explicit goal of communist society, and it permeated education, where co-operation and social awareness were seen as essential in children's learning. A typical classroom would be organised into teams, with members of each team helping one another to learn. Assessment was mainly team based, and helpful behaviour was deliberately praised and encouraged.

That social emphasis permeated intellectual thinking too. Although Soviet psychologists were aware of Western theories, they tended to disagree with their individualistic approach, regarding social influences as being important and under-acknowledged. So while Piaget was working on his grand theory of cognitive development in Switzerland, a very different perspective was emerging in the USSR. Lev Vygotsky was aware of Piaget's theory but thought it neglected the influence that other people, particularly adults, have on children's cognitive development.

For Vygotsky, cognitive development happened in two ways. General physical knowledge was acquired, as Piaget described, through practical interaction with the environment. Vygotsky called the opportunities this provided for the child's learning the 'zone of personal development'. But other people in the child's environment provided an extended cognitive environment, not just through direct teaching, but through conversations, through providing role models for imitation, and even indirectly through reading, theatre and other social institutions.

Vygotsky called this the 'zone of proximal development', and for him it was the key to understanding how children acquire the higher cognitive skills. A child growing up in a woodworker's family, for example, can learn quite a lot by simply handling tools and wood, and playing with them. But that child will only become really skilled when an adult shows them how to use those tools to the best effect. In the same way, a child can learn to solve basic practical puzzles, but it takes adults – teachers, parents and others – to help them to develop really sophisticated thinking. For Vygotsky, input from adults provides a kind of scaffolding, or support, which gives the child a framework for further learning and development, including the acquisition of complex cognitive skills. It doesn't always have to be adults, of course. It could be an older sibling, another child, or anyone else. But Vygotsky's important point is that cognitive development is a social process, not just an abstract individual one.

Vygotsky's work, while widely known in Soviet society, didn't really have an impact on the West until it was translated into English, which didn't happen until 1962. It gradually gained popularity, particularly as a number of challenges to Piaget's ideas emerged in the late 1970s and early 1980s, which also showed how he had failed to recognise the social dimension. Vygotsky's theory gave an alternative perspective from which to interpret those findings. It's unlikely that his work would have been fully appreciated when it was developed in Russia during the inter-war period, but it came into its own in the West later in the century.

That inter-war period was an active time for theory-building in developmental psychology, even though some theories didn't achieve their full impact until after the Second World War. 'It steam-engines when it's steam-engine time', as the saying goes, and that was the time of modernism, which maintained the belief that it was possible to create a brave new world in which scientific progress would eradicate the legacies of old social problems. People believed that science and technology would find the answers to all society's needs, as was happening with biological progress, like the eradication of disease through vaccination.

In the US, behaviourism, with its emphasis on the human being as a tabula rasa, offered new ways of understanding human beings; in the USSR, social influences were paramount, as exemplified in the work of Vygotsky; but both rejected the old and offered new approaches. It wasn't until after the Second World War, though, that those theories became widely accepted. Paradigm changes take time, but in psychology many of them were accelerated by the upheavals and challenges presented by the advent of the global conflicts of 1939 to 1945.

CHAPTER 15

The Missing Link
EXPLAINING MOTIVATION THROUGH NEEDS AND DRIVES, AND THE CHALLENGE FROM MASLOW

Means, motive, opportunity: Agatha Christie's formula has been the mantra for murder mystery writers for many decades. Means and opportunity – well, they're pretty straightforward: did someone have the wherewithal to actually commit the crime, and did they have a chance to do it? But what of motives? What motivates people to commit crimes such as murder? And can psychology help us to understand it?

If you'd been asking this question in the middle of the last century, the short answer would have been 'No'. It took a long time for psychology to get to grips with the more complex aspects of human motivation. Apart from Freud, that is, who had his own ideas about it. As we saw in Chapter 5, Freud saw much of human motivation in terms of hidden early traumas and unconscious wish fulfilment. We have the life-force of libido energising our actions towards pleasure, and the dark energy of thanatos, driving our behaviour and leading at times to dark and evil deeds.

It's a theory, but is it really an explanation? Freud developed the thanatos part of his theory in an attempt to explain the carnage of the First World War, and it's certainly been popular with thriller writers ever since. But if we all have this dark energy, then why are real-life murders so rare? And why do soldiers need so much training before they can actually kill other people? Most people – by far the majority – prefer to live a peaceful life, avoiding conflict and just getting along with others. In everyday life, we might get a bit irritated now and then, but actual hate and real aggression are nothing like as common as the dramatists portray. It's just that peaceful, co-operative behaviour is harder to make into a good story.

William James, in his influential 1890 text, *The Principles of Psychology*, followed Darwin in thinking that we are mainly motivated by instinct. It's instinctive, he believed, to seek food if we are hungry, to love our children, to find a safe home. We react aggressively if those things are threatened, and that's instinctive too. Which all sounds reasonable enough – until we really look at it. Because while saying that something is 'instinctive' implies that it is inborn and something we don't have to learn, it doesn't tell us anything about what people actually do. We might have an instinct for security, but to one person that might mean protecting their home against criminals, to another it might be earning enough money. Someone else might focus on the physical structure of their home, while a fourth person might find security from living in a friendly and supportive community. So to say something is instinctive doesn't take us very far if we want to understand what motivates people, or why people act as they do.

What all this boils down to is that motivation wasn't really something that the early psychologists paid much attention to. They took it for granted. Behaviourism, though, changed all that. The behaviourists dismissed Freud's ideas about unconscious motivation, and also James' instinct theory, in much the same way as they dismissed just about anything to do with the human 'mind'. For them, the whole idea of the mind was too vague and unscientific. Their new psychology was modern and not bound by tradition. It had to be objective, empirical and, above all, rigorously scientific. Which applied just as much to motivation as to any other aspect of human experience.

For the behaviourists, motivation, like everything else, came down to stimulus-response (S-R) learning. A hungry baby feels satisfied when it is fed, so the feeding and the comfort become associated with the mother's presence. That association produces a learned attachment to the mother, which later generalises to warm feelings towards other close people. Forget instinct, the behaviourists argued, all human (and animal) motivation can be explained though learned S-R connections.

This was the situation facing Clark Hull, a farm boy from New York State with only a patchy experience of school, who had taught himself to read as an adult, and eventually studied mathematics at college. It led him into aptitude testing, but his interest gradually shifted to hypnosis and suggestibility. In turn, that led him to psychology and the works of William James, Watson and Pavlov. Having bootstrapped his own education, Hull was particularly interested in learning and the behaviours that led to learning, and he became a firm behaviourist. His ultimate aim was to produce a mathematical theory of learning.

Hull could see that there was something missing in the learning theory of the time. Pavlov and Watson talked about learning as if it was a direct connection between the stimulus and the response. This is nice and tidy, but it leaves a bit of a problem, because we don't always respond to the same stimulus in the same way. Seeing a loaf of bread in the kitchen might result in making yourself a sandwich – or it might not. But the stimulus – the loaf – is the same. The difference is whether you feel hungry or not. Being hungry isn't a stimulus, and it isn't a response. It's a physical state, and it makes all the difference to how we respond to a stimulus.

It had been largely taken for granted that the animals used in experiments needed to be hungry for food rewards to be effective. But until Hull, nobody had taken much notice of what that actually meant. Hull saw it as important: that the basic state of the 'organism' makes all the difference to whether learning happens.

There is a stimulus and a response, but in between them is the state of the organism, and that state affects whether a learned connection is made or not.

It happens, Hull believed, through needs and drives. A need is a lack of some sort – for example, being dehydrated because of the lack of fluid in the body. That need generates a drive (being thirsty), which is a state of tension, so we perform actions that will reduce that tension (making a cup of tea, filling a glass of water from the tap, lapping water from a stream, and so on). This is how the link between the stimulus (lack of liquid) and response (drinking) is formed, and that, in essence, was Hull's drive theory of motivation.

So instead of S-R learning, Hull's model was S-O-R learning, with 'O' being the state of the organism. ('Organism', by the way, was the word the behaviourists used for animals, humans or any other living things. They wanted to emphasise that they were talking about the fundamental units of learning, the 'atoms' of psychology, which applied to everything that could learn. And, of course, it sounded much more scientific.)

Hull's work was published in the late 1930s. Around this time scientists were also exploring the role of the hypothalamus in maintaining bodily homeostasis. Homeostasis is the internal balance of the body, regulating things like temperature, fluid levels and oxygen levels, and so on. The hypothalamus is the part of our brain that controls that balance: if our blood sugars get too low, it stimulates feelings of hunger so we look for food; it stimulates sweating to cool us down if we get too hot and shivering to keep our muscles active if we get too cold; we breathe more deeply if our oxygen levels are being used up in vigorous exercise, and so on. These are all homeostatic processes that allow the body to rebalance itself when it needs to.

The discovery of how the hypothalamus regulates homeostasis gave Hull neurological support for his ideas, and he developed a complex mathematical formula to describe learning and motivation in an objective, 'scientific' way. His work earned him the prestigious position of professor of psychology at Yale University. And, not surprisingly, his drive theory became firmly established as the psychological explanation for why animals – and people – do things. For motivation, in other words.

But was it enough? It might explain why we get a drink when we're thirsty, but most of what human beings do, and why we do it, is more complicated than that. So the theory was rapidly adjusted to take account of more complex kinds of motivation. One of the key distinctions was between primary and secondary drives. Hull, like the other behaviourists of the time, believed that all motivation began with primary drives, which are straightforward reflections of physical needs. More complex drives were learned by association: for example, secondary drives, like attachment, were seen as developing through the association of food and comfort with the mother figure.

Something that offered the possibility of satisfying a drive, like food for a hungry animal, was known as an incentive. Hull distinguished between direct incentives like food, and indirect incentives that could motivate behaviour without directly satisfying a need – like money, and in one textbook, good music. The two ideas of secondary drives and indirect incentives meant that the theory could essentially bend itself to explain just about any aspect of human behaviour. The explanations sometimes became a bit convoluted in the process, but the general idea was rapidly accepted, leading psychologists to identify more complex human needs, such as a need for achievement (nAch), a need for power and influence over others (nPow), and – one of my favourite abbreviations – a need for affiliation (nAff). Psychometric measures of these rapidly became popular both with researchers and with applied psychologists.

But not all need theories came from behaviourism. The most famous need theory of all was developed by Abraham Maslow in 1954. He had been working with Harry Harlow, who had conducted a series of now-famous experiments, involving infant monkeys deprived of their mothers. They were fed from a wire mesh model but also given another model with a terry-cloth covering. The young monkeys spent most of their time clinging to the cloth model, only moving to the wire one to feed. When they were offered opportunities to explore, they used the cloth model for reassurance: if it wasn't there, they were timid and didn't explore, but if it was present, they were braver and showed more curiosity. As Maslow saw, these studies challenged the assumption that primary drives were at the core of attachment. If they had been, the young monkeys would have found the presence of the wire mother – the source of their food – equally reassuring.

Maslow distinguished between D-needs, or 'deficiency needs', which satisfied a specific lack or deficit, and B-needs, or 'being needs', which were all about the higher aspects of life. He proposed a hierarchical model, with higher needs becoming active only if the D-needs of the lower levels were satisfied. Physiological needs are basic: if they are not met, they become more important than anything else. Once they are satisfied, the next level becomes important, and if those are satisfied, then it's the next level that matters. The levels outlined by Maslow were, from lowest to highest: (1) physiological needs, (2) safety needs (shelter and protection), (3) love and belonging needs, (4) esteem needs (respect and self-esteem), (5) cognitive needs (curiosity and search for meaning), (6) aesthetic needs (beauty, order and symmetry) and, at the highest level, (7) self-actualisation needs, or realising one's full potential.

An oversimplified version of Maslow's theory became very popular in organisational psychology, and still is. Often represented as a pyramid of needs (although Maslow himself never produced such a diagram), it appeared to give managers answers to why their employees (or perhaps their trade union representatives) never seem to be entirely satisfied. According to this model, if adequate levels of pay have been achieved, attention would turn to working conditions; if those were OK, then employees would become concerned with their job satisfaction, and so on. We'll come back to Maslow's work in the next chapter, as he became an important founder of a significant challenge to behaviourism, in the approach known as humanistic psychology.

CHAPTER 16

The Humanist Movement
EMPHASISING THE WHOLE PERSON

Samuel and Rose Maslow had had enough. Despite murmurings of reform, Jewish life in what was then Kiev, like the rest of the Russian empire, meant living under constant threat. There were frequent anti-Jewish pogroms and other episodes of violence, which often resulted in murders. There was even a state law that conscripted all twelve-year-old Jewish boys into a special branch of the Russian Army, where they led miserable lives, overworked, underfed, and often abused. Boys as young as ten could be – and often were – forcibly taken from their homes, on the grounds that they looked twelve. Being Jewish in old Europe was to be constantly vulnerable to persecution; but hope for a better life was offered by the new country of America.

So almost as soon as Rose and Samuel were married, they immigrated to the promised land – to Brooklyn, New York, where their first child, Abraham, was born in 1908. They were part of the New Immigration: a wave of over 20 million immigrants to America between 1880 and 1920, mainly from southern, eastern and central

Europe. Rose and Samuel Maslow, like many of the 2 million Jews who immigrated to America at this time, settled in a multi-ethnic community.

The promised land wasn't all sweetness and light. Abraham Maslow's parents were poor and worked hard. They were strict and unloving, but they did value education. He was the oldest of seven children and a lonely child, often experiencing abuse from other children. The roving gangs of his impoverished neighbourhood were generally racist and antisemitic, so being Jewish made Abraham an easy target for stone-throwing. But despite – or perhaps because of – his unhappy childhood, he grew up as a caring, loving individual who believed firmly that the world could be a better place. That belief shaped his career, and eventually became his life's work.

Maslow didn't have many childhood friends, but he loved reading and learning, often visiting public libraries and studying hard at high school. On his father's advice, he made a brief attempt to study law, but it didn't suit him, and eventually he ended up at Wisconsin University studying psychology. There he worked with Harry Harlow in primate research and with Thorndike on human sexuality. He wasn't happy with the strict experimental/behaviourist approach dominant at that time. The Second World War further convinced him that the two main approaches in psychology – behaviourism and psychoanalysis – simply didn't deal with the positive aspects of human psychology. Maslow became convinced that an alternative approach – a third way – was not only possible but necessary.

He didn't totally disagree with the behavioural approach but thought that it over-emphasised the negative aspects of human behaviour, focusing on correcting deficiencies or faulty learning rather than bringing out the positive aspects. In the same way, psychoanalysis focused on problems and negatives rather than on the positive potential of human existence. His professional discussions with the anthropologist Ruth Benedict and the Gestalt psychologist Max Wertheimer, as well as his own life experiences, convinced him that there was much more to people than simply satisfying needs or dealing with childhood traumas. All this led him to develop what he called 'humanistic psychology' – an approach to studying people that explored positive human qualities like hope, creativity, love and health.

One of Maslow's theoretical contributions, as we saw in the last chapter, was his distinction between the needs that simply correct for deficiencies, which he called 'D-needs', and the needs that reflect a striving for something more positive, which he called 'B-needs', for 'being'. It opened up the idea that human motivation is about more than just physical needs: we can also be motivated by things like beauty, friendship and self-actualisation. Maslow's approach quickly became a major influence in organisational psychology, and the hierarchical model he proposed is still taught today. But his main contribution to psychology was his firm belief in the potential goodness of human beings and the continuing efforts he made to show that this should also be part of psychology.

Maslow found a kindred spirit in Carl Rogers, a clinical psychologist who had reached similar conclusions. Through his work, Rogers had come to believe that human beings have two absolutely fundamental psychological needs. One of these is a need for self-actualisation, and the other a need for positive regard from other people. A lot of the psychological problems he saw in his clinical work happened when those needs came into conflict.

Most people, Rogers argued, experience unconditional positive regard from their parents or other family members – they are loved and accepted no matter what they do or say. But for some, positive regard is conditional – for example, when people have parents who withdraw their affection if they fail to be 'good'. This means, according to Rogers, that as adults those people don't dare risk losing positive regard from others. If they were to take independent action to develop their own potential – in other words, to self-actualise – they might risk disapproval from others, so they suppress that need. So satisfying the psychological need for approval or respect means sacrificing the exploration and confidence needed for self-actualisation. And that, according to Rogers' clinical observations, leads to neurosis.

Like Maslow, Rogers believed that people are inherently good, but that their positive qualities are often suppressed or distorted by negative experiences and beliefs. All humans, he believed, strive to develop and to actualise (make real) their personal potential. People who manage to achieve this live happy, creative lives and should be what psychology, in Rogers' view, is all about.

Maslow and Rogers, then, both used the idea of self-actualisation, but they saw it in different ways. For Maslow, self-actualisation was a 'peak experience': a special state that was only achieved very rarely. So people who achieved it consistently were quite special and unusual individuals. For Rogers, though, self-actualisation was more of a process: action taken to satisfy an ongoing need rather than the achieving of a special state. He believed that the need for self-actualisation could be satisfied in any way, depending on the person concerned: music, model-making, gardening, or any other activity that led to a sense of personal achievement. What mattered was the person's own 'self', and that was the other important concept that Rogers brought to the party. The idea of the self had become entirely lost in the behaviourist era and was only regarded as a device for balancing internal tensions by the psychoanalysts. But for Rogers, it was the key to understanding the real person.

Other psychologists in the post-war era were also challenging the rigidity of behaviourism and psychoanalysis. Maslow and Rogers gave a focus to the new approach, showing that it was not only possible to study psychology from a humanistic angle, but that doing so addressed many of the questions about human experience that couldn't be answered – or even asked – within either a behaviourist or psychoanalytic framework. We might also note that this was a time when consumerism was growing and beginning to define Western society, so an interest in the self and ways of exploring different aspects of it was fully in accord with the times, in the same way that the rigid one-process-fits-all approach of the behaviourists fitted the modernist ethos of the first half of the twentieth century.

As interest in this 'third way' spread, people began to get together and share ideas, and Rogers and Maslow rapidly became regarded as the founding fathers of the new school of humanistic psychology. Pressure grew to create a formal association reflecting the new approach, and the American Association for Humanistic Psychology was inaugurated in 1961. Those ideas, though, spread far beyond America so, in response to widespread international interest, the association dropped the 'American' bit in 1963, and the organisation was renamed the Association for Humanistic Psychology.

Humanistic psychology, according to its journal, could be defined by five basic principles. The first principle is that humans are more than just the sum of their parts. We have ideals, beliefs and other qualities that are special aspects of being human, and not derived from basic elements such as trial-and-error learning. The second principle is that people live in a uniquely human context, as well as a physical one. Our experiences of other people are an important part of our lives, helping to shape our actions and beliefs as much as, if not more than, our physical contexts.

The third principle of humanistic psychology emphasises consciousness and awareness, not only of our immediate feelings, but of ourselves in relation to other people. This in turn leads to the fourth principle, which is that as conscious human beings we don't just respond to environmental demands: we make choices, so we are responsible for our actions and their consequences. The fifth principle is that, as human beings, we also have intentions. We direct our actions in terms of those intentions and, in one way or another, we look for meaning, value and creativity in our lives.

In its first few decades, the main impact of humanistic psychology was in psychotherapy. Carl Rogers became the champion of a totally new approach, which can really be summarised as respecting the one who is receiving the therapy as a person, rather than a patient. He began outlining his new approach in the early 1940s but really made it clear in his book, *Client-Centered Therapy*, which was published in 1951. He used the term 'client' deliberately, to emphasise that the person was not simply a passive recipient of treatment, but actively engaging in therapy by their personal choice. His methods, too, stressed the importance of respecting the individual concerned and maintaining a friendly, transactional relationship with them.

Rogers pioneered a number of novel methods that became very popular during the 1960s. One of these was non-directive therapy – the idea that, actually, the client is perfectly able to work out their own life-solutions. The role of the therapist isn't to tell them what to do, but to help them to recognise what would be best for them personally. Rogers did recognise that therapists do sometimes need to make suggestions, and so they can't be completely non-directive, but that whole idea ran completely counter to the I'm-the-expert-and-I-know-best power relationship that was normal at the time. According to Rogers and the many other clinicians who followed his example, the new approach was much more effective.

Another of Rogers' techniques was the 'encounter group': bringing a number of people with similar experiences together, so that they could share their personal experiences and potential solutions. The therapist would be part of the group, but their main role was to facilitate the discussion, not to direct it. Encounter groups became very popular, and there was even an extreme version, the T-group, in which participants were exhorted to open up their innermost thoughts and anxieties to the others. The aim was to break down established defence mechanisms and so achieve psychological 'healing'. T-groups eventually fell out of fashion, as people recognised that not all defence mechanisms are harmful, and that some can actually be useful. But the general principle of encounter groups still remains.

While its early influence was in psychotherapy, humanistic psychology has had a consistent influence on psychology as a whole. It showed the need for new research methods that emphasised meanings as well as behaviour, which eventually led to the methodological challenges that we will be looking at in Chapter 40. Its emphasis on a holistic approach to understanding people and the exploration of human potential provided a theoretical background for researchers interested in other aspects of mental experience, like self-efficacy, spirituality and mindfulness. Ultimately, too, it led to 'positive psychology', which we will be exploring in Chapter 37.

CHAPTER 17

Psychology Goes to War
A Turning Point – Applied Psychology
and Military Research

Britain is at war, and 10,000 people have been drafted in to work at Bletchley Park. They are billeted in local villages and working in a conglomeration of temporary huts, set up in the grounds of the estate. Everyone knows that their work is a massive codebreaking project, essential to the war effort. But not a single person talks about it. Not to their friends, their family, or even their spouses. Some of them don't mention it for the rest of their lives; others only reminisce about it over half a century later. Their landladies and landlords don't even ask; they too know that 'careless talk costs lives'.

The Second World War transformed Europe completely. Right across the continent, countries faced the upheavals of invasion, privation and even famine. Jews and Romanis were rounded up and herded into camps. Many fled, but most were murdered. And in Britain, the whole country became part of the war effort.

Psychology, too, was transformed by the Second World War. The First World War had stimulated new areas of enquiry, like the results of brain injuries or psychological trauma, but the Second put psychology to work. Almost anyone with relevant knowledge was expected to contribute.

In the UK, many psychologists worked on codebreaking at Bletchley Park, and many others worked with other aspects of the military. They helped to revise recruitment and selection procedures, to make the most of the talents and skills of military personnel, and they developed psychological techniques to boost morale among the troops. Some highly secretive units also worked on the opposite dimension: psychological warfare, consisting of ways to deplete morale, and to demoralise the enemy. None of these psychologists were forthcoming about their work. Most said nothing at all, and others didn't talk about it until many decades later.

Frederic Bartlett, for example, had previously conducted work on memory that had opened up the relationship between cognition, social psychology and anthropology. His famous 'war of the ghosts' study had shown how people adjust their memories to fit with their existing cultural and personal expectations, and he believed that stronger links between anthropology and psychology would strengthen social psychology. He acted as a consultant to the Royal Air Force during the 1930s, and his work continued through the Second World War. His primary research was the analysis of the psychological problems that had become apparent as the RAF expanded and their pilots' work became more demanding.

Bartlett was Chair of Experimental Psychology at Cambridge, which meant that a lot of war-related psychological research was carried out there. He worked closely with one of the most influential psychologists of that time, Kenneth Craik. Almost forgotten today, Craik was particularly interested in the challenges of real-world situations, and how psychology could help to resolve them. He was a talented engineer as well as a psychologist, and especially good at creating models and simulations, so that environmental and psychological stressors like fatigue and being faced with multiple choices could be studied experimentally. Craik joined with Bartlett in setting up an important research facility during the war: the Medical Research Council's (MRC) Applied Psychology Unit at Cambridge. The unit employed many psychologists who would later become famous, and Craik became its first director. He died in a motorcycle accident just before the war ended, but he left a powerful legacy.

Donald Broadbent was another of the many psychologists whose interests were developed at Craik's Applied Psychology Unit. Broadbent served in the RAF during the war and became interested in how people interact with complex technologies. He conducted extensive research into attention, developing a filter model of selective attention, which was later refined by his colleague Anne Treisman, another researcher at the MRC unit. He also looked into the factors influencing how long and how accurately people could keep up their attention without making mistakes, conducting research that has direct relevance today for complex work like air traffic control.

Richard Gregory served in the Signals Unit of the RAF during the war years and attended university in Cambridge after the war. His particular interest was in perception, which he saw as being all about hypothesis testing. That idea had first been put forward by Helmholtz, who had suggested that the brain makes sense of the information it is receiving by forming hypotheses based on prior knowledge and experience and checking them against evidence from sensory information. Gregory promoted that theory and went on to found the Department of Machine Intelligence and Perception (later the Department of Artificial Intelligence) at Edinburgh University. His RAF experience had given him a particular interest in visual illusions, stimulated by the mistakes people make and the way information is often misread. Among many other achievements, he founded the Bristol Exploratory, which gave ordinary people direct experience of scientific phenomena. He continued to share his enthusiasm through lectures on perception and illusions throughout his long and vigorous life.

Gregory wasn't the only psychologist interested in perception. In America, J.J. Gibson had begun his academic career in philosophy but became fascinated by experimental psychology instead, undertaking a PhD on the experimental study of visual memory. While teaching psychology a couple of years later, he met the Gestalt psychologist Kurt Koffka, who had always argued that perception is at the heart of psychology. Gibson didn't agree entirely with Koffka, but he did agree that perception was central to understanding the world. However, he also believed that it didn't involve complex cognitive activity – rather, he saw it as a much more direct process. Gibson's theory centred around why perception was useful for the animal or human doing the perceiving – why it evolved in the first place. That led him to the idea that we don't just perceive objects as entirely separate from ourselves, but that our perception of them is also shaped by the possibilities they offer us for action, such as whether we can eat them, or sit on them, or pick them up. These 'affordances' are an integral part of Gibson's theory of perception.

During the war, Gibson directed a psychological research unit for the US Air Force. One of his concerns was improving pilot selection. He applied his psychological expertise to develop a new approach based on how pilots interpreted and used the information presented in motion pictures. That then led him to an interest in how we interpret changes in texture or colour, for example, to assess distances, and also in how important movement is in everyday perception. Gibson distinguished between 'form' perception, the perception we use to make sense of static pictures or images, and 'object' perception, when either the perceiver or the object itself is in motion. After the war, he brought these insights together in his theory of ecological perception, generally rated to be one of the most significant psychological theories of the twentieth century.

That process was relatively typical of how the war influenced psychology. While most of the actual research was classified as military intelligence and therefore not published, once the war was over psychologists who had worked on various projects brought together and published the theoretical insights they had gained from their work. Many highly influential books were published between 1946 and 1955, establishing a strong foundation in cognitive psychology for the 'cognitive revolution' of the 1980s, and strengthening the theoretical basis of the discipline.

Other psychologists also made contributions to the war effort, in one way or another. In America, Alphonse Chapanis and Paul Fitts were called in to analyse the frequent crashes of the B17 Flying Fortress planes, which were seen as resulting from pilot errors. The psychologists realised that the crashes all seemed to happen in the same way. When they looked into it, they found that, rather than being the fault of the pilots, the problems were really in the design of the cockpit. The plane's controls were all very similar, both in look and feel, making it far too easy for a pilot who was concentrating on aligning his plane accurately for landing to reach out and pull the wrong lever, with disastrous results. They redesigned the controls so that those for the landing gear felt completely different from those for the wing controls, which significantly reduced the number of accidents.

J.S. Bruner also worked for the American war effort, but in a very different field. Bruner had graduated in psychology in 1939 and went on to take his PhD at Harvard. The title of his 1941 thesis was 'A Psychological Analysis of International Radio Broadcasts of Belligerent Nations'. So perhaps it wasn't surprising that by the 1940s he was working with what was officially called the Office for Strategic Studies, but generally known as Eisenhower's 'Psychological Warfare Division'. Bruner was particularly interested in rumour and propaganda, and the way that popular beliefs could be manipulated. After the war, he worked at both Harvard and Oxford and conducted extensive research into cognitive and educational psychology. One part of his work concerned how children's minds represent information through actions, icons and symbols. It became very influential in education, but also had another unexpected result when the designer Alan Kay presented him with an early Macintosh computer, saying that it was his work that had inspired the design of its friendly iconic interface.

The Second World War was a powerful influence on the development of social psychology as well as cognitive psychology. Persuasion and propaganda had been topics of interest for social psychologists before the war, but they became much more significant during those years, and that work was used to great effect by both sides. Other psychologists studied influences on motivation and morale, such as the camaraderie of a particular platoon or the support of work colleagues. The war also saw an increased recognition of the value of clinical psychology. The First World War had recognised shell shock – what we now call PTSD, or post-traumatic stress disorder. This time, psychologists were actively involved in the development of screening methods, aiming to identify those who were the most vulnerable. They weren't, of course, universally successful, but they also developed treatments that meant that soldiers with PTSD could return to active combat. Their work helped to generate an acceptance of psychometric testing as an important part of applied psychology in a clinical context.

The increased recognition of PTSD also began to change social awareness about stress itself. It became increasingly recognised that stress is not a clinical problem (although it can become so in more extreme cases) but a facet of everyday life experience. It brought home to people the idea that someone who is suffering from extreme stress, like PTSD, is not necessarily 'abnormal'. They are experiencing an understandable reaction to extreme and traumatic experiences, but that does not mean that they are mentally ill.

Those war experiences helped to firm up the discipline of clinical psychology itself. The first clinical psychology department in the UK was established at the Maudsley hospital in the immediate aftermath of the war, and training and qualifications in clinical psychology followed rapidly. The Maudsley was mainly focused on behavioural approaches to treatment, and it pioneered methods of treating phobias and of aversion therapy.

The Second World War, then, was a turning point for psychology, as the discipline became increasingly recognised as an applied science, with invaluable knowledge across a range of areas. Even psychologists who didn't work directly for the military were influenced by the war and its implications. Solomon Asch, who was later to become one of the most famous psychologists of all time, began his career in psychology before the war, studying impression formation and authority figures' influence. When Hitler initiated the Second World War, Asch adjusted his research focus to investigate propaganda, and the ways in which people can be influenced by it. His studies later led him to investigate conformity, and the impact people have on others, for which he remains famous.

The end of the war, and particularly the discoveries of the concentration camps, generated even more psychological research as people tried to come to terms with both personal and societal collusion with such crimes. This set a research agenda in psychology, some of which we will explore in the next two chapters.

CHAPTER 18

Explaining Nazism
PSYCHOANALYTIC AND BIOLOGICAL EXPLANATIONS
FOR AGGRESSION

Blood, pain, thunder, explosions! The man woke up screaming as he relived the horrors he had seen on the front line during the war. The terrible dreams happened every night, even though he was home and safe, and had been for many months. He dreaded falling asleep; even when awake he was haunted by flashbacks. Eventually, his wife persuaded him to go to one of the clinics run by that famous psychoanalyst, Sigmund Freud. Maybe he could help.

Freud had always maintained that dreams revealed the unconscious wish fulfilment of the unconscious mind. But after the First World War, many of his patients were soldiers troubled by repeated nightmares, in which they relived the traumas and horrors of their war experiences. In 1920, he wrote the essay 'Beyond the Pleasure Principle', in which he proposed that there must be another basic energy, the opposite of libido or 'eros', which became known as 'thanatos'. (Eros in Greek mythology was the personification of love, while Thanatos was the personification of death.)

As we have seen, Freud's original psychoanalytic theory had seen motivation as coming from eros, the fundamental drive for life and creativity. Eros generated the energy known as libido, which was then kept in check by the ego. But the First World War and its aftermath had made him re-evaluate. His revised thinking had also been stimulated by a 1912 paper by one of the first female psychoanalysts, Sabina Spielrein, who had proposed that destructiveness is also part of our unconscious motivation. Spielrein was an active member of Freud's Vienna circle and had worked with both Jung and Freud, making many contributions to psychoanalytic theory. Although Freud hadn't accepted her ideas immediately, he had acknowledged later that she had stimulated his train of thought, which had been further enhanced by his clinical work.

For Freud, thanatos was a primitive, elemental and destructive force: a complete contrast to the positive drive to survive, satisfy desires and procreate. He believed it was the only way to explain people's capacity for brutality and inhumanity, not just towards others but also towards themselves. Those energies were not only the source of aggression, Freud believed, but also the reason for some people's need for power and control over others. So, for Freudian psychoanalysts, this theory explained the political movement known as fascism, which had been growing steadily during the inter-war period. Far from being limited to Germany, fascist movements were evident right across Europe, including in the UK. Fascism had originated in Italy during the First World War, where it had rapidly gained popular support, and its leader, Benito Mussolini, had taken over the Italian government in 1922.

Fascism is a strongly nationalist movement characterised by highly authoritarian views, the suppression of opposition, and approval of the use of violence to achieve political aims. It is typically focused around one strong leader and is sometimes, though not always, strongly linked with racism. Italian fascism wasn't particularly antisemitic – there were many Jewish people in Mussolini's government who held high positions until Mussolini was forced by Hitler to remove them. But Hitler's fascism, as is well known, was strongly antisemitic, since one of his personal goals was the total eradication of the Jewish race

– a project that he put into action when he came to power, at first through repressive social laws, and later through the death camps.

The discovery of the concentration camps at the end of the Second World War showed how fascism could generate extreme social prejudice with tragic effects and raised a number of questions for psychology. For some, those questions were all about how social influences can dominate people, and we will be looking at that research in the next couple of chapters. For others, it raised questions about the type of personality that could embrace extreme ideologies to the point of sanctioning or supporting genocide. One of the most well known of these psychologists was Theodor Adorno.

Adorno was a multitalented individual – a musician and composer as well as a sociologist and psychologist – who, before the war, had been a member of the Frankfurt school, a group of academics who used Freud's ideas and also those of Marx and Hegel to analyse and critique the society of the time. Following harassment by the increasingly powerful fascist movement in Germany, Adorno moved to England and subsequently to America, where he continued to combine social research with work in the music industry. Together with a number of well-known sociologists, Frenkel-Brunswik, Levinson and Sanford, he co-authored a book, *The Authoritarian Personality*, which rapidly became popular.

The book drew on interviews with white Americans and identified some typical ways that people who held extreme right-wing beliefs thought. One of these was a characteristic rigidity, in that they held to their beliefs even in the face of contradictory evidence, and simply refused to change their minds. Another was intolerance of ambiguity: they didn't cope well with equivocal ideas but insisted on definite 'right' or 'wrong' answers. In arguments, they chose a side quickly and then kept to it no matter what anyone said.

For Adorno and his colleagues, these observations were part of a complete personality syndrome. They reflected a person who was highly authoritarian, believed in punitive social sanctions, showed high levels of prejudice towards 'outsiders', and held extreme right-wing personal beliefs. They called this the 'authoritarian personality'. Studies with such people showed that they had been brought up by rigid, authoritarian parents who didn't allow discussion or opposition or even the expression of disappointment. It wasn't a particularly uncommon child-rearing style at this time but, according to psychoanalytic theory, this treatment would generate a lot of suppressed anger in the child. Owing to their strict upbringing, though, the child wouldn't be allowed to express it.

Adorno and his co-authors suggested that this hostility to the parents' arbitrary authority became lodged in the child's unconscious mind, not accessible to conscious awareness. This would lead to the development of defence mechanisms, to prevent any hint of that buried rage from surfacing. It was these defence mechanisms, Adorno and his colleagues argued, that produced the authoritarian personality structure. Being open to new ideas, for example, might also open their minds to thinking the unthinkable – that they were actually angry with their parents. Keeping their thinking rigid and refusing to recognise ambiguities blocked any opportunity for these feelings to come to the surface.

Another characteristic of the authoritarian personality was a high level of deference to authority figures. The researchers saw this as a 'reaction formation' against their inner hostility. Reaction formation is a Freudian defence mechanism by which the behaviour being suppressed turns into its opposite. Suppressing aggression towards authority figures was important in case the child's hostility towards their parents became linked with it. Being exaggeratedly supportive of authority prevented any possibility of criticism or challenge that might extend to their parents. It was also the reason those people tended to be so hostile towards others – particularly those who did not share the same attitudes. It gave them a way of displacing their inner anger. By expressing their hostility towards another group (Black people, Jews, long-haired hippies, for example), they could release their anger 'safely' – that is, without having to acknowledge their own inner conflicts.

Adorno developed a psychometric test to measure authoritarianism, which became known as the F-scale – the F standing for fascism. It measured nine personality traits that Adorno believed were the direct result of those defence mechanisms. The traits were: conventionalism, or the tendency to be suspicious of anyone different from 'normal'; submissiveness, or the tendency to be deferential to authority figures; aggression, or hostility to anyone challenging authority or suggesting that it might be inadequate; a tough-minded approach to punishment, which Adorno called 'anti-intraception'; superstition, or a belief that outcomes are governed by 'fate' and can't be controlled; toughness, in the sense of a domineering and even bullying manner; a destructive attitude to new or challenging ideas; a tendency to project their own unconscious impulses onto others; and an exaggerated and hostile concern with sex and sexual behaviour.

Adorno's was not the only explanation of human aggression popular at the time. Konrad Lorenz was an Austrian biologist who was particularly interested in animal behaviour – not the laboratory behaviour that was studied so intensively in America, but the way animals behaved in the farms and villages of his childhood. Together with his colleague Niko Tinbergen, Lorenz became known as one of the founders of ethology – the study of animal behaviour in the natural environment. However, their work was interrupted by the Second World War. Lorenz was known to be a Nazi collaborator, while Tinbergen was Dutch and spent some years as a prisoner of war before moving to Oxford, so there was an understandable friction between the two for quite a few years.

Much of Lorenz's pre-war work was on imprinting – a form of attachment that we will explore more closely in Chapter 22. But he also wrote extensively on animal aggression, arguing that aggression was an inbuilt drive in both animals and humans. His idea was that mammals, including humans, continually generate an aggressive energy. If it isn't used immediately, that energy accumulates in a kind of 'reservoir'. It has to be released somehow, or it will spill over into other activities. In animals, that energy would be released by a specific sign stimulus – for example, a male robin will release aggressive behaviour at the sight of another robin's red breast. This hydraulic model of action-specific energies applied to other types of instinctive behaviour as well, in Lorenz's view, but it was particularly relevant to his understanding of aggression.

Where humans differ from other animals, Lorenz argued, is that other animals also inherit a set of appeasement gestures, to which other members of its species respond. For example, a dog being threatened by another dog might roll over on its back. This show of vulnerability is an appeasement gesture which means that the other dog will automatically stop attacking. Appeasement gestures limit the destructive power of aggressive behaviour, so that members of the same species don't just end up killing one another. But humans, according to Lorenz, don't have inherited appeasement gestures, which means that once their aggressive energy is released, they can continue attacking right to the death. And that, he argued, makes human beings particularly destructive and much more dangerous than other animals.

For Lorenz and many of his followers, this was the explanation for wars: they were the extension of a natural territorial instinct that was exaggerated by an excess of aggressive energy. But even in peacetime, men (Lorenz didn't really include women) still had that reservoir of aggressive energy constantly filling up. Lorenz believed that it needed to be diverted into safer channels, or it would find an outlet in violence. The only way to control it, he argued, was through catharsis – a concept developed by the ancient Greeks which is all to do with using that energy in safer ways. Sport and competitive physical activity were Lorenz's answer: they allow people to release these powerful energies in a safe context.

Lorenz's ideas were not particularly new – most human societies recognise that it is wise to allow young men some kind of outlet for their testosterone-generated energies, whether that is done through shows of strength at village fairs, team games like football, or extremely strenuous forms of dancing. What Lorenz did, though, was to create a biological theory, making his ideas appear to be scientifically based, and to equate individual energies with the mass destruction of war. His model suggested that (a) aggression was inevitable as a fundamental human instinct; (b) wars were simply manifestations of this; and (c) wars themselves were probably inevitable as part of the human condition. Other psychologists, of course, pointed to the level of conditioning and training required for soldiers to become able to kill other people, and the high levels of propaganda needed in wartime to get the population on side. But that was a debate for later times.

CHAPTER 19

Conformity and Acquiescence
ASCH AND MILGRAM ON OBEDIENCE

Sam wasn't happy. He'd volunteered for a psychology experiment and was sitting in a row with five other people. The experimenter had just shown them a card with three lines on it and asked the volunteers which was the longest. The answer was obvious – it was line A. Sam was second from last to be asked, and to his amazement, those before him said line C, which was obviously shorter. But it was definitely line A, and Sam said so. He was even more astounded when the last person in the row said C as well. The experimenter showed them another card. Again, the answer was obvious, but again, the others before him all gave the same wrong answer. As his turn approached, Sam found that he was sweating. What should he do? Maybe there was something he hadn't noticed? No, the right answer was still obvious, but again Sam was the only person who said it. His anxiety increased. It happened a third time, and this time he gave in. Rather than be the only dissident in the group, he gave the same wrong answer as the rest. Which didn't, actually, relieve his anxiety at all.

Sam was participating in a social psychology experiment carried out by Solomon Asch in the 1960s. Asch was a Gestalt psychologist who believed, firmly, that the dominant behavioural explanations of social behaviour just weren't enough. Asch, along with Max Wertheimer and Wolfgang Köhler, had taught at Swarthmore College in Pennsylvania, which had become a centre for Gestalt psychology in America. The Gestaltists emphasised the view that social acts can only really be understood in their setting, and trying to study them in isolation meant that they lost their meaning. It wasn't long after the Second World War, and Asch wanted to know how a whole nation could end up going along with Nazi policies, even when so many people disagreed with them.

He drew on the work of Muzafer Sherif, a Turkish psychologist who had immigrated to America during the Great Depression. Sherif had visited Köhler in Berlin in 1932 to attend his lectures on Gestalt psychology. The Nazi party was just gaining power, and not many people were openly disagreeing with them – although many disagreed in private. This interested Sherif, who began to investigate it experimentally. Using the autokinetic effect – the illusion of movement produced by a dot of light in a darkened room – he asked people to estimate how much the light moved. The important thing about this task is that everyone sees some movement, but it isn't the same from one person to another. When he tested people individually, each participant's results were consistent, but the answers of the group varied widely. But when he tested the whole group together, so that they could hear one another's judgements, they tended to settle on a group judgement. Not only that, but if they were then tested individually sometime later, they stuck to the group norm.

Sherif had shown how people conform in an ambiguous situation with no correct answer – but what about situations where the answer is obvious? That was the idea taken up by Solomon Asch. In what became a classic series of experiments, he showed that our tendency to conform with other people is so strong that some people will do it even when they know they are giving the wrong answer. Asch observed, too, that even those who stuck to the 'right' answer found it really stressful to disagree openly with the rest of their group. When asked, those who had given the wrong answer said that they believed that it was more important to get along with other people than to be 'correct' in a relatively trivial assessment.

For Asch, this helped to explain people's behaviour in German society. If simply disagreeing in the safe environment of a psychological laboratory was so stressful, how much worse would it be in the context of a society where open disagreement also brought the risk of job loss, imprisonment or even physical attack? Not only that, but the very brave few who did oppose Nazi policies openly were either forced to emigrate or ended up in a concentration camp.

In the 1980s, a set of replications of the Asch studies queried whether it was 'a child of its time' – that is, whether people in the 1950s were generally more conformist than they were now. Those replications showed a much lower tendency to conform, and for a while people believed that Asch's results had just come from a more obedient generation. However, in response to Asch's query, the researchers, Stephen Perrin and Christopher Spencer, confirmed that their participants had found dissent just as stressful. Further studies showed up methodological problems, caused by deliberately choosing participants who wouldn't have heard of Asch's original studies. Unfortunately, that meant that they were students drawn from physical sciences like physics and engineering, so they saw accuracy of measurement as being really important – more so than social acceptability. Studies using more typical populations showed that the 'Asch effect' was as strong as ever.

Other psychologists explored different aspects of conformity. They found that conformity to an obviously false result could happen even if the rest of the group were not physically present, but that just one other dissenter (even if they held a third opinion) was enough for someone to stick to their own view and not conform to the majority. That applied in abstract or definite tasks, like the one in Asch's original study. If the task was about political opinions, though, the research participant would tend to go along with the majority even if they disagreed with their views, and even when there was a dissenter with different ideas. But very self-confident people, or those who saw themselves as particularly competent in that area, rarely conformed to the group.

The Asch effect is one of the most robust findings of social psychology and helped to clarify how ordinary people went along with the increasingly extreme views and policies of the Nazi party in Germany. But for many others, their involvement was closer: as the Nuremberg war trials showed, thousands were involved in the operations of the Third Reich, in both military and civilian roles. It fell to Asch's student, Stanley Milgram, to explore the psychology underpinning that level of obedience.

Milgram's preliminary study was to ask a number of psychologists and psychiatrists how many people would be prepared to administer a lethal electric shock to another person. Their estimate was consistently low: fewer than 3 per cent. Then he placed a newspaper advertisement for volunteers to participate in a study of memory and learning. As each volunteer arrived at the laboratory, they were introduced to another person, supposedly another volunteer but actually an actor. They drew lots (actually rigged) to decide who would be 'learner' and who would be 'teacher'. The real volunteer was always given the teacher role but believed it had been a random allocation.

The 'learner' was then strapped to a chair, and told to expect some mild electric shocks, which wouldn't cause any permanent damage. He acted as if he was anxious and told them he had a weak heart. The research participant, looking on, was given a mild 15-volt electric shock to show what was involved (this was the only real shock in the whole study). They then sat in front of a console in the next room, with a microphone and speaker to communicate with the 'learner'. The console had a row of thirty switches, labelled from 15v to 450v, each switch increasing by 15 volts along the row. It also had descriptive labels beginning with 'slight shock', ranging to 'danger: severe shock' at 300 volts and finally 'XXX' at the highest levels.

The procedure was for the 'teacher' to read out a word and then four alternatives. The 'learner' had to identify the one that meant the same as the original, receiving a shock if they got it wrong. The shocks had to be increased for each wrong answer and were accompanied by (prerecorded) reactions from the learner, ranging from slight grunts to ever-increasing screams of pain, indications of severe distress and, finally, at 330 volts, an ominous silence. The supervisor pushed them to continue, saying things like 'The experiment requires that you continue' and 'You have no other choice. You must go on.'

Milgram's results shocked everyone. Instead of the 3 per cent the experts had predicted, Milgram found that all his research participants would go up to 300 volts. At this point, the learner refused to answer, but the teacher was told to take silence as a wrong answer and carry on increasing the shocks. In the experiments, 63 per cent of the time the teacher went right to the end, despite the silence from the next room. As far as they were concerned, the other person might have died.

Similar results were found in other countries, with a few cultural differences. The number of those who would continue until the end was slightly lower in Australia and slightly higher in Jordan, for example. Milgram himself carried out twenty-one different variations of the study, ranging from a condition in which the teacher had the free choice of shock level, when fewer than 3 per cent reached the maximum, to one in which there was no sound from the victim at all, when most people used the full range. A friendly supervisor reduced the level of maximum obedience to only 50 per cent of participants, while seeing another person disobey reduced it to just 10 per cent.

What was most apparent to Milgram, though, was the moral strain the research participants experienced. They were clearly distressed and argued with the supervisor, pleading to stop, but were always told, sometimes in quite a bullying manner, that they had to continue. Some participants coped by using psychological defence mechanisms like denial or avoidance – refusing to admit what was happening or pressing the switches only lightly, as if that could minimise the shock. Most tried to help the learner – for example, by stressing the correct answer as they read it out. But for many, the pressure to continue was too strong.

Not in every case, though. Gretchen Brandt and Jan Rensaleer were two of Milgram's participants who made disobeying look very easy. At 210 volts, Gretchen Brandt turned to the experimenter and calmly refused to continue; Jan Rensaleer also refused quite calmly, only becoming angry when the supervisor told him he had no choice but to continue. A choice, he replied firmly, was exactly what he did have. Both of these participants had experienced the implications of unthinking obedience: Gretchen Brandt had grown up in Nazi Germany, while Jan Rensaleer had been in Holland during the Second World War. For them, disobedience was simply their moral duty.

Concern with the ethics of research was stimulated by a paper criticising Milgram's studies, which gradually resulted in stringent ethical criteria preventing such research in the future. The core of the criticism was the possible psychological harm to the participants in his experiments, from finding that they were capable of 'killing' another person. Ironically, though, Milgram had been meticulous in that regard. He had conducted follow-up interviews with all the participants, not just soon after their involvement but also some time later, to make sure that they had not suffered in this way. Others were less careful, however.

The standard excuse at the Nuremberg trials was that people were only following orders. But those orders concerned the active participation in the murder of millions of people, and the Nuremberg judges ruled that this wasn't a sufficient excuse. Hannah Arendt wrote a book, *The Banality of Evil*, which was a detailed study of Adolf Eichmann, the person responsible for making sure that the Holocaust ran smoothly and that the death trains all arrived on time. At his trial, Eichmann came across as not self-evidently evil, and not even particularly hating Jews (although recent evidence challenges this). For the most part, those who were involved were ordinary people, who saw themselves as just doing their jobs. Milgram's work helps us to understand how that could happen.

CHAPTER 20

The Return of the Mind

Miller, Bruner and Neisser – Champions of the Cognitive Approach

Rats and stats! That's how some social scientists dismissed psychology in the mid-twentieth century. Although that insult was often politically motivated, given the intense competition for academic funding, and wasn't strictly true, there was nonetheless a grain of truth in it. A typical psychology student in the 1960s would receive a comprehensive grounding in learning theory, mainly based on the maze-running behaviour of the laboratory rat, and they would receive an equally thorough grounding in the statistical approaches that formed the basis of psychometric testing. Research methods were always based on the need to acquire measurable, quantitative data, and above all psychology was taught strictly as the science of behaviour. Any mention of the 'mind' was virtually heresy.

In the years immediately after the Second World War, both US and UK experimental psychology had become dominated by the behaviourist tradition. A large proportion of psychological research was conducted on animals, usually laboratory rats, following

Watson's assertion that stimulus-response learning was fundamentally the same in all organisms. Studies with human beings were carried out within the same rigid experimental paradigm, using only clearly demonstrated and quantifiable behaviour to provide data that could be regarded as valid, and regarding other types of information with deep suspicion. Behaviour, not thoughts, ideas or conversations, was the source material for psychology. That was unquestionable, and any attempt to suggest that there might be such a thing as a mind was seen as woolly thinking, unworthy of the name of science.

That approach met deep hostility from academics from neighbouring disciplines, such as sociology and anthropology, some of which still lingers today. They had no doubts that humans had minds, and furthermore that studying those minds was interesting – and necessary – in its own right. And they weren't alone. A general feeling of unease at the strict behaviourist approach was also growing among many experimental psychologists. George A. Miller was one of them.

In 1960, Miller was a professor of experimental psychology at Harvard, conducting experimental studies in speech and communication. These, however, had left him with a number of lingering doubts about the validity of the strictly behavioural approach. After a sabbatical year, which he spent exploring ideas from neighbouring disciplines, he realised that he just couldn't accept Harvard's narrow experimental approach any more. He discussed it with his friend Jerome Bruner, a social and developmental psychologist who shared his feelings and had been working in a related area. Together, they put a proposal to the university for the founding of a new centre, which became the Harvard Center for Cognitive Studies.

For Miller, even the use of the word 'cognitive' felt like heresy. Having worked firmly in the experimental tradition, he was aware of what a challenge it represented to the behaviourist model. The new approach suggested that (a) there was such a thing as a mind, (b) that the mind could process information, and (c) that it could affect what people did. Bruner was less disturbed – social psychology had never really accepted the behaviourist model, largely due to its Gestalt influences, so he was quite comfortable with the idea. Together, they became the leaders of a new movement in American psychology: one which retained the experimental tradition but investigated mental functioning like thinking, problem-solving, concept-formation and memory.

It helped that the two men were both eminent and respected psychologists in their own right. But it was also the right time. Doubts had been growing, and increasing numbers of psychologists became interested in cognitive functions. In this, they were able to draw on the early experimental research that had been dismissed by the behaviourists, such as that of James and Ebbinghaus, and their main focus was using objective, experimental methods to explore aspects of human thinking. Gradually, thinking became part of experimental psychology again. While animal studies of learning continued, studies of problem-solving, perception and memory also became regarded as acceptable by journal editors and other influential guardians of the academic world. But it's noticeable that almost nobody used the word 'mind'. 'Cognition' sounded so much more scientific, and dodged those years of prejudice.

Bruner had worked as a social psychologist in Eisenhower's Psychological Warfare Division, working on propaganda and popular attitudes, and immediately after the war he took up a post in educational psychology at Harvard. A classic study of his from that time involved asking poor and rich children to estimate the size of coins of different value. The poorer children, perhaps not surprisingly, consistently over-estimated the size of the coins – providing Bruner with empirical evidence that perception was more than the strictly neurological process that the behaviourists had assumed. Together with a colleague, Leo Postman, he performed several studies showing the influence of mental 'set', or preparedness. Their studies were unquestionably to do with the mind but were conducted rigorously within the experimental tradition. In 1956, he had published *A Study of Thinking*, which discussed these and other findings. So for Bruner, Miller's suggestion was both timely and appropriate.

One of the academics Miller had met during his sabbatical year was the psycholinguist Noam Chomsky. Although not strictly a psychologist, Chomsky had a profound influence on Miller, and subsequently on psychology itself, and he became known as one of the founders of cognitive science. His father had been an expert in the Hebrew language, which may have influenced the young Chomsky's decision to study how children become competent in language. He had begun by working in the behavioural tradition, which held that language was essentially acquired through experience: young children hear language around them and gradually decode the rules and principles of the language that is being spoken. Chomsky tried to make this idea work but found it couldn't really explain what was going on. His main problem was that competence isn't the same as performance: a child (or indeed any person) might only use a limited number of grammatical forms in their speech, but still be capable of understanding many more, including ways of saying things that they might not have encountered previously. Moreover, children all over the world acquire language at similar ages, and in similar ways.

As we saw in Chapter 13, Chomsky concluded that acquiring language must be an innate capacity in human beings. He suggested that the developing brain is structured in such a way as to produce a natural sense of basic grammar: that is, it can extract the essential principles of language no matter which language is actually being acquired. His impact on the new cognitive movement in psychology really began with his lengthy review of B.F. Skinner's book, *Verbal Behavior*, in which, as we know, he challenged Skinner's claim that language developed through operant conditioning. While psychologists have debated the ins and outs of Chomsky's model, and few would adopt it wholesale nowadays, it was a radical shake-up for the psychology of language. For Miller, it was yet another challenge to behaviourism, which helped his growing determination to stand up to its dominance.

The Harvard Center for Cognitive Studies was founded in 1960, and both Bruner and Miller used it as the centre for their subsequent research. Bruner continued his studies of mental set, while

Miller studied memory. The study that Miller is most famous for is his 'magical number 7'. This was how he described his findings that people are only able to keep a limited amount of information in mind at any one time. It might be single digits – letters or numbers – or it might be meaningful chunks, like 'BBC' or 'CNN', but most people can only keep an average of seven items in mind at any one time. That's an average, of course: some people might only manage five or six, while others can recall eight or nine, but there is a definite limit to how much we can stay consistently focused on – although we can remember a huge amount of stored information, and retrieve it when it becomes relevant.

Miller's paper stimulated several research programmes, and the resulting consensus was that there are three different types of memory: an immediate sensory 'buffer', which retains echoes of sensations; short-term memory of the sort one might use when inputting a verification code for online banking; and the long-term memory we use for the information we store throughout our lives. From there, psychologists went on to explore the precise nature of these memory stores and have identified several types of memory, such as procedural memory, which we might use when making a cup of tea, and episodic memory like the memory of your last holiday. We will come back to some of these ideas in Chapter 32, when we explore the impact of computer modelling on cognitive psychology.

Ulric Neisser was another major figure in the transition of American experimental psychology to include the cognitive domain. He had been a graduate student of Miller before Miller had nerved himself up to declare an overt interest in cognition, and he had also studied at Swarthmore after he graduated. This brought him into contact with Köhler and his associates and stimulated his growing interest in how psychological processes work in their social contexts. Later he moved to Brandeis University, where Abraham Maslow was engaged in challenging both behaviourism and psychoanalysis with his third way, as we saw in Chapter 15. He was particularly taken with Maslow's insistence that psychology should be primarily a force for good and should therefore emphasise the positive aspects of the human mind.

Neisser's own research was into how we process perceptual information, and especially how we search for particular things or people. In the experimental form, this meant searching for particular digits in arrays of numbers or letters, but even in using this abstract method, Neisser showed how perception is more than just a routine physiological process. Both the form of the letters and the mental readiness of the participant can make a real difference in what appears on the surface to be a fairly mechanical task.

In 1967, he published an influential book, *Cognitive Psychology*, which not only gave the new field its name, but also showed how it is possible to model the way that information flows and is processed in the mind. This naturally attracted parallels with how computers – then a new and fascinating innovation – process information, and studying information processing became a major focus for cognitive research. Researchers began to develop computational models, but importantly, they continued the experimental tradition of studying under rigidly controlled laboratory conditions, using material with as little meaning as possible so as to avoid 'contamination' by prior knowledge.

The focus on information processing made cognitive research more acceptable to mainstream psychology, but it worried Neisser considerably; he felt that it was important to take into account the social and personal contexts of cognition, and that the strictly experimental approach of the cognitive researchers missed the point. By adopting tight experimental control designed to remove all possible 'contaminating' factors, they were actually studying something quite artificial and divorced from everyday experience. He outlined this thinking in a 1976 book, *Cognition and Reality*, which described perception as being at the heart of cognition and saw it as a continuous cycle of perceptual search, informed by prior experience and the immediate context. Although it was far more relevant to what real human beings do, this book proved much less popular with cognitive researchers. Neisser himself remarked, sadly, that he supposed that he had been telling people that what they were doing wasn't really worthwhile, so perhaps their reaction was understandable.

That tension between cognition in the laboratory and cognition in everyday life has never really gone away. It influenced the perceptual theory developed by J.J. Gibson, also developed around this time, but which only really achieved full recognition in the 1990s, as we shall see in Chapter 33; and it informed a number of subsequent developments towards the end of the century. But the acceptance of cognition as a valid study in psychology was a major challenge to the dominance of behaviourism, and a milestone in the development of experimental psychology.

CHAPTER 21

Emotion and Stress
FIGHT OR FLIGHT, STRESS AND PSYCHOIMMUNOLOGY

Have you ever run for a bus or train and just missed it? You stand there at the bus stop or platform, breathing heavily. Your heart is pounding, and you feel a bit sweaty. It takes you a few minutes to get back to a calmer state. At these times, too, you're easily provoked. If someone says something that seems stupid or inane to you, it's much too easy to snap back, or to feel much more annoyed than you would usually be.

It's all to do with the state your body is in – a state that psychologists call arousal, although it's not the same as sexual arousal! It's a survival mechanism. When you feel frightened or threatened, or even anxious about missing the bus, your body tries to make sure that you have as much energy as possible. That's because, in primeval times, if you were frightened or threatened by something, it was probably something physical, which you would either have to fight or run away from. If you were going to fight, you'd need all the energy you could get, because losing might see you killed. And similarly, if you were going to run away, you'd need all the energy you could get, because if it caught you, you might still be killed. There was no point in holding energy back for later – there might not be a later!

This response is automatic, and it's called the 'fight or flight' reaction, for reasons that I hope are now obvious. It involves a number of physiological changes: you breathe more deeply, to get more oxygen into the blood; your heart beats faster and your blood pressure increases, so that oxygen reaches your muscles more quickly; your blood thickens so it clots more easily (in case you get wounded); and your digestion changes so it converts fats and sugars into energy very quickly, but puts digesting more complex foods like proteins temporarily on hold. If you're frightened, your skin becomes paler as blood is diverted towards the internal organs, you sweat and you get goosepimples, which are only vestigial in humans but in a long-haired mammal would mean its hair stood on end, so it looked bigger, and possibly less worth attacking.

The fight or flight syndrome was first identified as a full set of physiological responses by Walter Cannon in 1915. But of course, it was known before then. William James, often referred to as the father of American psychology, felt that this response was actually the explanation for how we feel emotions. He gave the example of tripping on the stairs and catching hold of the banister to save yourself. At the time, you do what's needed without thinking about it. But afterwards, you feel your heart beating faster, you breathe a little more quickly and your hands may feel a little sticky. It's only then, James argued, that you feel alarmed. Your mind interprets those physiological feelings as the fear of falling. In a famous quotation, James asserted that we don't cry because we feel sad, we feel sad because we cry. What he meant was that our emotions come from the mind making sense of the body's physiological reactions. It's easy to pick holes in James' idea – for example, asking how the body knows to generate that reaction in the first place. But his radical theory did generate research, and ultimately that research helped us to understand stress, and how it affects us.

In the modern world, people are not often faced with threats that call for running away or fighting. The things that make us feel anxious or frightened are more indirect, like the fear of being unable to pay the mortgage, or social anxieties. They also tend to be long-lasting, not going away quickly. Which brings us to the work of Hans Selye – a Hungarian-Canadian endocrinologist who had become interested in how cancer patients and others appear to experience particular symptoms, which he referred to as 'stress'.

Selye published *The Stress of Life* in 1956, and it became an immediate bestseller. He showed how arousal isn't an all-or-none response; there can be milder versions of the same set of reactions, to the point where quite a mild shock can set off the same physiological processes, but to a lesser degree. Your heart only speeds up a little, you do sweat a little more but not very much, and the other changes happen too although not as strongly. The reaction is still there, but it's almost unnoticeable.

Sometimes, too, it's beneficial. Athletes and other competitors find that a certain level of arousal is useful if they are to perform at their best. For most activities, there's an optimal level of arousal: it helps us up to a point, but if it gets too much then it starts to interfere with how we perform. Being annoyed might help you to speak freely in an argument, but if you get too angry you may find it difficult to find the right words. It's known as the Yerkes–Dodson Law, and it was first named in 1908, although it wasn't until much later that people really understood what's going on. That law states that the optimal level of arousal is higher for simple tasks than it is for complex ones. Being furiously angry while you vacuum the carpet is only likely to make you do it faster; but being in the same state while trying to compose a complaining email doesn't help at all. It's better to be a bit calmer – to reach your optimal level of arousal for that task, but not go over it.

Even an anxious or scary thought can trigger arousal to some degree, and it's this reaction that is spotted by the lie-detector machines known as polygraphs. They record several types of sympathetic response (arousal is caused by the action of the sympathetic nervous system), and they can identify even the very small changes that happen when someone tells a deliberate lie. The difficulty, though, is that what they are actually detecting is physi-

ological arousal, and it takes a skilled interviewer to tell the difference between an anxiety-producing true statement and a lie.

Selye showed that there is a relationship between the standard,
known forms of arousal and the similarities of the responses in
both animals that have been subjected to mild stressors for long
periods of time and cancer patients or people suffering from tuber-
culosis. These symptoms were definitely produced by stress, and
they were similar in animals and humans, but they weren't quite
like immediate arousal. Selye called this the 'general adaptation
syndrome', or 'GAS', and suggested that people (and animals) go
through a definite process of adaptation to long-term, continuous
stress.

Selye's general adaptation syndrome has three phases. The first
is an alarm phase, in which the arousal reaction is apparent. But if
the stress continues over time, it moves into the second phase,
the resistance stage. In this stage, the person (or animal) seems
to have calmed down, but there is still just as much adrenaline in
the bloodstream, and there is a tendency to overreact to stressful,
or perceived stressful, events. It's well known that constant anxiety
about money or work can damage personal relationships, and this
is a large part of the reason why. Because people in this state overreact, it's far too easy to get into arguments with loved ones, and
constant arguing will strain any relationship.

As Selye pointed out, the resistance stage is extremely damaging
for the body. It uses up the body's reserves of energy and also
significantly reduces our resistance to infection. If it goes on long
enough the person goes into the third phase, the exhaustion stage,
in which they finally give up the struggle. If they are fighting
cancers or other illnesses, that usually results in their death.

Since Selye published his book, a considerable industry has
developed around stress, ranging from academic research into
causal factors to recommendations for reducing stress, and ways of
managing stress positively. His work led to the development of two
new areas in psychology. One of these was the development of
psychoimmunology – that is, the relationship between psychological factors and the immune system of the body. The second was

the psychology of agency and control, which helped psychologists and psychotherapists to identify coping strategies to help people to deal with the harmful effects of long-term stress. We'll come back to that idea in Chapter 34.

There are different ways of looking at psychoimmunology. One is to look at it on a purely physiological level, and researchers have found that people with long-term stress have increased levels of chemicals known as glucocorticoids in the bloodstream. Over time, these attach themselves to the white blood cells that are the body's defence against infection, lowering their effectiveness. So someone under stress is more likely to catch an infectious illness, such as a cold or flu, and often feels tired and weak. A number of other illnesses have also been linked to long-term stress, including heart disease and gastric ulcers.

One of the more infamous animal experiments of the 1950s is referred to as Brady's monkeys, in which pairs of monkeys were given regular electric shocks. One monkey from each pair could press a lever that allowed it to hold off the shocks for twenty seconds at a time; the other could do nothing and just had to put up with whatever happened to them both. So both monkeys had the same physical pain, but only one had the additional psychological stress of having to press the lever at frequent intervals, for six hours at a time. After the experiment, several of the 'executive' monkeys died of duodenal ulcers, while their passive partners had no such problems. Joseph Brady explained this in terms of changes in stomach acidity brought about by long-term stress, and his study was regarded as 'proof' of a link between stomach ulcers and stress. Understandably, it attracted considerable criticism when animal welfare became a major concern in psychology, but that came later.

There are other ways of looking at psychoimmunology, though. The anthropologist Robin Horton, for example, showed how the way that non-technological societies deal with infectious diseases often acknowledges the importance of stress in a person's resistance to infection. According to Horton, traditional African medical practitioners, often derogatively called 'witch doctors', would begin their consultation with someone who had fallen ill with an infectious disease by asking them about recent social experiences: who they might have quarrelled with, or who they had been worrying about. They were particularly looking for sources of social stress, like recent arguments with friends or relatives.

To Western eyes, this seemed inappropriate. But, as Horton pointed out, in a society with a high level of infant mortality it makes a lot of sense, because anyone who survives to adulthood must already have a strong level of resistance to disease. The question isn't where the infection came from, but why the person's resistance was lowered enough for them to succumb to it. And in those societies, social stress is the most likely reason.

Selye pointed out that not all stress is negative; sometimes, it can be beneficial. He called positive stress 'eustress' and showed that there was actually no difference in the physiology of that and negative 'distress'. But eustress can have both mental and physical benefits. Sometimes, it's the way that the person understands what is happening that makes all the difference. Further research showed that the key concept here, in both humans and animals, is whether there is a sense of control over what is happening. We can cope with far more stress if we feel able to control it in some way. That insight had profound ramifications, not least in the way it eventually led to a whole new branch of psychology: positive psychology, which we will look at later in this book, in Chapter 37.

CHAPTER 22

Developing Relationships
IMPRINTING, RELATIONSHIP FORMATION AND THE
MATERNAL DEPRIVATION DEBATE

You'll probably have seen images of lines of ducklings following a mother duck, or young goslings following a human 'foster-parent'. The reason they do this is because of imprinting: a special, very rapid form of learning, which is distinctive in precocial animals – that is, animals that can move around soon after birth. Because they are mobile almost immediately, they could easily wander off and become prey to any predator in the vicinity. But they learn, rapidly and automatically, that they must stay close to their mother, and they become distressed if it seems they will be left behind. Experiments have shown that the underlying mechanisms are innate: newly hatched ducklings and goslings will follow the first moving object they see, and will even overcome physical barriers by climbing over obstacles or pushing through long grass to keep following.

Imprinting was studied in Europe by Konrad Lorenz before the Second World War, and several researchers assumed that this was the way that most mother–infant attachments were formed. In

America, though, the behaviourist tradition held sway, and the dominant assumption was that an infant developed an attachment to its mother because the mother was the food-provider. Feeding, it was thought, generated pleasurable sensations that were linked through conditioning to the presence of the mother. The behaviourists insisted that this was how infant–parent attachments were formed.

That idea was challenged, though, by Harlow's famous study of attachment in monkeys, which we looked at in Chapter 15, in which young monkeys preferred a cloth-covered model to a bare wire one, even though they were fed from the wire model. As those young monkeys matured, however, it was clear that their development was not normal. They were unable to interact effectively with other monkeys and were often bullied. Their artificial upbringing had deprived them of the opportunity to learn the basic skills of a social species. Later studies by Harlow, in which infant monkeys were brought up together, but with no adults, showed that social contact could go a long way in ameliorating that damage. While not completely normal, those monkeys interacted more effectively with others and were able eventually to integrate into a wider social group. Harlow had successfully challenged the behaviourist assumption that attachment only came from feeding, but he also showed that the nature of those attachments could have lasting effects. We'll come back to that idea later in this chapter.

Lorenz's model of imprinting rapidly became accepted as an explanation for attachment. It was, after all, still a form of learning and, for a while, it was taken as the basic process of attachment in all animals, including humans. Imprinting was the starting point for John Bowlby, the psychologist whose name has become pretty well synonymous with attachment theory. After a somewhat mixed career, including a stint in the Royal Navy, Bowlby had become interested in psychology. He was by then at Cambridge, attending lectures on biological psychology from Frederic Bartlett, and also reading psychoanalytic theory. He had been interested in attachment before the war, but his war work on officer selection helped him to develop his methodological and statistical knowledge.

When peace came, he joined the Tavistock Institute and established a research unit to look into the consequences of mother–child separation.

Bowlby had a strong background in psychoanalysis, and the work of the Tavistock Clinic was mainly based on the approach of Melanie Klein. But Bowlby didn't think that psychoanalysis offered a sufficient explanation for what happens in separation, when attachments are broken. He was friends with the ethologist Robert Hinde, who was also interested in relationships, and discussed recent ethological research on attachment with him. Having followed Harlow's research on infant monkeys with interest, Bowlby concluded that humans are biologically predisposed to form and maintain attachments with their primary caregivers – that is, the people who look after them and see to their day-to-day needs. This leads to the development of a two-way affectionate relationship between parent and child, which becomes the foundation for later adult relationships.

Bowlby outlined his theory in the 1950s, and his basic model of attachment has remained reasonably well accepted ever since, although with refinements to include other types of family relationships such as fathering and grandparenting. But he saw attachment as a single process, and the infant's relationship with their mother as special: a process he called monotropy. Research by his colleague Mary Ainsworth, though, showed that attachments could be of different kinds.

Ainsworth used the 'strange situation technique' to study attachment. This involved facing very young children with strangers, either with or without the presence of their mothers. She also did research on the behaviour of orphaned and hospitalised children, and identified three basic attachment styles: secure, insecure-avoidant and insecure-ambivalent/resistant. Children with secure attachment styles were confident in the presence of their mothers, not particularly distressed if they were absent, and easily soothed. Children with other types of attachment were more likely to reject the mother on her return, or to only approach her tentatively. Ainsworth also found that the mothers of securely attached infants tended to be more sensitive and more responsive to their babies, even during the first few months of their infant's life, and that they held their infants more carefully than mothers of infants who had been classified as either avoidant or ambivalent.

These findings connected with research by Rudolph Schaffer in the mid-1960s, who undertook ethological studies of parent–infant interaction in the infant's own home. He found that infants' strongest attachments were not necessarily with the person who looked after them most of the time. Instead, they attached most strongly to the person who responded most sensitively to their signals. That would usually be the mother, but sometimes it was someone who only spent an hour or so with the infant each evening. Sensitive responsiveness to the infant was the key. Shaffer's observations allowed attachment theory to explain seemingly unusual situations, like the infant forming its primary attachment to a working father rather than to a full-time mother.

Full-time mothering had actually become quite an issue in the post-war decades. As we've seen, Bowlby held to the belief that close and protective mothering was important, and in his best-selling book, *Child Care and the Growth of Love*, he discussed the potential emotional damage to children that could result if their relationship was disrupted. This generated a widespread social debate, partly stimulated by post-war studies of orphaned or hospitalised children, but also fuelled by a growing social concern about juvenile delinquency. Society's anxiety about beatniks, rock and roll, and the apparent disrespect for old-fashioned law and order among young people was generating a moral panic at the time.

Bowlby drew on his research with disturbed young people to suggest that it was maternal deprivation in the early years that disrupted the juvenile delinquent's capacity to form healthy relationships with others, and that this led to their delinquency. In extreme cases, he argued, it could even produce 'affectionless psychopathy' – a complete absence of any sense of social attachment or social responsibility.

The debate was intensified by a list in Bowlby's book which described situations likely to damage the child's attachment. It included the item 'Mother working full time', generating a political, as well as social, debate. At the time, employment was needed for returning servicemen, and women who had worked during the war were encouraged to become full-time 'housewives'. Many objected to being 'forced back into the kitchen', and some families simply couldn't afford to have just one adult income. But the idea that a mother with a full-time job was somehow damaging her child took hold of the popular imagination and became a very real social pressure.

In the 1960s, Michael Rutter reassessed Bowlby's evidence and the question of maternal deprivation itself. He found that juvenile delinquency was usually a reaction to the immediate situation: adolescents from stressful homes were more likely to become delinquent, and those from homes where the stress had been resolved usually returned to a less rebellious life. Rutter's book challenged maternal deprivation concerns and remained in print for many years – mainly because the debate about working mothers continued to rumble on in society at large.

The maternal deprivation debate also focused attention on the effects of severe deprivation and continuing neglect. Stories of feral children – children who were found wild, apparently never having experienced human contact – have abounded through the centuries, like the story of the twins, Romulus and Remus, who were supposed to have been abandoned as babies but stayed alive by being suckled by a female wolf and grew up to become mighty warriors and the founders of Rome. Most of the more recent accounts, though, described feral children as being wild and untameable, and incapable of becoming civilised.

Like many others, Bowlby shared Freud's belief that damaging early experience causes lasting effects in adulthood. But case studies of severely deprived children showed that, with the right kind of care, a remarkable degree of recovery was possible. One of the most famous cases was the child Genie, who was discovered at the age of fourteen. She had been kept confined by her father since she was only twenty months old, tied to a chair and fed only on baby food. She was not spoken to and was punished if she made any noise. When she was found, she couldn't talk or understand language. But with care and training from a team of psychologists, she learned quickly and, after a couple of years, she could use language quite competently.

Sadly, however, Genie was to fall victim to the methodological straitjacket of the time. Although the researchers had masses of data – film of Genie and recordings of interviews with her – that data was all qualitative, not numbers. This, to the psychological establishment of the time, meant that it was anecdotal and unscientific, so not real evidence at all. Their research funding was therefore stopped, and Genie returned to the care system, where she was fostered and again abused. The researcher who had cared for her, Susan Curtiss, was repeatedly refused contact even decades later.

Other cases were more positive. Two sisters took on the fostering of a pair of severely neglected six-year-old Czech twins who had been locked in a small cupboard or in the cellar of the house, with no social contact and no toys. When found, they could barely walk and only had a few words, which they had picked up before their father was given care of them. But with loving care and stimulation, they progressed rapidly, developing new skills and abilities. They were cheerful and popular at school and had warm and loving relationships with their foster-mothers.

In another case, a child who had been kept in an attic and suffered severe neglect was discovered at six and a half years old. Isabelle was given loving care and prolonged and expert attention. When first found, she couldn't speak and didn't recognise objects or people. But eighteen months later, she had made a rapid recovery. When examined by a psychologist, she came across as a bright, happy little girl who was doing well at school and was popular with schoolmates. She learned more quickly than other children of her age, and made up the skills that she had lacked before. Far from her being irreparably damaged, the care she was receiving had produced an accelerated recovery. As we saw in Chapter 5, Anna Freud had found a similar effect in the Bulldogs Bank children. These studies suggest that children can show an amazing amount of resilience, and that even damaging early childhood experience can be overcome with loving care and appropriate learning opportunities.

Attachment theory, then, had moved from a rigid behaviourist insistence on stimulus-response conditioning, to a biological 'instinctive' model, to a psychoanalytic approach emphasising maternal bonding, and eventually to a recognition of the importance of social interaction and loving care in both early experience and for repairing early trauma. That gradual recognition of the importance of social interaction was reflected in many other areas of psychology throughout the latter part of the twentieth century.

CHAPTER 23

Social Learning
GROUP CONFLICT, NORMS AND LEADERSHIP STYLES

As we saw in Chapter 20, George Miller had to nerve himself up to challenge the dominance of behaviourism. But in the meantime, another psychologist was quietly getting on with it. Albert Bandura – justifiably one of the most famous names in psychology – also wasn't happy with the behaviourist insistence that all learning derives from trial-and-error S-R (stimulus-response) connections.

Bandura consistently maintained a practical approach, possibly stemming from the way that, after finishing high school, he had spent some time working in Canada's Yukon Territory. The hard-working, hard-drinking and gambling culture that he found there was very different from that of his Albertan village upbringing and helped him to gain a wider perspective on life in general. At university, he fell into psychology almost by accident. He shared a carpool with medical and engineering students who all had early starts. Since his own lectures didn't begin until later, he looked for another early course to take, found psychology, and was hooked from then on. After graduation he went to the University of Iowa for his doctorate, working with Arthur Benton, who had been a student of William James and Clark Hull: the former was an experimentalist who recognised the importance of mind, and the latter a strict behaviourist, representing the dominant approach of the time.

Bandura was interested in learning, but he felt that the behaviourist insistence that learning could only happen from direct trial and error was too limiting. In fact, he believed, we do most of our learning second hand, by observing and imitating other people. Bandura began research on what he called 'observational learning' in the early 1960s and conducted the now-famous 'bobo doll' experiments. In these, children were shown films of adults acting aggressively towards, and even attacking, a large punch-bag-style model known as a bobo doll. They were then taken into a playroom that contained a number of toys, including a bobo doll. Repeated studies showed that the children would copy what they had seen on screen: they had learned by observing someone else's behaviour, not by their own trial-and-error experience.

Bandura was careful to make sure that his research was carried out in strict accordance with behaviourist and experimental principles. His demonstrations of observational learning became widely accepted, quietly incorporating a small bit of mental representation into the strict behaviourism of learning theory. That's why he is sometimes (quite rightly in my view) regarded as one of the founders of cognitive behaviourism. Bandura continued to study different aspects of imitation and identification, focusing particularly on the effects of modelling and self-regulation. By 1977, the cognitive movement was gaining ground in America, and he was able to be upfront about cognitive influences. His book, *Social Learning Theory*, openly discussed how social influences affect both cognition and behaviour. Quietly, Bandura had made a massive impact on psychology's knowledge of learning processes. But his legacy didn't stop there. He went on to explore the various mechanisms of personal agency, which we will come back to in Chapter 34.

Social psychologists, though, had always been a little less influenced by behaviourism, largely due to the influence of those Gestalt psychologists who had moved to America. At this time, concern about social issues was on the increase. By the 1960s, Martin Luther King was leading the civil rights movement, Angela Davis was openly advocating Black rights and communism, and Malcolm X was promoting African-American unity. Understandably, American society was becoming increasingly worried about social prejudice, and this concern was reflected in the research projects that emerged at this time.

Muzafer Sherif, whose work on conformity had stimulated Asch's famous studies, had married his research assistant Carolyn Wood in 1945. Together they went on to explore some of the factors influencing the development of group norms and inter-group hostility. Muzafer Sherif became well known for this research, but in fact, as he insisted indignantly, it was Carolyn who was really the driving force and theoretician behind most of it. But the prevalent sexism of the day, combined with academic elitism, meant that she was unable to publish in her own name, so the research papers had to be attributed to her husband. It is only recently that Carolyn Sherif has received the credit she was due.

One of their most famous studies was the 'Robbers' Cave' experiment, reported in 1961. It was conducted in a boys' summer camp, in which the Sherifs picked two carefully matched groups, each consisting of twenty-two twelve-year-olds. The first stage allowed the Sherifs to explore how group identities form: the two groups were kept separate, and the boys were encouraged to support their own groups. They developed their own status hierarchies, named themselves – the 'Eagles' and the 'Rattlers' – and made their own flags. Leaders emerged, and the groups developed their own informal rules of conduct and norms for their behaviour. And as they became aware of the other group, they began to become competitive.

In the second stage of their research, the psychologists arranged competitive activities between the groups, with attractive prizes for the winners. Immediately, members of each group began to show hostility towards members of the other group. During this phase, they ate together for the first time, and those occasions frequently

produced derogatory name-calling and singing. Hostilities intensified over the next five days: they raided each other's cabins, burned
the other's flags, and complained to the supervisors about eating at
the same time as the other group.

In the third phase, the researchers created joint activities that
were deliberately designed to bring the two groups together, like
Fourth of July celebrations. But these didn't seem to work: inter-
group hostilities were as strong as ever. It was only when the two
groups had to work together to solve a serious common problem,
like repairing the pipeline that supplied the camp's water, that the
groups began to co-operate with one another. This was reinforced
with other joint activities, such as when the groups combined to
pull down a partially felled and dangerous tree that was preventing
them from using their playing field, and the time that all the boys
contributed to buy a film to watch that evening. These joint activities were so successful that the groups were fully integrated by the
time they had to go home. They asked to share a coach, and even
pooled their prize money to buy everyone drinks during the
journey.

The Robbers' Cave study was an influential demonstration of
how group norms can develop, and how intergroup contacts could
be managed. It led to an interest in social processes, leading to
research into both leadership and prejudice. However, by contrast
with the group studies emerging in Europe, the individualistic
assumptions that dominated American culture, society and
psychological theory meant that attention focused on individual
behaviour in the group, rather than on the general impact on the
group itself.

This trend applied in other studies too. A number of researchers
drew upon older work such as LaPiere's 1930s report of a trip
across America with two Chinese friends. They visited several
hotels, the owners of which were known to have strongly prejudiced attitudes, which they expressed openly. But the Chinese
couple were made as welcome as anyone else. A plethora of laboratory studies explored the apparent discrepancy between attitudes
and behaviour and developed a variety of complex explanations to

account for it. What they didn't seem to take into account, though, was Asch's work on conformity, which showed how people's social natures make them unwilling to contradict or confront other people in a face-to-face situation. Instead, most of the theories put forward to explain the apparent contradictions, attitudes and behaviour focused on how the individual was processing their information.

Not all research into prejudice was equally limited, though. In 1968, a teacher, Jane Elliott, was spurred on by the assassination of Martin Luther King to discuss what it was like to be Black in America with her third-grade pupils. The class agreed to try an exercise to see what it felt like, so Elliott separated them into two groups on the basis of whether their eyes were blue or brown. In the first week, the blue-eyed children were deemed to be the 'favoured' group; in the second week it was the brown-eyed children. Each time, those in the 'inferior' group wore distinguishing fabric collars and were given less favourable treatment, while the children in the 'favoured' group were given special privileges and favoured treatment in the classroom.

The study had more dramatic effects than she had perhaps expected. The children in the 'favoured' group began to act arrogantly towards the others, often talking to them in a superior and bullying manner. They also did better at their schoolwork, sometimes even managing to succeed in tests they hadn't been able to do before. Those in the 'inferior' group, on the other hand, became timid and subservient. Their schoolwork suffered, and they tended to separate themselves as a group from the others. Elliott's study, although not the first of its kind, became widely publicised, and has been regarded as a 'milestone' in American social psychology.

Her study was a clear example of what the Sherifs had referred to as 'realistic conflict theory', as an explanation for how group prejudices develop. This theory argued that conflict between groups, and the subsequent prejudice from group members towards others, was likely to develop if there was real competition for privileges. When two groups are in competition for privileges, the group that has them will become defensive and protective of their advantage, while members of the group that doesn't have them feel frustrated and envious. The outcome is intergroup hostility and, in an unrestrained situation, conflict. This theory was an important precursor to Tajfel's theory of social identification, one of the core theories in European social psychology, which we will come back to in Chapter 28.

The study of group processes only had a limited impact on mainstream psychology, but it became a major influence in organisational psychology. Before the Second World War, the Gestalt psychologist Kurt Lewin had conducted research into leadership styles. His work became particularly influential after the war as a model for management and organisational leadership. Lewin's classic study was conducted with groups of children in a boys' after-school model-making club. The psychologists organised them into three groups: one with a strictly authoritarian leader, one with a democratic leader who would chat with the boys and discuss their work with them, and a third with a laissez-faire leader who left the boys pretty much to themselves. After seven weeks, the leaders were rotated, and then rotated again after another seven weeks, until each group had worked with each type of leader.

Lewin found that the three styles produced very different patterns of behaviour. Those with the authoritarian leader worked hard, but they didn't really co-operate with one another, and if the leader was absent they didn't do much work at all. Those with a laissez-faire leader didn't do much work anyway and tended to be a bit aggressive and quarrelsome. The group with the democratic leader, however, worked consistently and cheerfully, regardless of whether the leader was present, and often helped one another out.

Lewin's research was published in 1939, and it had – and continues to have – a tremendous impact on management theory. It also stimulated more research into group processes, such as the different types of roles people adopt in group discussions, and how leader expectations can become self-fulfilling, coming true because people believe them. Douglas McGregor, for instance, distinguished between Theory X leaders, who hold the general view that people are lazy and will only work if you make them do it, and

Theory Y leaders, who believe that people usually like to work and will work hard if they are respected and trusted. These beliefs, too, can be self-fulfilling: people working for a Theory X leader feel less appreciated and so become less motivated. They are more likely to take sick leave and generally don't work as hard. McGregor's approach continues to influence organisational psychology and management theory today, although its impact on mainstream social psychology was more limited.

As psychology developed in the post-war period, then, it developed a focus on the way that people and groups interact. Psychologists explored how expressed prejudice was not always reflected in individual behaviour, how group norms could develop that encourage or minimise prejudice, and the way that different types of leadership could produce very different types of behaviour. In the next chapter, we will look at psychological research that aimed to understand how attitudes can be changed.

Changing Attitudes
COGNITIVE DISSONANCE, ATTITUDE MEASUREMENT
AND THEORIES OF PREJUDICE

'Flee the Flood!' read the headline. Lake City and large parts of the rest of the world would soon be swamped by a massive flood – to be precise, on 21 December 1954. This was the message from medium Dorothy Martin (aka Mrs Keech), who said that she had received the warning from aliens from the planet Clarion. At this time, America was in the grip of a UFO mania, and the aliens, apparently, had offered to rescue survivors in a flying saucer. Mrs Keech gathered a group of believers and retreated to high ground overlooking the city. Many of these believers had taken drastic action preparing for the catastrophe: some had sold their houses and possessions; some had left their jobs or ended relationships; and all of them expected the end of the world to come on that day.

22 December dawned, no flood had come, and the world didn't end. This was perfect research material for Leon Festinger, Henry Riecken and Stanley Schachter, a small group of social psychologists who had joined the group professing to be believers. They had chatted with the group members before the event, during the

waiting period and afterwards, exploring how they would deal with the contradiction of their beliefs. Some, who had been less committed to the group, simply left. But the most committed members argued that it was their actions and demonstrations of faith that had caused God to relent and save the world after all. They had modified their beliefs in order to rationalise and justify their actions.

For Festinger and his team, it was a clear example of cognitive dissonance. Admitting that the original prediction was wrong would have given those people uncomfortable mental conflicts. Not only would they have to admit that they were wrong, but they would also have to acknowledge that the extreme actions they had taken were entirely unnecessary. Changing their beliefs to justify their actions meant that they could avoid the cognitive tension caused by the contradictions in their beliefs. Festinger's study came at a time when research into attitudes was particularly popular, and it attracted attention as a clear example of attitude change.

American psychology in the post-war era, as we have seen, was largely dominated by the behaviourist perspective. From starting off as a minority movement, its main ideas had become accepted implicitly, dominating mainstream psychology through assumptions rather than by individual psychologists explicitly allying themselves with behaviourism. A major element of that acceptance was to do with quantitative research and the growing idea that any true science should have a mathematical base.

Statistical techniques had been part of the psychometric field since the early days of Galton and Spearman. J.P. Guilford had published a comprehensive statistical handbook for psychology and education students in 1942, and by the 1960s this was in its fourth edition. The emphasis on statistical analysis had several effects: one, as we saw in the tragic case of Genie, was to dismiss qualitative forms of analysis as not being 'valid' evidence, and another was to encourage a growing perception (and sometimes hostility) from the other social sciences as psychology being just 'rats and stats'. But it also enabled psychologists to conduct research into psychological processes like attitudes – as long as they were measured quantitatively.

As we saw in Chapter 9, attitude research began before the Second World War, but it really came into its own in the post-war decades. Researchers explored various aspects of attitudes: how to measure them scientifically, how they connect with the individual's personal values, what attitudes are for, and whether people are consistent in their attitudes. There was also an ongoing debate about the precise relationship between attitudes and behaviour, and a plethora of theories designed to explain what attitudes are and how they come about.

Measures of attitudes took various forms, as researchers tried to capture the more subtle aspects of attitudes. Charles Osgood's 'semantic differential', for example, used pairs of adjectives as similes or metaphors, inviting the respondent to indicate how much they felt that a particular event or object was, say, warm or cold, friendly or hostile, and so on. Imaginative though it was, the analysis of the semantic differential was problematic for two reasons. It assumed that everyone attributed the same meaning to the same words, and, above all, it relied on qualitative interpretations of the results.

What was really considered to be important, at this time, was numerical data. A scaling system developed by Rensis Likert provided one type of answer. Likert proposed a five- or seven-point continuum, which could give a graduated response. People could be invited to say, for example, how much they agreed or disagreed with a specific statement. This didn't give precise numbers, but it did give ordinal data – that is, data that indicated whether a particular score was more or less than another; and there were statistical techniques to deal with that type of data. Likert scales are still used extensively, in opinion polls and consumer research as well as in the measurement of attitudes or beliefs.

Attitude theories ranged in scope, from the idea that attitudes simply reflect social judgements, to the idea that they are all about maintaining cognitive balance. The Austrian psychologist Fritz Heider believed that there is a strong tendency for people to prefer their attitudes to be consistent with one another, and that inconsistency (or, at least, inconsistency that the person becomes aware of) leads to a kind of cognitive stress. It was this idea that formed the foundation for Festinger's research into cognitive dissonance.

Other studies explored the functions of attitudes and identified at least four different ways that people use them. Firstly, they can give meaning to our experiences, helping us to understand the world and how we should react towards people or events. They have a utilitarian function, helping our social interactions by making us appear socially acceptable. They allow us to express our personal values, and what we see as the more positive sides of our inner selves. And their fourth function is that they serve unconscious purposes: some attitudes are useful for people because they cover up unconscious conflicts or motives. For example, the reaction formation seen in some people who express highly prejudiced attitudes might really be covering up their own conflicts on that issue.

Another branch of attitude research explored how people's actions often don't match with the attitudes they claim to have. One popular explanation was that there was an important difference between attitudes in very specific situations and attitudes about the world in general. This might, for example, explain why the hoteliers in the LaPiere study we looked at in the last chapter expressed prejudiced attitudes towards Chinese people, but were nonetheless welcoming to the Chinese couple when they arrived at the hotel. Martin Fishbein and Icek Ajzen conducted a meta-analysis of the various studies of attitudes and behaviour, and developed what they named the 'theory of reasoned action'. This was based on the assumption that people usually behave in a sensible way, considering the implications of their actions, so if you want to predict how people will behave, it is more useful to look at their intentions than to try to predict their behaviour from the attitudes.

The interest in attitudes also led to theories designed to explain prejudice, which had become a hot topic in America in the postwar decades. We looked at some of the explanations developed immediately after the war in earlier chapters, but many other theories were generated in the following decades. By the 1970s, for example, psychologists were beginning to develop cultural theories, like pointing out that prejudice against Black people was much more widespread, and also more extreme, in the southern United States than it was in the north, and noting how this reflected the general cultural differences between the two.

That idea was supported by other research. A study that looked at changes in attitudes from white immigrants to Zimbabwe (then Southern Rhodesia) found that the longer they stayed the more prejudiced they became. And another study of the time compared racial prejudice in the Netherlands and the UK, countries that had a similar proportion of Black to white people, and found that it was much lower in the Netherlands. The difference was a culture that explicitly frowned on such prejudice, and regarded racist discourse as being socially unacceptable, which wasn't the case in the UK at that time. Overall, it became apparent that social and cultural norms were much more influential in prejudice than personality traits.

That didn't account for everything, of course. Some people remain prejudiced even in highly tolerant societies, although there is evidence that this tends to be encouraged by the mini-cultures that exist in families. But the link between prejudiced attitudes and real social discrimination is harder to pin down. Gordon Allport proposed five stages by which social prejudice can move to the kind of extreme annihilation policy shown in Nazi Germany and in other 'ethnic cleansing' pogroms. A society would move, he said, from 'antilocution' – that is, hostile talk and verbal denigration – to avoidance of the target group without specific harm. That is followed by active discrimination in employment, housing and social participation, which readily leads to the fourth stage, which is an increased frequency of physical attacks, both on people and on their property. The fifth, and final, stage is where attempts are made to get rid of the group altogether, as in the Holocaust, the Rwandan massacres and, sadly, many other examples. It is for this reason, Allport argued, that tackling prejudice on what appears to be a superficial level, like everyday talk, is important. Left untackled, it can so easily lead on to more extreme actions.

One particularly influential study was published by Carl Hovland and Robert Sears in 1940. They documented how measures of economic wellbeing correlated with the frequencies of lynchings of Black people in the southern United States and found that a significant increase in lynchings went along with a decline in economic conditions. This is the process of scapegoating, where a minority group or out-group is blamed for changes in economic circumstances or other forms of unwelcome social change, even though it is nothing to do with them. The typical argument of immigrants 'taking up our jobs' or consuming the country's resources in other ways is how scapegoating works. Scapegoating doesn't explain all prejudice, but it remains a robust explanation for changes in the levels of prejudice in society.

But the really important question, of course, is how to change people's attitudes. Leon Festinger's theory of cognitive dissonance offered one possibility. Before he and his research team infiltrated the group of Mrs Keech's followers and witnessed their reactions to the non-ending of the world, they had already been investigating dissonance in the laboratory. Their research programme had begun with Fritz Heider's ideas of attitudes as reflecting a search for cognitive balance: Mrs Keech's predictions and the behaviour of her group of believers show what happens when people's beliefs are obviously disconfirmed, but that was a particularly dramatic example.

Festinger's laboratory research showed that, for the most part, we can cope with a small amount of imbalance. Cognitive dissonance only really comes into play when two beliefs or attitudes directly contradict one another, and the person becomes aware of it. The response is either to change one of the cognitions, or to add an extra one to 'explain' the apparent discrepancy. The prejudiced hoteliers in LaPiere's study could rationalise the discrepancy of their attitudes by adding an additional belief that the Chinese couple were particularly 'nice' people. Mrs Keech's followers didn't change their main cognitions; they simply added the belief that the actions they had taken had made the difference.

Cognitive dissonance theory was backed up by a lot of experimental evidence and remains one of the major factors in attitude change. It was one of the gentler theories of the time: as the Cold War progressed, some researchers investigated rather more extreme methods of attitude change, through drugs and methods of brainwashing.

CHAPTER 25

Psychology in the Cold War
The Minnesota Starvation Studies and the CIA Mind-control Experiments

Would you be prepared to starve in the name of science? Thirty-six men did. In fact, more than that were prepared to: those thirty-six men had been selected from a larger pool of volunteers. In this study, which is known as the 'Minnesota Starvation Experiment', they were put on extremely low diets for twenty-four weeks, designed to produce severe weight loss. Then their food was increased, but the levels of proteins and vitamins were varied, so researchers could find out which foods would help them to recover most effectively. Finally, they were allowed to eat what they wanted for another eight-week period.

During their semi-starvation period, the men were required to walk 22 miles a day and were given only the kinds of food available in famine times – basically, bread and potatoes. Understandably, they became obsessive about food: some of them would cut their food up into tiny pieces and eat it very slowly. Others collected recipe books or eating utensils. Their mental health declined significantly, with increases of hysteria, hypochondriasis and depression, and feelings of dizziness and sluggishness. The last two symptoms vanished when they began receiving more food, but not the other symptoms. Some of the participants reported that it was years before they felt normal again.

This research has been cited as an example of questionable ethics, but the men were carefully monitored throughout and the researchers were careful to adhere to the ethical principles being discussed at the time. The information gained from these studies was circulated in a pamphlet advising care organisations how to help people to recover from semi-starvation, which was a significant proportion of the western European population in the years immediately following the Second World War. Those findings are still used to help those recovering from periods of anorexia or other eating disorders. Perhaps most importantly, when the men were interviewed fifty-seven years later, all but one of them said they would do it again.

A set of ethical principles known as the Nuremberg Code was produced as an outcome of the 1945 Nuremberg trials of war criminals, which followed the discovery of the concentration camps. Before the Second World War, it was generally assumed that research conducted in the name of science was entirely justified, regardless of the wellbeing of the subjects. As the extreme and inhumane experiments that had been conducted on concentration camp victims came to light, those being prosecuted argued that these experiments were intended to further knowledge about the human condition, and were in principle no different from other research that had been conducted before the war. The judges disagreed, and the result was the Nuremberg Code, which established standards for research with human subjects.

A central tenet of the code was that research should only be carried out with volunteers, and not with coerced subjects like prisoners. It should also be for the good of society and conducted so as to avoid unnecessary suffering – although the key word here is 'unnecessary'. The Minnesota starvation studies were initiated because of the recognition of the danger of famine across Europe in the post-war years. Although the researchers were careful to adhere to the current ethical principles, not everyone was as meticulous.

During the post-war years, relationships between Russia and America, never great at the best of times, became gradually worse. By the 1950s, they were in a state of outright hostility: the two sides represented entirely different economic and political approaches and, while not directly warring with one another, supported opposing sides in a series of smaller wars across the globe. In America, anti-communist feelings were manipulated into virtual hysteria by politicians like Senator McCarthy, who initiated a number of 'witch hunts' designed to remove those with communist sympathies from positions of authority or influence.

During this time, rumours abounded about the use of 'brain-washing' techniques in Russia, brought about by people who defected to the Soviet Union for ideological reasons. They were augmented by accounts from returning prisoners from the Korean War, who described lengthy and torturous experiences designed to make them confess to ideological 'wrongdoing' and to convince them that communism was superior. Towards the end of the 1950s, a British psychiatrist, William Sargant, described these techniques in his book *Battle for the Mind*, in which he not only showed the similarities between these 'modern' methods and earlier methods of religious conversion, but also drew on Pavlov's conditioning experiments with dogs. Sargant argued that, given enough stressors and systematic starvation, just about anybody would eventually give in to these brainwashing techniques.

But that came later. What Sargant didn't say in his book was that he had been involved – albeit peripherally – in a massive American Intelligence project known as MK-Ultra. This began in 1953 and was a systematic and wide-ranging series of illegal experiments.

The project had several aims: one was to identify methods for achieving brainwashing; another was to see if it was possible to create an assassin triggered by a post-hypnotic command like that described in the novel *The Manchurian Candidate*; a third was to discover whether there were combinations of chemicals that could reliably act as a 'truth drug', and so on. MK-Ultra systematically violated the Nuremberg Code, despite America having signed up to it at the time it was developed.

The MK-Ultra project research explored many different ways of disorienting people, including verbal denigration, electric shocks and sexual abuse. One significant practice was sensory deprivation, in which people were deprived of sensory input (sight, sound and even touch) by being cocooned in padding so movement was impossible, or floated in tanks, or in several other ways. These experiments often left people with lifelong problems, ranging from depression to severe mental illness.

The MK-Ultra project was huge, involving universities, hospitals and prisons. It has been said that just about anybody who was anybody in the American behavioural sciences was funded in some way by the CIA at this time. Most of those scientists were unaware of the real source of their funding, though: it was dispensed through front organisations which didn't reveal where the money was actually coming from. Others only discovered that their own research had been part of it much later. Among them was Dr Timothy Leary, a clinical psychologist conducting research into the use of the psychedelic drug LSD as a therapeutic medium. Leary had become interested in the power of psychedelics during a visit to Mexico in 1957, when he had taken mescaline, which he described as a turning point in his life. When he returned to America, he set up the Harvard Project, in which his own research programme investigated the effects of psychoactive drugs, including LSD.

From his results, Leary argued that these drugs could be of positive benefit in psychotherapy, as long as proper attention was given to set and setting – set being the person's frame of mind, and setting being the context in which the drug was taken. He also conducted the 'Concord Prison Experiment', which showed that the reoffending rate could be reduced by a third if prisoners received a carefully guided experience with these drugs. However, Leary, perhaps unwisely, was absolutely evangelical about his findings, recommending LSD as a mind-expanding drug for everyone, and inspiring many young Americans to drop out of school and join the new counter-culture. His extreme views were too much for Harvard, and he was eventually fired as a professor, but he continued to advocate the use of mind-expanding drugs publicly, to the embarrassment and later anger of the more conventional American establishment. LSD was made illegal in 1968 (it had been legal up to that time), following which Leary was arrested many times for drug offences.

In the meantime, however, the CIA had been observing his research with interest. They purchased large supplies of LSD from the Swiss laboratory where it was manufactured. They were possibly funding that laboratory too, since they funded almost any research into psychoactive drugs that they could find – as well as many other projects. The CIA experiments into LSD included such bizarre investigations as exploring what would happen if elephants were given the drug – on the rather odd grounds that, since it seemed to simulate psychosis in humans, perhaps it would simulate a similar condition, 'musth', in elephants. It had already been shown that spiders on the drug would spin extremely regular webs, goats would make stereotyped geometric patterns as they walked around, and cats would adopt strange positions. So why not try elephants? To my mind, the real question is why; but nonetheless an elephant in Oklahoma City Zoo, Tusko, died from an overdose of the drug. That created a press furore, but two others, in a secret location, were given a much lower dose in their drinking water and just spent their time rocking and swaying until the drug wore off.

The CIA also conducted a number of other clandestine experiments, ostensibly investigating the potential of LSD as a 'truth' drug, but more often simply observing how it generated mental disorientation. Thousands of Americans and Canadians were unwitting participants in these experiments, and in Lexington, Kentucky, hundreds of drug-addicted prison inmates were bribed with heroin to participate in experiments with LSD and mescaline. In Edgewood, Maryland, nearly 7,000 soldiers were systematically exposed to various chemicals: not just psychoactive ones but also organophosphates and mustard gas. The men suffered long-term physical and psychological consequences: a third of them died in their forties, and those who survived were permanently disabled by poor health. In 1975, Congress finally investigated Edgewood and it was shut down.

During this period, LSD was often administered without warning, even to members of the CIA themselves. Timothy Leary's warnings about 'set and setting' were entirely ignored, and unsuspecting subjects – even visitors – might be given it in a cup of coffee or through some other clandestine method. They were only told that they had been given the drug, if at all, about twenty minutes later. These experiments continued for a further decade, producing a range of outcomes including amnesia, paralysis, depression and schizophrenia, but these were never reported to medical personnel. In one famous case, one of the scientists involved, Dr Frank Olson, jumped out of a thirteenth-storey window, ostensibly from drug-induced depression. Did he fall or was he pushed? Opinions are divided: the official verdict was suicide, but his family insisted that he had been having doubts about the project, and that a subsequent autopsy showed evidence of a blow to the head before the fall.

Such questions are not uncommon, owing to the secrecy of the project and the fact that, when the Watergate files were uncovered in 1973, the director of the CIA ordered all documents relating to MK-Ultra to be destroyed. It was only because some documents had been mis-filed in another building that the project became known. Among other things, they gave evidence of inhumane experiments on children, using those whose parents were involved in child pornography so couldn't complain. Various lawsuits happened in the 1990s, and a few victims of the MK-Ultra programme were compensated – but only those who could prove definitively that their ill-health or psychological damage came from the experiments. It's a fruitful ground for conspiracy theorists, because so much of what happened really was clandestine and secretive, and affected so many people.

At the same time, and not unrelated, a range of increasingly severe 'treatments' for mental patients were being developed, spearheaded by the same psychiatrists who were linked with the CIA studies. William Sargant was one of them. The treatments included insulin shock therapy, in which patients were given such high doses of insulin that they went into a near-death coma and were sometimes kept like that for long periods. Electroshock therapy, which involved passing an electric current through the brain, was another source of experimentation. It produced severe convulsions and temporary amnesia, which worsened and eventually became permanent if the treatment was repeated, which was sometimes daily. The apparent success of electroshock treatment at lifting depression (possibly because of the amnesia, as people forgot their problems temporarily) meant that it continued as a psychiatric treatment until well into the 1970s, although it was administered less often. Such treatments became less extreme, as mind-suppressing drugs, such as chlorpromazine (Largactil), emerged, but their brutality generated its own reaction, which we will look at in the next chapter.

Challenging Psychiatric Orthodoxy
CRITICISMS OF THE MEDICAL MODEL AND THE
ANTI-PSYCHIATRY MOVEMENT

It's the 1960s, and the world is new. Challenging ideas are popping up all over the place, and young people are making their own statements, in fashion and music but also in how they see the world's problems and what we should be doing about them. Their movement is fuelled by radical ideas, from philosophers like Nietzsche and Sartre, from feminists like Simone de Beauvoir and from Black radicals like Frantz Fanon. Their ideas have even penetrated into psychiatry, and the whole medical approach to mental illness is being questioned.

The 1961 book *The Myth of Mental Illness* by Thomas Szasz opened up that particular debate. He questioned the idea that people who were psychiatrically disturbed were actually ill in any medical sense. Szasz had become increasingly concerned about the use of forced psychiatric treatments, which, as we saw in the last chapter, had become increasingly severe, and often quite brutal. He was also bothered about how psychiatric diagnosis was conducted, and the difference between that and medical diagnosis.

Szasz's argument was essentially that the term 'mental illness' was inherently misleading. If what was described as a 'mental illness' had organic or neurological origins, then it was a physical illness, and it was misleading to call it mental illness. And mental illnesses that didn't have organic origins were not illnesses at all, but reflected difficulties that people have in living their lives. For Szasz, 'problems in living' is a much more useful way of looking at these issues, because it directed attention towards how people could be helped to come to terms with their problems.

The term 'mental illness' actually began as a metaphor, suggesting that people with these problems should be treated as if they were ill. But the recognition that it was a metaphor was lost, and the idea became firmly established in medical thinking. It wasn't just as a result of the power of the medical profession – although that was one factor which Szasz identified – but also because people themselves found it comforting to regard their problems as illness. It removed their personal responsibility by implying that it was something they couldn't help, and that other people could deal with and possibly cure.

At the heart of Szasz's criticisms was how 'mental illness' is diagnosed. The diagnostic criteria for mental illness, such as those in the *Diagnostic and Statistical Manual of Mental Disorders* (DSM), are social, not medical – like how well the person is coping with family and friends or keeping up with their social responsibilities. People are judged to be mentally ill on the grounds of not fitting into accepted social behaviour patterns, making inappropriate communications or feeling unable to cope with everyday life. These, Szasz argued, are problems in living, not illnesses. But the medical profession assumed they were physiological disorders and that medical methods would be sufficient to treat them.

In addition, these diagnostic criteria tend to rest on the psychiatrist's own definition of 'normality', and these are also social judgements. Szasz cited the psychiatric syndrome 'drapetomania' – the tendency of slaves to try to escape from their plantations – which was used as a diagnostic category for mental illness in the southern United States. In the early part of the nineteenth century, some middle-class girls who had illegitimate babies were deemed to be mentally disturbed and 'put away' in psychiatric institutions by their families. Some remained in the institution for forty years or more after their pregnancies.

It would be nice to think that Szasz's criticisms were effective, but sadly, his message was dismissed by the psychiatric profession – although not entirely by psychotherapists. He has been described as one of the most disliked people in modern psychiatry, and the tendency for psychiatric diagnosis to reflect social judgements shows no sign of easing off. The DSM continues to list new disorders, often describing behavioural 'syndromes' that are regarded as perfectly normal in other cultures or in different parts of the Western world. Many of the everyday variations in children's temperament have been medicalised in this way. There have always, for example, been children who need high levels of physical activity and quickly become restless in the classroom. It wasn't uncommon for such children to be sent outside to run round the playground a few times to 'work it off', and then return to class. But in more recent years, there has been a tendency to give such children drugs to make them more quiescent in the classroom.

There isn't space here to list the many other examples of psychiatric diagnosis as social judgements. But these are not trivial. In Chapter 6, we saw how diagnosing people as 'mentally defective' or disturbed led eventually to their systematic murder in Nazi Germany. The great mathematician Alan Turing, who had contributed so much towards the Allies winning the Second World War, committed suicide after a particularly brutal series of psychiatric 'treatments' for his homosexuality in the 1950s. And there have been many examples across the world of political dissidents being classified as psychiatrically disturbed and removed from society on the grounds of their needing psychiatric treatment. Psychiatry's capacity to silence dissident voices has been a convenient solution for too many repressive regimes.

Szasz's ideas were much discussed at the time and formed part of the basis for a new challenge, which journalists dubbed the 'anti-psychiatry movement', although many of the professionals involved in it rejected that name. It had come from David Cooper, a psychiatrist originally from South Africa but living in London. Like a number of others, he had become disturbed by some of the excessively brutal psychiatric treatments of the time, particularly the abuses of electroconvulsive therapy (called electroshock therapy in the US) and insulin shock therapy, which had become alarmingly common.

Cooper was also influenced by Michel Foucault's history of madness in his book *Madness and Civilization*. This discussed how the separation of 'mad' people from society was relatively recent: it had only happened with the 'scientific' approach of the Renaissance. Before that, disturbed people were simply accepted as part of society. In London, Cooper became involved in a radical therapeutic project called 'Villa 21', in which the medical approach to schizophrenia was minimised, the idea being to break down the professional/patient distinctions and to restore power and autonomy to the patients. The treatments were mainly group therapy, with the occasional use of the new calming drug chlorpromazine if a resident became excessively excited or disturbed, but only with their consent. The experimental community was ended in 1966, not because it was unsuccessful, but largely due to opposition from the more conventional parts of the psychiatric establishment.

Cooper concluded that psychiatric institutions are really not able to deal with mental illness, and that the social roots of such problems, such as those within the family, are of paramount importance. He published *Psychiatry and Anti-Psychiatry* in 1967, which questioned the distinction between sanity and madness, and explored alternatives to the conventional methodology for treating patients. Cooper described himself as an existential Marxist and came to the conclusion that madness and psychosis are basically all about the difference between the person's 'true' self, and the self that other people impose on them, and which they then internalise. His view on therapy was that it should be all about paying close attention to how people treat one another in everyday life. He also explored the use of consciousness-expanding drugs, as part of the process for opening up alternative ways for people to perceive their own problems.

Cooper had become friends with R.D. Laing, another psychiatrist, when he first moved to England. The two held similar views about psychiatry, although not necessarily about politics – Laing had no time for Marxism but was a firm believer in Sartre's existentialism. Laing had spent some time working in one of the British Army's psychiatric units, where he had also witnessed the inappropriate and often cruel use of insulin shock therapy and electroconvulsive therapy. In 1956, he moved to the Tavistock Clinic in London, where he worked with John Bowlby and others, and received training in psychoanalysis.

Like Szasz, Laing challenged the validity of psychiatric diagnosis, on the grounds that medical diagnosis was made on biological evidence, while psychiatric diagnosis was made on the basis of social behaviour. He disagreed with the idea of schizophrenia as an illness, or as a genetically inherited syndrome, seeing it, like Szasz, as being a problem of communication and social interaction. Laing and a colleague, Aaron Esterson, published a number of case studies showing how dysfunctional communications in families could sometimes result in the person's eventual retreat into schizophrenia. The disturbed communications made by those people were then taken as evidence of their madness, but were often metaphors for the distress they were experiencing. One example, for instance, was that of a girl whose schizophrenic symptoms included watching an imaginary tennis game. Enquiries into the family dynamics showed a division between the parents, with the girl herself being used in arguments and to carry unpleasant messages to each side.

Laing also drew on work by the anthropologist Gregory Bateson, who had developed similar ideas about schizophrenia. In the 1950s, Bateson had identified a pattern of communication known as the 'double-bind'. This has four conditions. The first is that the victim receives contradictory messages, either verbal or emotional – for example someone saying 'I love you' while their body language indicates aversion or even hatred, or a child being told to speak freely but then criticised or silenced if they do. The second is that the situation makes any kind of metacommunication impossible – like asking which of the contradictory messages is right. The third is that the person can't withdraw from the situation, and the fourth is that failing to do what is being asked results in some kind of punishment or sanction. In other words, the person finds themselves in a situation where whatever they do is wrong: any action they make will be disapproved of or punished by their significant others – usually other family members.

The movement that became known as the anti-psychiatry movement grew in strength throughout the 1960s, bringing together ideas and knowledge from many different countries. Apart from Szasz, Cooper and Laing, it included, among many others, the American psychiatrist Theodore Lidz, the Italian physician Giorgio Antonucci, the French psychoanalyst Félix Guattari and the Italian psychiatrist Franco Basaglia. The movement, which was always more of a loose affiliation than a formal organisation, also included other well-known names like the clinical psychologist Timothy Leary and the sociologist Erving Goffman. In the mid-1960s, they formed the Philadelphia Association – an international group devoted to promoting alternative approaches to the treatment of schizophrenia and other forms of mental illness. The group set up another therapeutic community, Kingsley Hall. The project was supported by Cooper but, perhaps because of his previous experience, he didn't become directly involved in it. Laing, however, did, and his open media discussions and filmed reports of the project meant that it became internationally famous.

Although the anti-psychiatry movement didn't achieve the goals of its members in redefining mental illness, it did open up a more humane approach to psychiatric treatment. This was partly assisted by the advent of chemotherapy in the form of new drugs, which meant that violent patients could be suppressed chemically rather than physically. The old methods continued to be used for some decades, but to a lesser extent.

But while the idea of treating mental patients as autonomous people was never quite achieved in psychiatry, it had a major influence in the world of psychotherapy, which we'll come back to in Chapter 34. One of the spokespeople for the new approach was George Kelly, the founder of Personal Construct theory. Like others of his time, his therapy reflected the increasing respect for the individual, which was becoming a major feature of approaches to psychotherapy.

CHAPTER 27

Social Psychology in America

PERSONAL SPACE, MEASURING ATTRACTION, BYSTANDER INTERVENTION AND AN INDIVIDUALISTIC APPROACH

Janet was getting irritated. She had an exam coming up and was trying to concentrate on her revision. She was sitting in her usual place in the library, and someone had placed themselves right next to her. There was plenty of room around the table, so why was this woman sitting so close? It wasn't reasonable. Or comfortable. Janet sat on the very edge of her chair and leaned away from the intruder, trying to get as far from her as possible. She tried to focus on her books, but it was getting hard to concentrate. The intruder was just too close. She felt pressured and uncomfortable, even though there was no actual physical contact. Finally, Janet gave up. She packed up her books and went to sit somewhere else. An observer, sitting a few tables away, quietly noted down the time she moved, as he had noted the time when the intruder arrived.

Janet had been an unwitting subject in a psychological investigation of personal space, inspired by the work of sociologist Harold Garfinkel, whose ethnomethodology involved deliberately breaking the unwitting 'rules' of everyday behaviour in order to make them apparent. Nancy Jo Felipe and Robert Sommer's 1966 library study used the same approach, as they explored the various degrees of closeness that would produce reactions from other people. Their study became a classic in social psychology, as an exploration of personal space.

It was fairly typical of many of the social psychological experiments taking place in America at the time. The college campus provided a reasonably controllable environment in which they could be carried out. While learning theorists and cognitive psychologists needed highly controlled laboratory facilities, social psychologists had the advantages of student common rooms, canteens, classrooms and even student accommodation as their potential laboratories. And they had a ready supply of subjects: both volunteers and others, like Janet, who were unaware that they were even participating in an experiment.

The result was a plethora of studies exploring aspects of student life. Identifying the factors in attraction was a favourite topic: various researchers explored the effects of physical attractiveness, similarity and complementarity, physical closeness (for example, sharing a flat) and reciprocal liking. Some of these were conducted around the student campus; others, such as studies of physical attractiveness, were conducted in the laboratory using ratings of photographs. The research outcomes generated and explored a variety of theories, which reflect the different approaches common in the psychology of the time. The behavioural explanation, of course, was that attraction arises from positive reinforcement, through personal affirmation as two people interact. Cognitive explanations favoured the idea of cognitive similarity: mutual agreement on ideas and opinions. Psychologists with an interest in social exchange and reciprocity asserted that attraction is essentially a form of evaluation, as a possible relationship is weighed up in terms of its potential benefits or disadvantages.

As the second half of the twentieth century went on, an increasing number of challenges to this research emerged. There were doubts, for example, as to the validity of some of the measures involved: did the ratings of photographs really demonstrate the same feelings of attraction as when meeting real people? These doubts were fuelled by some real-life studies, such as Theodore Newcomb's study of proximity, in which students were offered free accommodation and allocated roommates according to various factors, such as similarity or dissimilarity in their attitudes. What Newcomb found was that simply sharing a flat or being roommates for an extended time was by far the main factor in determining friendships between the students – regardless of whether they held similar attitudes or not.

Other challenges, which really came into their own several decades later but began to be voiced in the 1970s, were to do with the ethics of experimentation. Both the American and British psychological associations developed guidelines for research with human beings (this was when the term 'participants' came to be preferred to 'subjects'), and these guidelines included the unacceptability of deception and the use of uninformed participants. They took some time to have any effect, being largely disregarded on the grounds that the real-life studies were essentially observational in nature and, in any case, the deception was relatively trivial. But concern about these matters grew, and although deception continued to be needed, and ethically justified, in some research contexts, the unthinking and routine use of deception gradually faded out.

Another set of concerns, originally voiced in the 1970s by critics like Irwin Silverman but only gradually becoming more accepted, concerned the representativeness of American psychology students as examples of universal human behaviour. That challenge has been taken up more strongly in recent times, reflecting both the increasing concerns about diversity and inclusivity and the growing awareness of, and challenges presented by, psychology in other parts of the world. We will be looking at these issues more closely in Chapter 40.

The emerging balance between cognitive and behavioural approaches in American psychology was also reflected in social psychology, as researchers explored aspects of non-verbal communication and person perception. The study at the beginning of this chapter was an investigation of proxemics, or personal space; other investigations of the topic showed how it varies from one culture to another, and between personal and impersonal conversations. Studies of gestures and facial expressions, too, showed cultural variability, although the facial expressions showing basic emotions do seem to be universal, the same across all human cultures. Research included other aspects of interaction, such as the various meanings of eye contact, from expressions of intimacy to the hostile stare of aggression; the nature of conversational exchanges, like the accepted timing of eye contact and verbal exchanges; and the use of paralanguage, such as tones of voice and 'um' and 'er' type fillers.

Many of these studies adopted a behavioural perspective. They measured, for example, the extent of pupil dilation or length of gaze as people in the laboratory looked at images of desirable objects. Some, as in the library study at the beginning of this chapter, used behavioural indicators in more real-life settings. But studies of, for example, the impressions given by how we dress or hold ourselves were more cognitive in their orientation. They led naturally to research into how we perceive other people, and that also linked in with the growing interest in attitudes that we looked at in Chapter 24.

Although personality tests and trait theory had been established for a long time, the focus here was on the traits that we assume in other people. It came from the way that we can develop whole theories about people's personalities from very little information. Knowing that one person is a librarian and another is a forester, for example, can generate entirely different assumptions about them. They would be considered to have different, distinctive personality traits. Whether these traits reflect core features of how we judge personality or just peripheral ones, and whether they are evaluative or not, was disputed by academics for many years. But almost everyone working in this area assumed that trait descriptions are always understood in the same way: that 'kindness' or 'aggression' would always have the same meaning for everyone who uses those words. Later research by George Kelly into how we use personal constructs challenged this idea, as we will see in Chapter 34.

Other aspects of social psychology developed in response to events happening at the time. News reports of the brutal murder of a young woman, Kitty Genovese, stated that several people in the nearby apartments had witnessed the murder, but nobody had called for help. Although later investigations showed that these reports were not accurate, they were widely believed in America at the time, and replicated in psychology textbooks. Research into 'bystander apathy' became renamed as 'bystander intervention' as psychologists continued to explore the factors that encouraged or inhibited people in helping strangers, since those studies showed that, in general, people are more prepared to help others than to stand by.

Several theories were suggested to explain bystander intervention, including the alienation resulting from living in cities, which it was suggested might make people less likely to help strangers. But this wasn't really borne out by the evidence. In one study, for example, people were asked to choose whether they wanted to be 'experimental' or 'control' in a learning experiment, and told that the 'experimental' condition involved receiving electric shocks, while the control condition did not. They were told that they would be paired with another research participant, who would be given the other condition. Over 90 per cent understandably chose the control condition. But when they were told that the other participant had asked to have the control condition because they were 'really scared' of the shocks, nearly three-quarters chose the experimental condition. And if they were told that the other person had decided to stand back and let them choose, nearly 90 per cent chose the experimental condition. People were acting against their own interest to help someone they hadn't even met.

Other studies showed that even if people saw that someone was drunk, rather than ill or disabled, they were inclined to help them. Not equally likely, though. In a series of field experiments, Bibb Latané and others showed that fewer people would help someone who seemed to be drunk than someone who had collapsed for another reason – although the majority would still help. In another study, people in the street were approached and asked for a small amount of money. Sometimes, they said it was to make a phone call, sometimes they were told that it was because the person's wallet had been stolen, and sometimes no reason was given at all. Even then, a third of the people approached gave some money, while more than half gave money if a reason was offered.

There are factors working against helpful behaviour, though, including how much television people watch. Studies have repeatedly shown that people who watch a lot of television tend to rate the world as being much more dangerous than it really is. This suggests that they might be less likely to step in to help someone else, because they imagine, not particularly realistically, that it might pose a personal danger. Laboratory studies suggested other factors too: in one study, college students were asked to sit in a waiting room, either in groups of three or alone. Suddenly, smoke began to pour through a ventilation grille. Those waiting alone reported it quite quickly, while those in groups took much longer. When asked, the group members said that they had judged their behaviour by others: nobody wanted to be the first to react, because the fact that the others weren't reacting suggested that it didn't matter. Other studies found similar results, and Latané and his colleagues argued that it was a combination of what they called 'pluralistic ignorance' – a shared denial that the apparent problem actually matters. There was also a sense of and diffusion of responsibility – a feeling that the other people around were equally responsible for taking action.

Latané went on to develop the 'Law of Social Impact', which outlined a number of different social forces that people are faced with at any one time. These, Latané argued, work like a set of light bulbs shining on the person concerned. Using this metaphor, the light bulbs could vary in their brightness, having a stronger or weaker effect – for example, someone's mother or sister might be more influential than someone who was just a stranger. It would matter how many bulbs there were, in that more people would tend to have a greater influence. And it matters how close the light bulbs were to the person, either physically, in the sense of being actually close by, or mentally, as in whether the person needing help was personally known, or perhaps particularly needy.

Social Impact theory provides a plausible explanation for how people might respond. But it sees social influences as external forces on the individual. A very different way of thinking was being developed by European social psychologists, who had experienced somewhat different social influences during and after the Second World War.

CHAPTER 28

Social Psychology in Europe
THE IMPACT OF GROUP MEMBERSHIP ON
UNDERSTANDING AND BEHAVIOUR, AND THE SHARED
CONSTRUCTION OF MEANING

While American social psychology was determinedly individualistic, following Floyd Allport's insistence that social psychology was simply a part of the psychology of the individual, perspectives in Europe were rather different. This was historical: Europe had been dramatically exposed to the way that social movements could perpetuate themselves, capturing minds as well as behaviour and eventually dominating whole societies, even when they started off as small minorities. It was clear that individualistic explanations of social behaviour were simply inadequate.

As we've seen, many European psychologists fled to America or Britain because of the Nazi threat, but what they had to say was not always accepted. Bruno Bettelheim, for example, survived the concentration camps and went to America, but the paper he wrote about his experiences in the camp was largely ignored. Conventional social psychology had neither the theoretical orientation to deal with those issues, nor the willingness to confront such unpleasant realities. Also, in Europe whole countries had become dominated by beliefs that many individuals were sceptical about. How had that happened? Gradually, social psychologists in Europe began to develop theories that were robust enough to explain the realities of social life. A new form of social psychology emerged, spearheaded by two key theories: 'Social Identity theory, formulated by Henri Tajfel, and Social Representation theory', initiated by Serge Moscovici.

Social identity is all about group membership and how 'them and us' permeates our awareness of the world. Our personal identities also contain the social groups we belong to, and they can become part of how we think about ourselves. If I speak as a psychologist, I am identifying with that, not just playing a role: I see myself as a psychologist, but I also belong to many other social groups – both formal, like organisations, and informal, like being part of my local community. Each of them contributes to my sense of who I am – to my identity. But they are mostly unconscious, only becoming apparent when the situation makes them relevant. An argument about who does the washing up can shift from being a personal quarrel to an intergroup conflict if gender becomes a relevant issue in the argument.

Social Identity theory is firmly located in reality, recognising that real social groups vary in terms of their power and influence, and their access to social or economic resources. Those differences affect how people behave towards one another and can underlie major social conflicts, and even wars. It didn't start that way: it began with a series of studies conducted in the 1970s by Tajfel and his team, who were looking at how group membership influences decision-making. They allocated research participants into completely arbitrary groups, based on meaningless criteria like whether they were sitting in a blue or a green chair. When people were asked to allocate a set of counters to the various groups in the study, they consistently favoured their own group above others, even if they had no real reason to do so.

Naturally, this led to further investigation, and Tajfel, together with his colleague John Turner, explored how group membership helps people to define who they are in relation to others. They eventually published their Social Identity theory in 1979, in a paper called 'An Integrative Theory of Inter-Group Conflict'. They argued that the process of group identification rests on three fundamental psychological processes: categorisation, social comparison and the need for self-esteem.

Categorisation is fundamental to our everyday cognitive activity. We are surrounded by information all the time, and if we didn't sort things out mentally, we'd never be able to cope with it all. So we automatically develop categories which organise that information, helping us to group together things and people.

But we don't just categorise groups of people, we also compare them with each other. That might be in terms of whether one category is 'better' than another, or it might just identify differences between them without evaluation. The early minimal group studies suggested that categorisation in itself could generate rivalry and hostility; but further research showed that it only happens if there is competition for resources. If there is no such need, diverse groups can co-exist quite amicably, both in minimal group studies and in the real world.

The third psychological process is the emotional dimension of identification. Social groups differ from one another in terms of power and status, and that affects how people belonging to those groups feel about themselves – how that belonging builds or damages their self-esteem. We need to feel that belonging to our own group is a positive thing; if we see it as negative, we have to deal with that somehow. That gives us four choices. We can try to leave the group altogether, through social mobility or in some other way. We can make our personal comparisons with different groups instead, like comparing our own village with other villages rather than with large cities. A third strategy is to distance ourselves from the group, insisting that 'I'm not like the others' and trying to make sure that we are seen as an individual and not just as a group representative. Or we can try to change the status of the group itself. That might seem unrealistic, but we have only to look at recent changes in society's perceptions of gender roles, or at how society in general regards disabled people, to see how successful it can be. What's happening in that fourth process is that the social representations of the group are being changed, which brings us to the second major theory in European social psychology.

Social Representation theory was developed by the French psychologist Serge Moscovici during the 1970s. Moscovici had been interested in the various ways that psychoanalysis was talked about and also how it was reported through the press. It was a popular theory in France at the time, attracting a lot of discussion, but different political groups regarded it in very different ways. Those newspapers that addressed themselves to the professional and educated sectors of French society tended to present psychoanalysis in a neutral style, while those representing the Catholic right wing censored the theory, reporting only those aspects of it which they felt were consistent with orthodox Catholic beliefs, and avoiding controversial topics like libido and sex altogether. The communist press, on the other hand, represented the theory as an example of bourgeois ideology and typically capitalist, seeing it as a rival to the Marxist approach. These differences were so profound that they were, for Moscovici, clear examples of the way that styles of communication express underlying belief systems.

This led him to develop Social Representation theory, which is all about the routine explanations and theories that people use in everyday life. Social representations are the taken-for-granted information held by society, by individuals and sometimes by specific social groups, allowing people to explain their personal experiences and also providing the shared understanding for them to communicate with one another.

Essentially, social representations make sense of ideas or experiences that are unfamiliar, partly through anchoring them in knowledge that is already familiar, and partly through 'objectifying' them through metaphors. These metaphors are often unnoticed, being embedded in everyday language, for example, talking of 'pruning' the economy or making necessary 'cutbacks'. Gardening is familiar territory for many people, so these metaphors help them to develop an understanding of what is going on. But the metaphors themselves represent an underlying worldview. Whether they reflect 'truth' is irrelevant. What matters is that they become widely shared and generally accepted as explanations.

Social representations are directly linked to social identification, because people are much more likely to accept the meanings or interpretations that are shared by the other members of their social group. Nobody grows up in a vacuum, and we are all influenced by our cultures, our families, and the people we surround ourselves with – and that includes what we hear through mass and social media. It doesn't just shape our beliefs about other people; it even shapes our knowledge of the physical world, in that we tend to accept what we are told. As London School of Economics professor Rob Farr pointed out, most of us accept that glass is fragile without feeling the need to resort to the hammer.

All this helps us to understand why we so often find people talking past one another, and not really connecting at all. They are each making sense of the world through their own social represen-tations, which might have nothing in common with the explana-tions used by the other person. It happens in all kinds of situations: from arguing couples who become so hung up on gender roles that they don't really hear what the other person is saying, to industry leaders and trades unions trying to negotiate industrial disputes, or medical personnel talking at people with a very different under-standing of health issues. We saw some amazing examples of social representations in the 'anti-vaxxing' beliefs which circulated during the pandemic of 2020–22!

Social Identity theory and Social Representation theory became the core of European social psychology. They were brought together in the early 1970s, partly through a specific journal and partly through a paper by Henri Tajfel called 'Some Developments in European Social Psychology'. That gave a focus to the new approach and, by placing the theories firmly as the framework, made a clear distinction between this approach and the pragmatic, response-driven American type of social psychology.

The two theories reflect the importance of understanding how different group membership impacts on our social understanding as well as on our behaviour. Together, they could explain how the various different societies in Europe had responded to the Nazi threats and to other social movements. It generated a form of social psychological research that could explain, on an individual as well as a social level, issues such as intergroup relations, social prejudice and interpersonal conflicts. But that was only one part of the story: the psychoanalytic school had never been dismissed in Europe in the way that it was in America, and, as we've seen, it came back into prominence during the 1960s, particularly in France, while other approaches to social psychology were also emerging.

A different alternative, 'social constructionism', became particularly strong in UK social psychology. Drawing on the work of European intellectuals like Foucault and Ferdinand de Saussure, this approach is also about how people interpret their worlds. Its central tenet is that the meanings people use are collective in nature, constructed through discourse, rituals, and also through interactions that have deeper meanings than the simple behaviours that they might seem to be on the surface. Social constructionism was part of the wider post-modernist movement, strongly influenced by the work of the philosopher Nietzsche, which emphasised relativism and the unreachable nature of 'objective' reality.

The social constructionist approach in social psychology tended to focus on how meanings become manifest in everyday interactions, for example through analysing discourse of one form or another. Psychologists working in this field would typically analyse conversations or other forms of discourse, looking for the deeper meanings underneath the surface conversation. A discussion between a social worker and a parent looking to regain custody of their child has underlying issues of power and control, and the nature of the conversation would reflect those issues. In another example, a family discussion about a royal wedding showed how interpretations were evaluated and shared by the group, eventually producing a consensual account of the event.

There are a number of similarities between this approach and Social Representation theory, which are not entirely coincidental given their shared theoretical heritage in European intellectualism.

But Social Representation theory, like Social Identity theory, was located firmly within the experimental (although not the behaviourist) tradition, exploring these issues empirically, while the social constructionists were deeply suspicious of empirical research of that type. The fact that they came to similar conclusions about the shared construction of meanings and reality tells us something important about how human beings make sense of their experience. It also helps us to understand how and why some very different perspectives in psychology were emerging in the rest of the world.

CHAPTER 29

Global Psychology
FROM JAPAN AND CHINA TO RUSSIA, INDIA
AND SOUTH AMERICA

As we've seen, psychology as a scientific discipline was largely developed in Europe and America. But what was happening in the rest of the world? Strong international activity meant that it wasn't just trade that linked countries together: ideas and knowledge were major influences too. Asian universities have been established for many years and, as philosophical and other works became translated into other languages, curiosity grew, and people from other parts of the world went to study in Europe and America.

China and Japan were perhaps the first of the non-Western countries to embrace the new discipline of psychology. Both countries had a tradition of philosophical thought that went back many hundreds of years and addressed similar psychological and personal questions, and intellectuals in both countries became aware of Western philosophical precursors to psychology through an 1875 Japanese translation of Joseph Haven's *Mental Philosophy*.

The first professor of psychology in Japan was Yujiro Motora, who had studied psychology in America with G. Stanley Hall, the first president of the American Psychological Association and a committed psychologist and educator. Motora returned to Japan in 1888 and became a part-time lecturer in psychophysics at Tokyo Imperial University. In 1903, in collaboration with one of his first students, Matataro Matsumoto, he opened the first psychological laboratory in Japan. Matsumoto had also studied in America, at Yale University, with one of Wundt's graduate students, Edward Scripture. Between them, Motora and Matsumoto, Motora at Tokyo and Matsumoto at Kyoto Imperial University, established a firm foundation for experimental psychology in Japan. The first seven Japanese psychology students graduated from Tokyo Imperial University in 1905.

At first, Japanese psychology was widely diverse, but an early milestone set it firmly into the experimental tradition. Tomokichi Fukurai had studied with Motora and became an associate professor of psychology at Tokyo University. His initial research was in hypnosis, but he went on to develop a strong interest in psychical research, especially clairvoyance. His research, understandably, generated considerable public interest, but his procedures were controversial and felt by his colleagues to be unacceptable. After several hints and warnings, he was dismissed from his position in 1913. His dismissal reflected an increased commitment to establishing psychology on a fully scientific basis.

The Japanese Psychological Association was founded officially in 1927, following an All-Japan Psychological Meeting, which was organised by Matsumoto, who was by now professor at Tokyo Imperial University. Psychology was taught in several different Japanese universities, so psychologists welcomed this opportunity to share their research. The new organisation started the *Japanese Journal of Psychology* and established Matsumoto as its president, a position he kept until his death. At this time, Japanese psychology was strongly influenced by Gestalt psychology, and most research in the country reflected this influence, being particularly concerned with social and cognitive processes and their application in education.

Things changed dramatically with the onset of war. Although attempts to hold meetings and publish the journal were made, it wasn't until 1947 that Japanese psychology really began to get back to normal. By now, a new generation was taking over, and Japan was rebuilding itself following the devastation of the country during the war. Japanese psychology had always been closely linked with education, and the Japanese educational system rapidly established some of the highest literacy and technology standards in the world. Applied psychology, too, flourished as the country industrialised, and its concepts were widely used in manufacturing industries. In modern days, Japanese psychology is still notable for its expertise in applied psychology, but cognitive, social, educational and clinical psychology are equally highly developed. Japanese psychology generally follows the American model but has a much stronger emphasis on emotional experience and positive wellbeing – for example, Japanese psychologists have conducted extensive research into wellbeing at work, which has only recently come onto the agenda in Western occupational psychology.

In China, as in Japan, psychological thinking was part of a long-standing intellectual tradition, exemplified in Confucianism, Taoism and Zen Buddhism. Modern psychology as an independent subject was introduced by Cai Yuanpei, an educational reformer who had studied at Wundt's laboratory in Leipzig and had encouraged the teaching of psychology in Chinese pedagogical institutions. He went on to set up the first Chinese psychological laboratory at Beijing University in 1917. Three years later, the first independent psychology department opened its doors at the South Eastern University in Nanjing, and the Chinese Psychological Society was founded in 1921. Chinese psychology at this time tended to adopt the Western approach, studying both behaviourism and psychoanalysis, and also cognitive processes such as learning and memory. However, China's turbulent history in this period meant that psychology's formal development was interrupted by the war with Japan in 1937, and not re-established until the People's Republic of China was founded in 1949.

One of the more influential Chinese psychologists of those early years was Chen Li, who had studied with Spearman in London. He became known as the founder of industrial psychology in China and was also a notable figure in research into intelligence. The developing field of psychometrics was entirely congruent with Chinese social policy: China had introduced national testing for entry to the civil service in ancient times, and test batteries were used routinely from the time of the Han Dynasty (205 BCE to 220 CE). It is believed that the testing systems for appointment and promotion that were adopted so successfully by Britain's East India Company in its colonial activities were copied directly from the Chinese system.

Under the People's Republic, psychology in China took a different turn. It was expected to follow Marxist-Leninist and Maoist thinking, and independent psychology departments were abolished as Western psychology was regarded as another manifestation of capitalist ideology. Psychologists were expected to follow the Russian model, particularly the work of Pavlov, and to work in education or philosophy departments.

Psychometrics itself became regarded with suspicion, with its unwelcome focus on the individual's abilities. Houcan Zhang, who is now regarded as the 'mother' of modern Chinese psychometric measurement and its educational applications, was a professor at Beijing Normal University in the mid-1950s. When higher education was suspended during the Cultural Revolution, she was imprisoned for several years and subjected to 're-education', including, like other academics, working long hours in semi-starvation in the fields. She survived and returned to psychology and was eventually able to establish a testing research group in the psychology department in Beijing Normal University. Her work revised and revitalised the area and renewed its application in Chinese public examinations, promoting additional research into cognition and the Chinese language.

Modern psychology in China has largely recovered from the turbulence of those years, and psychology is an expanding subject. There is an ongoing interest in developing an indigenous psychology, which can address China's unique heritage and modern society, but there is also a strong research programme into behaviour genetics, along with psychological research in cognition, developmental and social psychology. The pace of change, though, is rapid, and it seems likely that this account will already be outdated.

Russian psychology, like that of China, began with close involvements with other European developments: Pavlov visited Wundt's laboratory in Leipzig, Sabina Spielrein was an active member of Freud's psychoanalytic circle, and there was close correspondence between Russian, European and American psychologists. By the end of the nineteenth century, there were thriving psychology departments in almost all Russian universities. Following the Revolution, however, things changed as Western psychology became regarded as a tool of capitalist ideology.

Marxist-Leninist ideology permeated scientific administration and directed academic work. Darwin's theory, for example, was rejected in favour of the evolutionary theory put forward by Jean-Baptiste Lamarck, who argued for the inheritance of acquired characteristics – in other words, that abilities or other characteristics acquired by a person or animal during their own lifetime could be passed on to their offspring. The implication – that people could be trained into new ways of being that would be passed on through the generations – was the basis for an educational programme designed to produce the 'New Soviet Man' (and presumably the 'New Soviet Woman' as well). But the insistence on Lamarckian genetics was an ideological straitjacket for many biologists and psychologists working in that area.

Not for all, however. The work of Ivan Pavlov, which showed how learning can happen even at a basic neurological level, could be fitted into this paradigm, as could the work of other eminent psychologists such as Alexander Luria and Lev Vygotsky. We have already seen how important Vygotsky's theories became in Western developmental psychology, although that was not until fifty years later; and Luria's research into brain functioning was deeply influential in Western neuropsychology. The study of psychology continued within the Marxist-Leninist paradigm and in the context of Soviet ideology. Space psychology, for example, flourished, and the book *Psychology and Space*, by the pioneering cosmonaut Yuri Gagarin and the psychologist Vladimir Lebedev, became a bestseller.

In more recent years, Russian psychology has been concerned with the study of cultural influences and, even more recently, has aimed to develop and articulate a distinctively Russian psychology. That reflects a global movement in this direction, as psychologists in other countries, too, re-evaluate Western approaches in terms of their relevance for their country's particular culture and history.

That movement is particularly apparent in Indian psychology. India, like China and Japan, has a tradition of historical thinking which was directly concerned with personal existence and being. Modern psychology was introduced in India during the British colonial period and drew on the work of both British and American psychologists as it was taught in universities. Since independence, however, and particularly in the current century, the focus of interest in psychology has become increasingly reflective of Indian culture, and a distinctive Indian psychology has emerged. Indian psychology in this sense is characterised by its concern with traditional Indian beliefs and practices, such as ayurveda and meditation, and has a particular emphasis on exploring those aspects and applications of psychology which are concerned with positive aspects of the human condition, such as wellbeing and achievement.

Indian psychology doesn't reject Western psychology. Rather, it adopts those concepts and theoretical developments that are pertinent to Indian culture. So there is active research into areas like perception, cognition, emotion and creativity, but also into the deeper aspects of personality, values and spirituality. It is not limited to strict experimental methodology, but embraces multiple methods, including narrative and account analysis and the use of both qualitative and quantitative ways of analysing research data.

In many ways, Indian psychology reflects the direction of travel for psychology in other parts of the world too. There is an increasing emphasis on multiculturalism and developing ways of using psychology to explore, respectfully, the beliefs and knowledge of Indigenous people. In many cases, this involves a rethinking of psychology itself, as psychology moves towards decolonising its theoretical assumptions – that is, identifying those theories or applications of theory that simply reflected the assumptions made in the colonial era, and those which could still be considered to have validity in other contexts or could be adapted appropriately. Social Identity theory, for example, reveals a different emphasis when applied in South-East Asian cultures: the underlying psychological processes are essentially the same, but how they impact on people in their everyday lives is quite different.

The move to develop an indigenous psychology is also evident across South America. Formal psychology as taught in universities tends to reflect each country's colonial history, with approaches ranging from European psychoanalysis to American behaviourism. The increasing adoption of applied psychology across South America has highlighted its wide diversity, so professional psychologists have formed networks across the continent, to bring together information and to discuss the rationalisation of professional qualifications and standards. But South America also encompasses a huge number of different indigenous peoples, and psychologists in those countries are looking to develop ways of integrating established psychological ideas with indigenous knowledge and approaches.

This chapter is inevitably limited in what it can cover, but similar trends towards adapting psychological knowledge to reflect traditional or indigenous cultures are happening across the globe. And in North Africa, a radical new approach to the psychological understanding of self and identity was developed in the work of Frantz Fanon, which we will explore in more depth in the next chapter.

CHAPTER 30

Culture and Self
FRANTZ FANON AND COLONIAL PERSPECTIVES
ON IDENTITY

Psychology as a scientific discipline may have originated in the nineteenth century, but its real growth came after the Second World War. Partly, this reflected an expansion in educational institutions, but it also reflected the growth of consumerism, leading to an increasing interest in how people's behaviour could be influenced so they would buy more. In the Westernised countries, that is. But changes were also happening across the rest of the world, with global changes in culture and economics, and the powerful impact of political ideas like Marxism and socialism. While these egalitarian ideas were hated and feared by the leaders of capitalist countries like the US, they were quite attractive in colonised countries, possibly for similar reasons.

These issues were also reflected in psychology, particularly in theories about self and identity. In the US, psychological research into the self-concept focused almost entirely on the individual: researchers investigated motivational drives such as the need for achievement, or looked at factors that might influence someone's personal self-concept. The underlying implication was that the self is independent, sometimes influenced by social factors but essentially separate and autonomous.

Individualism was a fundamental assumption in American society, but those ideas weren't exactly shared by the rest of the world. Americans became dimly aware of this with the youth culture of the 1960s, as young hippy travellers to India brought back alternative ideas to the West. Among these was the Hindu approach to the self, which sees selfhood as having external layers around the *atman* – a state of perfect unity with the innermost 'true' self. Although everyone contains it, not everyone can reach this state: it involves self-discipline and internal meditation; but the condition of their self is each individual's responsibility.

The challenge was the belief that external layers of self – involving unconscious qualities like avarice, lust and egotism – are often a hindrance to achieving one's true self, known as *jiva* in Hindu writings. *Samsāra*, the concept of reincarnation, is the belief that an individual may cycle through many lives, human or animal depending on the *karma* they have accumulated from positive actions in their quest to achieve the true selfhood.

That concept of self still emphasised the individual, but in a very different way, and it found a tiny home in the psychotherapeutic world through the efforts of Timothy Leary and less controversial psychologists and psychotherapists. But it didn't really influence mainstream American psychology. In Europe, as we have seen, the major social psychological theories were able to conceptualise the self in a way that could explain how and why ordinary individuals were swept along in the mass prejudice and social action that led to the Holocaust. But again, the main issue was how these impacted on the individual: it was still in some ways an individualistic approach.

In most of the world, though, individualism isn't as dominant. The individual self is not seen as independent, but as part of a complete social matrix of family and friends within that society's culture. In Indigenous Australian societies, for instance, it is the society as a whole that makes decisions, which the West would see as individual ones: whether someone should go on to university, for example, or take up a particular career. Those decisions are made by the group as a whole, taking into account the person's own wishes and nature, but also considering the impact it will have on their social group or society. The Australian rock band Yothu Yindi, for example, whose Aboriginal members were keenly aware of themselves as part of their Indigenous Australian culture, always discussed their progress and opportunities with the tribe's elders. Although they had some individual success in the music world, their perception of themselves was primarily in terms of their identities as members of their social group.

In most traditional societies, the self is seen as firmly embedded in its society: social membership is a fundamental aspect of personal identity, and not one that can be separated out. People are still recognised and acknowledged as individuals, different from one another and with their own distinctive personalities and talents, but it is understood that those have been shaped by their culture and social context.

The way that the culture is embedded in the self varies, as does culture itself. For example, in Japanese culture, children are social-ised from infancy into an awareness that their actions have an impact on other people. This means that the Japanese sense of self is highly sensitised to social shame and internalised guilt, and in turn that generates a strong importance attached to the socially rewarding aspects of membership and 'belonging'. As a result, Japanese people are more inclined to keep their individual thoughts private, in case they disturb social consensus, and to regard social acceptability as a consistent part of regulating their public behaviour.

The idea of the independent individual doesn't apply in tradi-tional African societies either. Psychologists and anthropologists have shown how the self in many of the countries of southern Africa is seen entirely in the context of the ongoing life of the people and their existence in the natural world. The idea of a completely independent self is seen as an unrealistic myth, which, if it could be achieved at all, would produce an individual who was mentally unbalanced, and not really properly human. People from traditional African societies who come to study in Western universities often describe an acute loneliness and a sense of being only half present: a vivid example of how important their home context and culture are to their self-concept.

These, and similar observations, were also made by psychologists from other cultures who attempted to show the limitations of traditional Western ideas about the self, and how they impacted on other aspects of psychology. Although some of them did at least achieve publication in academic journals, their contributions to mainstream psychology were regarded more as curiosities – items of interest – than as the radical insights into human identity that they really offered. The idea of the individual as independent, and social influence as external, remained dominant, even though that extreme individualism made Western culture unique and far from representative of the majority of human beings – that is, those living in the rest of the world.

It's questionable, incidentally, whether pure individualism is really representative even of Western cultures. Although traditional Greek philosophy (and thence mainstream psychology) assumed that there is an independent self, in reality our everyday lives are much more embedded in family, friends and society than is formally recognised. Family, for example, is regarded as paramount in both American and UK cultures, as exemplified both in media dramas and in news reports. Not just families, but friendship groups, interest networks, religious groups and other sources of interpersonal bonding are crucially important in how we see ourselves. European social psychology provided a theoretical context for acknowledging that, but the importance of culture and context for the self-concept was – and still is – seriously underplayed in Western mainstream psychology.

Not in other parts of the world, though. One of the most influential books in non-Western psychology throughout the second half of the twentieth century was Frantz Fanon's *Black Skin, White Masks*. Written in the 1950s, it made a massive impact, not just in North Africa, but in colonial systems all over the world. There is even a Frantz Fanon University, in Somalia.

Why such an impact? Fanon was a psychiatrist and political philosopher who had grown up in the French colony of Martinique. He was Black, and acutely aware of the social distinctions between the colonisers and the colonised. He was fifteen in 1940, when France fell to the Nazis and Martinique was taken over by French sailors, who expressed their racism and complete contempt for the residents in forceable ways. His later participation in the war on the Gaullist side reinforced these impressions. After the war, Fanon went to France to complete his education and qualifications, and subsequently published *Black Skin, White Masks*. It was originally intended as his doctoral thesis, discussing the psychological implications of the racism he had experienced both in France and previously; but it was rejected for its political content. So he published it as a book instead.

Black Skin, White Masks discusses how Black identity and self-concept in colonial or post-colonial society is qualitatively different from that of white people, even when those people seem to come from similar backgrounds. Fanon wrote about the way that language is used to reinforce those distinctions. Any form of language contains its own worldview, with social assumptions and covert meanings that assume that the speaker is part of that world. In French colonial society, the use of Creole forms of language was regarded as an illustration of lack of education or intelligence, as the use of Pidgin English was in the British colonies. At the same time, though, the mastery of 'white' language by Black people was viewed with suspicion, even as predatory. Black people in Martinique and other French colonies were nonetheless encouraged to speak 'white' French – and this, Fanon pointed out, meant that they had to take on a very different worldview from their personal experience of reality.

Fanon's book challenged several commonly held assumptions about the nature of Black people in colonised society. One view, for example, was the idea that social distinctions were partly maintained by a dependency complex on the part of Black people: a sense of personal inferiority. Fanon challenged this, pointing out that the nature of day-to-day contacts between white people and

Black people consistently reinforced a message of inferiority: it is the racist, he argued, who creates the inferior. Psychiatric vulnerability was another consequence: Fanon, as a psychiatrist, was explicit about the way that the treatment of Black people caused emotional trauma and was very scathing about Freud and the other famous psychoanalysts, arguing that their approach completely failed even to acknowledge, let alone deal with, these issues.

Fanon's central message for psychology was about the way that being Black in colonial society involves an entirely different type of self-concept. Even the basic body-schema, he argued, wasn't unified, because people's bodies – specifically the colour of their skin – were not just about themselves, but were also inevitably linked with what he referred to as a 'historical-racial' schema. The Black person, he argued, was inevitably seen as a representative of their race and social condition, which prevented them from being seen as an individual.

A later book by Fanon, *The Wretched of the Earth*, discussed the processes of colonisation and decolonisation. Fanon had already shown how colonial racism had seeped into people's individual psyches, and in this book he explored how class, race and economics supported the subjugation of minority groups. Fanon's work was, perhaps inevitably, totally ignored by Western psychologists. I was lucky enough to be introduced to them as a psychology student in the 1970s – but by a radical Marxist friend, not by a psychologist. Fanon's work influenced anti-colonial organisations around the world, and also Western Black militant groups like the Black Panthers. But it also opened up further analysis of how race influences the self-concept, generating a consciousness-raising process that continues to this day.

Fanon's work, and that of others from non-Western parts of the world, challenges the universality of many widely accepted concepts in mainstream social psychology. That doesn't mean that Western psychology has no validity at all. It's likely, for example, that some processes are universal, like self-efficacy, which we will look at in Chapter 37, but that they manifest themselves in different ways depending on the culture and context. Another example might be our need for affiliation, which can be linked with Carl Rogers' theory of the need for positive regard, and which may well be universal. Other ideas, though, are more questionable, such as whether all humans experience the need for achievement, which has been so strongly demonstrated in American culture. We'll be coming back to this issue in Chapter 40.

CHAPTER 31

The Growth of Neuropsychology
Neurotransmitters, Drugs, Sleep Deprivation, and the Surgical Identification of Brain Structures

Chris was feeling a little puzzled. He'd volunteered for this experiment, had the injection, and was waiting for it to take effect. But the other research subject in the waiting room with him was acting rather oddly. Chris wondered if he was drunk, but there was no evidence of that. The man batted pieces of paper around as if they were balls, smiled and laughed, and generally seemed to be really happy. More, it was infectious: Chris couldn't help smiling at some of his antics, and even felt a bit happy himself.

Unknown to Chris, he was a participant in a set of studies carried out by Stanley Schachter and Jerome Singer in 1962. Their study involved giving people injections, either of a harmless saline solution or of adrenaline (epinephrine), and then putting them in different social situations. The study was investigating William James' idea that our physiological responses determine our emotions (see Chapter 21), but the researchers found that the social setting had a real influence on the emotions that people felt. In another condition of the study, the actor appearing to be another research subject would pretend to be angry, seeming impatient and hostile towards those who were keeping him waiting. Those waiting in the room with the actor tended to feel angry themselves – only mildly so if they'd had the placebo (the saline solution) but more strongly if they'd had the adrenaline injection. Those in the 'euphoric' condition, on the other hand, felt happier, and again more strongly if they'd had the stimulating drug.

Their study attracted a lot of criticism: people said it hadn't been well controlled, and some even claimed that it had never happened at all. But, despite the challenges, it had a lot of influence. It expressed a relationship between our physiological state and our environment which fitted with people's everyday experience. We all feel more irritable if we are highly stressed, and, if we've just been exercising vigorously, we might feel either happier or more angry, depending on what we hear or have to do next.

This study reflected a growing interest in the biochemical influences on human psychology. In the 1950s and 1960s, researchers were making great strides in understanding the chemicals that pass electrical information from one nerve cell to another, known as neurotransmitters. Different neurotransmitters produce very different effects. Noradrenaline (norepinephrine) and serotonin were known to be involved in emotional reactions and were used in treating depression. Dopamine seemed to be associated with what at the time were called 'pleasure centres' but eventually became identified as 'reward pathways' in the brain. Endorphins and enkephalins produced feelings of wellbeing after exercise but were also activated by opiate drugs like heroin, while acetylcholine was known to be the chemical the brain uses to transmit messages to the muscles for movement. Researchers found that it is partly blocked by the drug nicotine, which is why smoking makes people feel more sluggish (although they sometimes interpret this as feeling more relaxed), and why giving it up gives them more energy. Nowadays, of course, we are aware of many more neurotransmitters, but this was transformative knowledge for psychologists in the 1960s, showing the first definite links between brain chemistry and psychological experience.

Another discovery was that neurotransmitters can inhibit as well as transmit information. Serotonin and adrenaline, for example, prevent sleep. In 1959, American DJ Peter Tripp decided on a stunt in which he would go without sleep for eight days, to raise money for charity and also to create a world record. He installed himself in a glass booth in Times Square and began his continuous live broadcast. For the first couple of days, he was fine, but by the fourth day he began to experience hallucinations, like mice scampering over him and spiders in his shoes. As the days went on, he became increasingly paranoid and, by the eighth day, he couldn't tell the difference between his hallucinations and reality. When it was over, he slept for twenty-two hours, and seemed to have recovered, but there was lasting damage: he continued to have psychotic episodes for the rest of his life. Both serotonin and noradrenaline are known to be involved in the actions of psychoactive drugs like LSD, and parallels were drawn between the result of Tripp's venture and the ways that long-term drug use affects people.

This period of psychology also saw the identification of biological rhythms, like the way that our levels of alertness change systematically through a twenty-four-hour cycle. This is partly stimulated by 'zeitgebers' like daylight, but also happens to people in enclosed environments where those cues aren't available. It hadn't really been apparent before, but the increase in intercontinental air travel produced jet lag, as people had to adjust to different time zones much more quickly than when they travelled by sea or rail. More, there has always been an increase in industrial (and later road) accidents in the early hours of the morning, when people are at their least alert, and psychologists began to be clearer about the reasons why that happens.

Sleep itself was also shown to go in cycles. As psychologists used electroencephalograms (EEGs) to measure brain activity through the night, they found that sleep ranges from a light 'surface' sleep through three more levels down to a deep sleep. These levels produce different EEG patterns, and also sometimes reflect how difficult it is to wake people up. The exception is a paradoxical pattern in which people appeared from their EEGs to be in light sleep but show rapid eye movements (REM) and don't wake up easily. When they are woken up, they report dreaming. Although there have been many wild and wonderful theories of dreaming, most psychologists see it as the brain sorting out and consolidating the huge amount of information we receive during the day, which is why problems often sort themselves out after a good night's sleep.

Other aspects of brain functioning also became clearer in the post-war era. Back in the 1930s, Egas Moniz had shown that an aggressive ape could be rendered docile by the entire removal of its frontal lobe. After the war, this procedure – lobotomy – began to be performed on violent mental patients. It certainly stopped their violence, but also rendered them pretty well incapable of making decisions. A slightly milder version of the operation, known as leucotomy, involved severing the nerve fibres connecting the rest of the brain with the frontal lobe, but leaving the frontal lobe intact. It had similar effects, although not quite so extreme, and remained an accepted psychiatric technique right through to the 1980s.

Understanding how the surface of the brain – the part that does the thinking – works was significantly advanced by the Canadian brain surgeon Wilder Penfield during the 1950s. Because the brain has no sensory nerves, Penfield's operations were carried out on conscious patients. He would use small electrical probes to stimulate different areas and ask the person to describe what they experienced. This allowed him to map out the motor and somatosensory areas – two strips running across the top of the brain – and to show how more of the motor area was used for the more agile parts of the body, while more sensitive areas took up more of the sensory area. His 'homunculi' of distorted bodies reflecting the relative sizes of the sensory or motor areas still feature in many psychology textbooks.

There were other ways that brain operations changed neuropsychology. Penfield had shown that the right side of the brain controls the left side of the body, and vice versa. A new operation for people with extreme epilepsy allowed researchers to investigate what happens when the two sides are separated. Typically, an extreme epileptic seizure begins with a burst of electrical activity on the left side of the brain, which then spreads across the whole of its surface. So surgeons reasoned that if they cut through the corpus callosum – the band of fibres that joins the two halves – the seizure would be limited, allowing the person to keep control of half of their body at least. When they actually performed the operations, the seizures dwindled to almost zero, which was a great relief to the patients.

Sperry, a neuropsychologist, investigated the psychological differences that these operations had made, and his 1961 paper became the talking point of the psychological world. He showed that the two halves of the brain can act like two separate brains, sometimes with different ideas, shown by one hand directly contradicting what the other was doing. One of these 'split-brain' patients described how he was unbuttoning a shirt with one hand, but the other hand was following and buttoning the shirt up again. Another reported going to her wardrobe intending to pick out a particular dress, only to find that her left hand had taken out a totally different one.

These differences showed in experimental trials as well. Split-brain people could only read words presented to the left side of the brain, and not to the right. As language areas are generally on the left side of the brain, that wasn't really surprising. But the right hemisphere did seem to have a basic understanding of spoken language. The person might not be able to describe in words something presented to the right side of their brain, but their left hand could reach out and choose it from a set of objects on the table. Or if they were shown separate images, such that each image went only to one eye, they would only describe the image that had gone to the left eye (that is, to the right side of the brain), but they could point with their left hand to the item on the image shown to the right eye. What the mouth said and what the left hand pointed to were entirely different.

Other brain operations offered even more scope for neuropsychologists. In the 1950s, Henry Molaison (known as H.M.) underwent a brain operation in an attempt to control his severe epilepsy. The surgeon destroyed an area called the hippocampus, on both sides of his brain. It removed the epilepsy, but it also gave him extreme amnesia. He could only remember his life up to the age of sixteen, and he was entirely unable to store new memories, which persisted for the rest of his life. He was unable to remember where he was living, who was looking after him, or even recognise himself in the mirror – although he could recognise himself in photos from his childhood.

Similar effects were shown by the musician Clive Wearing, who caught an infection in the 1980s that also damaged the hippocampus areas of his brain. This gave him both retrograde amnesia (he couldn't remember any of his past before the operation) and anterograde amnesia (he couldn't store new memories, or at least only with great difficulty, and he would often forget them later).

Other neuropsychologists used electrical stimulation to investigate the brain. In a series of studies of the brain's visual cortex, for which they shared a Nobel Prize with Roger Sperry, David Hubel and Torstein Wiesel used microscopic electrodes to stimulate single cells in the visual cortex of cats and monkeys. This allowed them to identify the specific functions of individual neurones, and to see how they responded to different aspects and areas of the visual field. Their observations showed how our visual system becomes able to recognise lines and shapes, and that neurones respond to similar messages from our two eyes arranged side by side, which gives us the comparisons we need for accurate distance viewing.

Although Phineas Gage, Paul Broca and Carl Wernicke had begun the study of neuropsychology in their separate ways, it was the period from the 1950s to the 1980s that really established neuropsychology. Advances ranged from identifying the biochemical action of neurotransmitters to the identification of specific areas of the cortex and the differing roles of the two halves of the brain, and even the way that individual neurones work. It would get another a boost in the next century, as brain scans showed the living brain in action.

CHAPTER 32

Enter the Computer
INFORMATION-PROCESSING MODELS OF COGNITION, ATTENTION AND MEMORY

In 1974, my psychology department received its first computer. It had been allocated its own air-conditioned room, with fans and filters to minimise dust, and it consisted of several large cabinets. Information was input through reels of punched tape, and only a handful of people were able to use it. This was the latest technology, and the whole department was very excited about it. No more laborious calculations of research data by hand, or competition with other academics for precious computer time on the university's huge mainframe computer, down in some basement somewhere.

How times have changed! Now, even the most basic of smart watches has more computing power than that computer did. Computers developed very rapidly after that: during the next decade desktop computers became available, and a further decade later they were becoming common in people's homes.

The increasing acceptance of computing also had its impact on psychology, as cognitive psychologists began to adopt the metaphor of the human brain as being like a computer. That development was helped by the increased acceptance of cognitive processes in American psychology, which grew steadily in the post-war era and slowly eroded the dominance of strict behaviourism. As we saw in Chapter 20, Jerome Bruner, a cognitive psychologist at Harvard from 1945 to 1972, was a key figure in this trend. He was interested in how we think and, in particular, how we group things together to form concepts – things like animals, furniture and trees. He experimented by presenting people with cards covered in un-familiar symbols and observing how they would group these together into categories. One of his findings was the way that, if we are faced with unfamiliar things, we begin by developing hypoth-eses, or guesses, about what their relationship might be. Then we rule those hypotheses out, one by one, until we find one that fits. So it isn't just a question of passively observing the groups: people are actively trying to work things out, even in simple laboratory tasks.

Most of the academic psychology at the time was laboratory based. Eleanor Rosch continued this trend, but looked at how we really use concepts in everyday life. She argued that in the real world not all concepts are equally powerful. There are three levels of concepts that we habitually use: a superordinate, general level, like 'animals' or 'furniture'; a basic level such as 'dog' or 'chair', and a subordinate, or more specific level such as 'poodle' or 'rocking chair'. The basic level represents things we actually do, like the way that chairs are all for sitting on: they have an everyday meaning for people, which makes them easier to acquire and readily brought to mind.

Research into concept formation also led to other areas, such as the use of words as symbols, how children learn to read, and how they acquire language. Following Chomsky's critique of behav-iourism (see Chapter 13), Roger Brown argued that children develop a form of early grammar, which he called 'telegraphic speech': two-word utterances with open words indicating objects or nouns, and pivot words indicating actions or possessions ('My ball', 'More milk'). In each case, it was personal experience that determined the concept or grammatical link being acquired.

In Britain, the focus was on different aspects of cognition. Donald Broadbent, a leading figure in cognitive psychology during the post-war years, had studied psychology at Cambridge under Frederic Bartlett and joined the Applied Psychology Unit at Cambridge in 1949. He had been in the Royal Navy during the war, officially working on personnel selection, although there was a consistent rumour that he had worked at Bletchley Park. Since people never talked about that time, though, that rumour was never confirmed. Regardless, his experience in the Navy had given him a particular interest in attention – both selective attention, which is how we focus on specific information and filter out the chaff, and sustained attention, such as how long air traffic control or radar staff can maintain constant and accurate vigilance.

Broadbent developed filter models of attention, which proved invaluable both to designers and to those trying to achieve optimal working conditions for those engaged in complex tasks. He established an interest in cognitive models, which steadily gained strength during the post-war years, and set a firm foundation for what later became known as the cognitive revolution: a massive expansion of cognitive psychology during the 1970s and 1980s.

Both US and UK psychologists were interested in representation: how information is stored in the mind. Earlier, Bartlett had used the model of the schema to describe the whole complex of knowledge that an individual holds around a particular idea. Schemas are broader than concepts, in that concepts are factual or informational knowledge, while schemas include personal understandings and physical or sensory associations. This, of course, is what makes schemas difficult to define. Some cognitive psychologists defined schemas very tightly, and then argued that those definitions weren't adequate to explain different kinds of memory, while others used a more general definition, looking at how schemas are used in everyday life.

Other psychologists focused on how we use schemas, like Robert Schank and Robert Abelson's model of the 'social script', which directs how we should act in particular situations, which is directed by social cues and expectations. The classic example is the sequence of actions involved in having a meal in a restaurant. You sit down, the waiter comes, you give your order, the food is brought, empty plates are taken away, further courses are brought, and so on. All of this is organised by a shared understanding of who should do what, in what manner, and in what order, just like the script for a play. Schank and Abelson identified three different types of script: situational scripts, like the restaurant example; personal scripts, like those we act out in our jobs or with friends; and instrumental scripts for achieving goals, like the way we go about travelling to work.

Psychologists have always been interested in memory, despite behaviourism, and William James' original assertion that we have two kinds of memory resurfaced. James had distinguished between long-term memory, lasting for months or years, and short-term memory, which fades quickly, like the way we remember and key in a one-time security code. In 1968, Richard Atkinson and Richard Shiffrin proposed that incoming information first goes through a sensory buffer, which filters out irrelevant information, then into short-term memory. From there, it only transfers to long-term memory storage if it is rehearsed: in their model, consistently repeating something would be enough to transfer information from short- to long-term memory.

Their model attracted considerable criticism. Researchers showed that rehearsal was not enough, that meanings matter, and so does the amount of mental processing that we do. Long-term memory could last for different lengths of time: some memories last only for an hour or more, some last weeks, months or years, and the memory involved in exam revision may last for a few weeks before the exam but typically vanishes very quickly afterwards. Some psychologists argued that there is just one memory store, but we do different amounts of processing with our information, and that is what makes the difference.

With short-term memory, we don't try to do much with the information: we only keep it until we have used it, usually by repeating it, and then we forget it. Repetition, Fergus Craik argued in 1972, is the most superficial level of processing. Talking about information, like describing what something looks like, involves more processing, since we are changing the sensory mode involved from visual to words. But the deepest level of processing is to explore the meanings and applications of the information. According to Craik's model, the level of processing determines how long information will be remembered, not just rehearsal as implied by the Atkinson and Shiffrin model. Despite the inevitable academic disputes, the central core of this theory has remained a useful guide to student revision ever since.

In the 1980s, Alan Baddeley and Graham Hitch proposed a model that replaced the short-term memory store with a more sophisticated version. They had worked on it for several years, and their final model was that we have a kind of working memory, similar to the processing chip of a computer, which co-ordinates several different types of input. These include a visuo-spatial scratchpad, which collects and codes visual information; an acoustic store, for sounds; a phonological loop, which decodes the meanings of speech; and an articulatory loop, which rehearses words. All this is brought together by a central executive, which is used for cognitively demanding tasks which need a lot of attention. It's an active store that is closely linked with attention, as the brain actively deals with and sorts out information, and not a passive store as the old idea of short-term memory maintained.

Other researchers explored different types of long-term memory, partly through experimental studies, and partly through clinical neurology. This involved case studies of people who had experienced various forms of brain damage and lost a particular type of memory as a result. One distinction that was made, for example, was between procedural memory, which is concerned with our basic skills and schemas, and declarative memory, which is our memory for specific facts and episodes. People who have suffered amnesia as a result of accidents often lose declarative memory but can still remember how to do everyday things like making a cup of tea or dressing themselves.

Another distinction was between episodic and semantic memory, proposed by the influential Canadian neuropsychologist

Endel Tulving. Episodic memory is all about the changing, temporary experiences that constitute our daily lives, like remembering a visit to an elderly aunt last Christmas. Semantic memory, on the other hand, is our organised knowledge of the world, like knowing that velvet is soft, or that dogs and cats are both types of animal. It also includes knowledge that we might not be able to put into words very easily, like knowing that an action would be right or wrong. Effectively, episodic memory is more factual, about things that have happened, while semantic memory is more to do with meanings and implications.

We all experience our memories as if they were factual records of what happened, but this really isn't true. Elizabeth Loftus conducted research into eyewitness testimony. In her most famous study, people were shown a film of a car accident, and asked either 'How fast were the cars going when they hit each other?' or 'How fast were the cars going when they smashed into each other?' When they were asked to remember the film a week later, those in the 'smashed into' group distinctly remembered seeing broken glass, but in reality there hadn't been any. This showed, vividly, how what we remember is subtly adjusted by our own interpretations, and by later events.

Ulric Neisser was also interested in real-world memory, like the way that two people can remember the same event differently. He carried out a number of studies of autobiographical memory – how we remember our own lives – including how particularly special events can generate a kind of 'flashbulb memory' in which we recall all the details of where we were when the event happened. These memories are strong and vivid, but not always accurate, often including details that actually happened later.

In a particularly clear example of constructed memory, Neisser compared real-world tape recordings of conversations with the testimony from someone who had been there. John Dean gave evidence at the Watergate trials which led to the resignation of President Nixon in 1974. He was known to have an extremely accurate memory, and in his testimony he described conversations word for word as they happened. When tapes of these conversations came to light later on, it was found that, although Dean had been entirely accurate regarding the meanings of the conversations, the words he remembered were often different from what had actually been said. This, Neisser argued, showed how memory isn't a factual recording, but is interpreted through our own schemas. As Bartlett had shown several decades earlier, memory is an active, not a passive, process. A similar message was becoming evident in studies of perception, as we will see in the next chapter.

CHAPTER 33

Understanding Perception
THEORIES OF HOW WE MAKE SENSE OF WHAT WE PERCEIVE

Have you ever been travelling in a train, or a car, and while you were looking of the window at the landscape noticed how objects outside seem to move as you travel? Things that are nearby flash past quickly. But things that are a long way away seem to be moving in the same direction as you are, only more slowly. But nothing stays still, not even objects in the middle distance. It's a puzzle, like so many other aspects of our perception, and one that attracted the interest of many psychologists in the post-war era.

One of the major differences between the American and British approaches to cognitive psychology in the late 1900s was the emphasis given to theories of perception. The basic principles of perceptual organisation that had been identified by the Gestalt psychologists during the 1920s and 1930s were generally accepted, but other research into perception wasn't much noticed in America. In Britain, possibly because of the work of the Applied Psychology Unit at Cambridge and Broadbent's focus on attention, and possibly because of the strong interest in computer modelling and the development of computer simulation, theories that psychologists had developed to explain perception were given much more prominence.

One of the key figures in this was Richard Gregory, who, as we saw in Chapter 17, had served in the RAF during the Second World War, and afterwards studied at Cambridge with Frederic Bartlett and the neuropsychologist Oliver Zangwill. He spent a couple of years doing research into methods of escape from submarines, and then moved on to establish the Special Sense Laboratory, where he explored a variety of problems, ranging from individual cases of people recovering sight after blindness, to working for the US Air Force on the perceptual problems posed by the moon landing and docking.

As well as his interest in psychology, we have seen that Gregory had a keen mechanical aptitude. He invented a number of new instruments, including the special camera that was used in the moon project to minimise the effects of atmospheric turbulence during re-entry and landing. In 1967, he moved to Edinburgh University, where he developed one of the first intelligent robots, 'Freddie', which could recognise and handle objects. But at the time there was little funding for research into artificial intelligence, so he moved again, this time to establish the Brain and Perception Laboratory at Bristol. He combined his interest in perception with his mechanical gifts to establish the Bristol Exploratory science centre – one of the first interactive science exhibitions.

This wide-ranging background led him to develop a theory of the 'perceiver as scientist' – the idea that human perception is largely based on developing hypotheses from our past experience to make sense of what we are looking at. In his model, the brain uses perceptual cues, like the depth cues it gains from binocular vision or cues that imply that figures are in front of their backgrounds. Using these, the brain makes educated guesses about what it is looking at. Sometimes it gets it wrong, creating visual illusions, and those mistakes, Gregory felt, can tell us a lot about perceptual processes.

Gregory drew on his broad experience, from the study of underwater perception to early steps in artificial intelligence. Sometimes, he argued, visual illusions work because they apply everyday depth cues inappropriately: cues like things in the distance seeming smaller than those nearby, or shadows indicating three-dimensional shapes. Sometimes we apply perceptual rules, known as constancies, like the way that we still perceive a car as white even if we are looking at it under an orange streetlight. His work on visual illusions was extensive, and his contribution to the public understanding of science through the Bristol Exploratory gained him public as well as professional recognition.

Not everyone agreed with his theory of perceiver as scientist, though. The American psychologist James Jerome Gibson was highly dismissive of the idea that the brain develops hypotheses to make sense of what it sees. Gibson argued that perception takes place in the real world. We don't perceive things as isolated objects, but with plenty of background and context. Not only that, he argued, we are active in the world, and it is unrealistic to try to separate perceiving from movement.

Perception has evolved, Gibson argued, because it helps animals and humans to survive from day to day. So it has an ecological basis: the animal's survival is taking place in a real world where it is active and moving around. That creates a visual experience that is quite different from looking at static images on paper or screen. The movement of the perceiver means that their visual field is always changing, in what he referred to as the 'optical flow'. Things are seen from different angles, some of the background becomes covered or revealed as we move, the surfaces show different textures and gradients of light, and our whole visual field changes. These things happen with even minor head movements, let alone whole-body actions. The ability to see things from different angles and interpret visual information using our own movement was a crucial aspect of perception for Gibson, since it means that there is no need to infer anything. All the information that is needed is there in what the eyes are receiving.

Gibson described his theory as 'direct perception'. He viewed theories that needed cognitive inference, like Gregory's model, as being only necessary to explain perception in limited artificial situations, such as in geometric illusions or the stimuli in perceptual laboratories, where people have to develop hypotheses because the available information is so very limited. In the real world, information is much richer. We have more than enough information, and it is constantly updated by our own physical activity. Our nervous system is attuned to these changes, so we automatically notice the implications of differences in the optic array.

Not only that, but part of our automatic visual processing is the possibilities that objects offer us: what we can do or how we could use them. A log, for example, affords sitting on it as a possibility; a stick affords the possibilities of support, of digging, of a missile, or whatever else is relevant at the time. For Gibson, real-world perception automatically includes these 'affordances': they are simply part of the process of perceiving. Gibson's ecological theory of perception is all about surviving, which means actively engaging with the world.

Gibson's theory was taken as a starting point by Ulric Neisser although, unlike Gibson, Neisser did acknowledge the usefulness of someone's own knowledge. Perception, Neisser argued, is all about making sense of our immediate experience. Neisser had conducted research into many different aspects of cognitive psychology in the past and had studied or worked with Köhler and Maslow, among others. From them he had gained the conviction that psychology should be a force for good and should therefore emphasise the positive aspects of human nature. This led him to a consistent interest in how people interact with the real world, both in remembering, as we saw in the last chapter, and in perceiving.

Neisser began his perceptual research with visual search. He rejected popular filter models, arguing like Gibson that we are surrounded with rich sources of information from all of our senses, and that we use that information to make perceptual choices. If we want to explain why someone picked an apple from a tree, he argued, we don't need a filter that stops them picking all the other apples on that tree: they just pick the one they want. In the same way, we choose what we pay attention to, based on our immediate situation and what we expect to be important. Human beings select what they will notice because we are active in the world, and some items of information are more relevant to our activity than others.

Like Gibson, Neisser argued that there isn't much perceptual uncertainty, because the optic array usually provides more than enough information for the perceiver. Instead, we sample that information, using other senses like touch and sound as well. We use an anticipatory schema that directs what we should search for or sample from the information available to us. The sample directs our actions, and their results modify the anticipatory schema, so it can direct what we should look for next. Perception, Neisser argued, is a continuous cycle. Think of crossing the road: the anticipatory schema prepares us for the idea that there may be traffic, so we search for traffic-relevant information, sampling what we can see and hear. That sample directs what we should do, so we act accordingly, and the result of that action modifies our anticipatory schema for the next move.

For Neisser, perception is a skilled activity that takes place over time. He was highly critical of traditional laboratory studies that expect people to react to a stimulus taken totally out of context in the same way as they would react to something in their everyday lives. The stimulus is not a 'pure' version of the real thing, as the laboratory scientists assumed, but is something else altogether. As Neisser pointed out, real-life events are rarely completely unexpected: even if a total stranger arrives, they still go to the door rather than come through the window, and their knock or the doorbell tells us that there is someone there. Neisser contrasted this with laboratory studies, in which stimuli are shown out of context and appear as if they were ghosts.

Real-life perceptual events also involve several different anticipatory schemas at the same time. We can interpret a smile on a number of levels: socio-cultural, personal, communicative, and so on. That means that we use several different perceptual cycles simultaneously, as we link our past experiences with the present situation and our predictions about our future behaviour. It doesn't mean that we only see what we are expecting to see, because real-world information is constantly changing what we anticipate. But it does make us more prepared to see certain things at any one time.

Other research into perception was focusing on entirely different aspects of the process. As we saw in Chapter 31, Hubel and Wiesel had identified a neural basis to the basic forms of perception. Their findings were used by David Marr in a model of how visual perception works at the most basic level. Marr's theory, which was published posthumously in 1982, showed how basic processes like figure ground perception could result just from the way that basic neural input was used by the brain.

Marr argued that we have all the information needed for perception in the light that reaches our eyes. Cells in the retina of our eyes provide us with information about contrasts and contours, and that can tell us about concave or convex surfaces and about areas of similarity which can indicate shapes or outlines. We use these to build up a basic image, which Marr called the 'raw primal sketch'. If we then add in Gestalt principles like proximity and similarity, we can get an image similar to an artist's rough draft, which Marr called the 'full primal sketch'.

Neural processing then adds information about depth and distance, telling us whether one part of the image is in front of another. Marr called this the $2\frac{1}{2}$D sketch because it's not quite 3D, but it's getting there. Then changes in the optic array from movement and action, together with the texture and colour gradients in the image all help to make a full 3D image. Specific images, like human beings or trees or animals, are seen as stick-like figures that become clearer as more detail is added – for example, as we move closer to what we are looking at. Marr suggested that this might be why stick-figures and silhouettes are such powerful images in drawing and art. Marr's computational theory doesn't contradict others, but it explained how basic visual processes can produce useful visual information at a neural level. And his theory made a significant contribution to the developing world of artificial intelligence.

CHAPTER 34

Control and Agency
LEARNED HELPLESSNESS, LOCUS OF CONTROL AND ATTRIBUTION THEORY

It all started with the dogs. In the 1960s, most psychologists had conducted animal experiments at one time or another: usually learning experiments, in which rats or other animals were taught to run mazes or engage in similar tasks. In many UK universities, carrying out an animal experiment of this kind was a required part of the students' assessment, and the argument that this might not be desirable only gradually became accepted towards the late 1970s. The arguments were given prominence by a number of extreme acts by the Animal Liberation Front, and by the end of the 1980s the practice had more or less died out. From then on, animal experiments in psychology were only conducted in a few specialised departments, although they continued in medical research. And they all required compliance with explicit ethical standards.

Not all those experiments were totally pointless, although most of them did seem to be. But psychologists had learned about conditioning from Pavlov's dogs, about how much more effective reward is than punishment from Skinner's rats and pigeons, and about attachment from Harlow's monkeys. And another important insight – possibly even more than these – was the idea of learned helplessness. Studies with dogs had shown how they would learn to jump from one box to another to escape from a mild electric shock, and back again if they saw the light that signalled that the shock was about to happen. But, asked Martin Seligman, what would happen if the signal was wrong or didn't happen, and they couldn't escape from the shock after all?

What happened at first was that the dogs would jump from one box to another repeatedly. However, as they learned that escape wasn't possible, they would become passive and lethargic, looking depressed, although the researchers didn't say that in public because it didn't sound scientific enough. More to the point, though, when the experimental situation changed back so that they received an accurate signal and could escape from the shock if they wanted to, those dogs didn't bother. They stayed passive, just putting up with the shocks. They had, Seligman said, learned to be helpless. While, at first, they could respond to a challenge and avoid the problem, their experience had taught them that there was nothing they could do. So, they did nothing and carried on doing nothing even when the situation had changed, and they might have been able to do something to help themselves.

Seligman and others drew a parallel between that and the way that people who have experienced too many of life's kicks often also become passive, not taking action that would help them even if they have an opportunity to do so. Learned helplessness doesn't just happen in animals: it can happen in human beings too. These insights sparked off an interest in the whole question of personal agency, and how important it is for people to feel that they have some level of control over what happens to them.

Psychologists began to investigate various aspects of control, and how people respond to it. Seligman's findings about learned helplessness quickly became linked to research into locus of control. This was an idea about personality which was being developed by Julian Rotter at about the same time. Rotter saw people's sense of control as being on a continuum. At one end was the belief that the person had no control at all over their lives, and that what happened to them was in the hands of powerful external agencies like governments or fate. At the other end was the belief that they could always exert some control over what happened to them: that control over their lives was entirely in their own hands. Rotter saw it as a continuous scale, not a dichotomy, and that most people's beliefs fall somewhere in between but tend towards one end or the other.

The belief that events could be controlled, Rotter showed, made a significant difference to the amount of stress people experience. People's beliefs about control can be identified by the attributions they make – the types of reasons they give to explain why things happen. People with an external locus of control tend to see causes as unavoidable: something they can't challenge or influence; while those with an internal locus of control attribute what happens to things they could influence, believing that their own efforts could eventually make things better.

Rotter's theory was extended by Bernard Weiner, who proposed another attributional dimension, which is whether the attributions that people make – that is, the causes they identify – are likely to last or not. A stable attribution would be effectively permanent, or at least not likely to change in the foreseeable future, while an unstable one would be just temporary. Later researchers added another dimension: that of global or specific. A global attribution is whether the cause is seen as having wide impact, affecting lots of other things, while a specific one is when the cause is seen as only relevant to that particular situation and not really affecting anything else.

Attributional analysis – that is, identifying the different patterns of attributions that people make – became a valuable tool in psychotherapy. The typical depressive attributional pattern, for example, was external, stable and global. Peter Stratton and his associates showed how attributional patterns could be used in family therapy to identify problems of dysfunctional families, and others used it to analyse ongoing beliefs in organisations. It became one of the bedrock techniques contributing to other developments in psychotherapy, which had begun in the second half of the twen-tieth century and gained real momentum in its final two decades.

As the twentieth century and consumer society progressed, psychology began to reflect society's growing interest in the indi-vidual, including how people deal with their problems. Psychologists like George Kelly began to focus on how people make sense of their worlds, mirroring the growing interest in cognitive processes. Kelly's quintessential approach to understanding mental issues was expressed in his remark, 'If you don't know what's wrong with the patient, ask him. He may tell you', and his work reflected a growing awareness of agency on the part of the client. This was a funda-mental change: people were being regarded as active agents in their lives, rather than just as the victims of 'disorders'.

Kelly argued that we think like scientists, developing theories to make sense of our own worlds. But the sense we make is our own unique understanding, not necessarily the same as other people's. (We're talking about everybody here, not just psychiatric patients.) We each, according to Kelly, develop our own personal set of constructs – personal ways of interpreting events or people – from our experiences in the world. These constructs are bipolar in nature, like 'kind'–'cruel' or 'thoughtful'–'careless', and we use them to weigh up the people we know or meet. Kelly's work was widely used in therapy, but also quickly applied to the commercial world, as market researchers became interested in exploring how people see new or existing products.

Another significant development was proposed by Aaron Beck in the 1960s. This was cognitive therapy: the idea of working with people to identify and change unhelpful styles of thinking, so they can tackle their problems in a more constructive manner. He had come to this approach through working with depressed patients who had very negative ways of thinking about their problems. Beck believed that they needed to restructure how they thought, so that they could begin to approach life more positively. His cogni-tive restructuring ideas became linked with other techniques, including a practical approach to training people to adopt different behaviours, emphasising new ways of acting as well as new ways of thinking. It became known as 'cognitive behaviour therapy': a complete cycle of thoughts, feelings and behaviour, all working together to address problems.

A similar, though not identical, approach to therapy was developed by Albert Ellis during this period. Ellis, like others, had become concerned with how people's psychological problems were linked with, and often derived from, negative beliefs and ways of thinking. His distinctive approach to therapy was to challenge those beliefs directly, confronting patients and showing through reasoned argument how irrational those beliefs were, while at the same time providing emotional support. 'Rational emotive therapy', as it was called, soon became extended with behavioural techniques to train people into new habits and ways of acting, and was known as 'rational emotive behaviour therapy', REBT for short.

These approaches were very different from either the psychoanalytic approach or the psychiatric models of earlier times, focusing as they did on the idea of personal agency. Other psychologists also explored the question of agency, but in a rather different way. Stanley Milgram, for example, had explained his findings on obedience (see Chapter 19) by proposing that we have two different states of mind. Mostly, he argued, we make our own decisions, but we are also capable of entering what he called an 'agentic' state, in which we abandon our sense of personal responsibility and just see ourselves as agents acting for another authority. He used this idea of the agentic state to explain why people can surprise, or even horrify, themselves by discovering that they are capable of acts of extreme cruelty. But as we've seen, 'I was only obeying orders' wasn't considered a sufficient excuse in the Nuremberg trials, and further psychological research also challenged the agentic state idea.

A similar approach was put forward by Philip Zimbardo, who conducted a number of studies into what he called 'deindividuation'. His research addressed the old idea of mob psychology – the belief that people in a crowd can lose their personal sense of identity so the crowd effectively just becomes a mob, capable of extreme actions that individual people wouldn't participate in if they were truly themselves. Zimbardo modernised and rationalised the theory on the basis of research that showed how people whose identities were disguised would act more aggressively than those who could be clearly identified. But the disguises he had used carried their own social messages: he used hoods and suits reminiscent of the violent Ku Klux Klan, which subtly communicated what was expected from the people wearing them. Later, Zimbardo conducted studies of torturers, and showed how keeping their anonymity was important, not just as added stress for their victims, but also for the torturers themselves. It allowed them to see themselves as deindividuated: as an anonymous person doing a 'job' that was completely different from other aspects of their personal identity.

Deindividuation isn't always a bad thing. People can develop a powerful sense of shared identity from being part of a crowd. That's a lot of the attraction in going to football matches, festivals and other mass events. Those involved often describe a sense of one-ness and belonging when they are part of a crowd that acts as a unified entity, with everyone spontaneously acting together. Psychologists have studied that shared experience in religious crowds as well as in sports and musical events, and, for many, it is really something special.

But participating in a shared experience is very different from becoming a mindless member of a violent mob. 'Mob psychology' was a popular idea in the nineteenth century, particularly with politicians, who used it to explain away the actions of angry crowds. More recent research, though, has shown how social riots and collective action of that sort aren't people reverting to an animalistic state, as the 'mob psychology' model suggested, but instead are almost always a shared reaction to a real sense of injustice. Stephen Reicher and his associates explored several examples of urban riots and found that either a sense of social injustice or a clash between social groups with opposing social representations would always be an underlying factor. What Zimbardo described as deindividuation they saw as a lessening of self-awareness, mainly coming from the way that people's attention is elsewhere, and not on their own selves.

The idea of deindividuation is a controversial perspective, partly because it has never ceased to be an attractive political explanation for the behaviour of crowds. But that tends to divert attention away from the underlying causes of the unrest. It may be an explanation in some situations, but it doesn't really help us to understand the special nature of shared experiences. To explain that we need to look more deeply into our social natures. In the next chapter, we will see how even small children are often more socially sophisticated than we used to believe.

CHAPTER 35

The Social Child

RE-EVALUATING PIAGETIAN THEORY AND THE SOCIALLY AWARE CHILD

Three-year-old Chrissy liked playschool. She got to do painting and play with the special toys, and every day the teacher read them a story. One day a new person came. She smiled at Chrissy and asked her to sit with her.

She spread out two rows of buttons on the table. 'Which row has the most buttons?' she asked. Chrissy looked, but they were both the same, so she said so. The woman spread out one of the rows, and asked again, 'Which row has the most buttons?'

She didn't want my first answer, Chrissy thought. I have to say something else. So she pointed to the longer row and said, 'That one.'

The woman nodded and smiled. 'Let's try a different one,' she said, and put two water glasses on the table. She poured water into both of them, and asked Chrissy which one had more water in it.

Chrissy told her they were both the same. Then the woman poured the water from one glass into a long, thin one and asked her the same question. Again, Chrissy thought she must have got the answer wrong, so she changed it. 'That one,' she said, pointing to the taller glass. Again, the woman nodded and smiled.

In the post-war decades, as we've seen, psychology was in a period of transition. Behaviourism gave ground to cognitive experimentation, and war experiences had set the agenda for much psychological research. By the 1980s, though, new perspectives were emerging as the post-war 'baby boomer' generation was producing new theories and insights. It wasn't a sudden change, of course. Some insights and theories were new, but many areas that flowered from the 1980s onwards came from psychologists reaching back to resume and re-evaluate work from the inter-war period.

Piaget's theory of cognitive development had been firmly based on studies like the one opening this chapter, and his theory was by now hugely influential in the educational world. But it, too, was being re-evaluated. This was partly because the idea of stages (which Piaget regarded as a minor and unimportant part of his theory) provided a rationale for teachers to justify why some children didn't progress in the same way as others. In the UK at least, the belief in innate intelligence was strong and was reinforced by influential psychologists such as Cyril Burt, who acted as a significant educational advisor to the UK government. Selection for grammar schools, geared towards university entrance, or for a more basic education designed for future factory workers or similar took place at the age of eleven, because it was believed that the child's innate intelligence would be apparent by that age. As we saw in Chapter 14, Piaget's theory was structured around the idea of genetic maturation, and education was seen as essentially allowing the child's innate abilities to mature.

A very different picture was evident in the Soviet countries. There, the official belief was that the ideal person was formed by social influences, not innate qualities, so social skills and mutual help were deliberately fostered in school. Children in each class were organised into teams, or links, and expected to help one another with their schoolwork. Individual competition was frowned on, but team achievements were highly praised. That didn't mean that all children were seen as the same: those with exceptional talent, for example in sport, science or music, were sent to special academies designed to nurture that talent, but the principle that such opportunities were open to every Soviet child was much publicised.

As we saw in Chapter 14, in 1962 an English translation of a major Soviet book on the child's cognitive development was finally published. The book itself had been written in 1934, but it wasn't until Jerome Bruner spearheaded its translation that Lev Vygotsky's ideas became available to Western psychologists. Partly, this was because of the intervening war years, and the disruption of interactions between Soviet and Western academics; but partly, too, it was because Vygotsky had been a supporter of Trotsky, and Stalin had banned his books, as he banned Trotsky's own writing, in the 1930s.

Vygotsky was aware of Piaget's work and agreed with him on many aspects. But where he really disagreed was on the way that the child learns and develops. For Piaget, cognitive development was based entirely on the child performing operations on the environment: learning by doing things that had an effect. According to Piaget's theory, people were essentially just part of the child's environment, not much different from their physical surroundings in terms of their influence on cognitive development. Vygotsky saw it very differently. The child's interaction with other people, he argued, was crucial for cognitive development. A child can acquire basic knowledge by interacting with the physical world, but it is other people who extend and develop that knowledge.

Children learn from other people in many ways: through imitation, by direct questioning, by listening and observing, and indirectly through books and other sources. For Vygotsky, contact with adult understanding is essential for full cognitive development in providing what he called 'scaffolding', allowing the child to build its knowledge through further learning. A child can learn from direct interaction with the environment, as Piaget had proposed, but they could learn much more with social support. Vygotsky referred to this extended area of cognitive development as the zone of proximal development – a concept which only gradually seeped into the educational world and didn't become fully accepted until the 1980s.

Piaget's work – the gospel for many educationalists – was challenged by others as well. One aspect was the idea that babies don't know that objects continue to exist when they are out of sight. Piaget argued that this cognitive ability, which he called the 'object concept', only developed when the child was between eighteen months and two years old. But researchers using infra-red photography showed that infants much younger than that would reach out for a toy even in total darkness, when they obviously couldn't see it.

Piaget's ideas about cognitive development were backed up by easily replicated demonstrations, which appeared to prove that certain types of thinking were limited at certain ages, but could be easily managed as a child grew older. One classic study, for example, suggested that young children were unable to see things from another person's perspective. Piaget used a model of mountains on a table, and placed dolls at various points. Then he invited children to choose what a particular doll could see, from a set of photographs. Younger children would consistently pick out their own view. For Piaget this was evidence that they were too self-focused (he called it egocentric), to see things from someone else's perspective. But a modern reconstruction, involving walls on a table and a boy doll hiding from a police doll, found no such effect: even quite young children could predict which hiding place would work. The researcher, Martin Hughes, argued that Piaget's findings were because the 'mountain' problem was irrelevant to small children, not because they lacked cognitive ability.

Piaget believed that young children could only focus on one attribute at a time and conducted experiments to demonstrate it. Children shown the same amount of liquid in a short fat glass and a tall thin one would say that the taller one held more; or that the longer of two rows containing the same number of buttons contained more. These experiments were tightly scripted, and gave very reliable results, but they too were re-evaluated. One criticism had to do with the child's social knowledge. In everyday life, if an adult asks a child the same questions twice, it's because they aren't satisfied with the first answer. So researchers argued that the reason why children change their answers is because they think they have given the wrong answer the first time. When they replicated Paget's experiments but only asked the question once, children were much more likely to give the correct answer. Those experiments hadn't been showing what the child knew, but how they thought they should interact with adults.

Further support for this challenge came in what became a classic set of experiments by James McGarrigle and Margaret Donaldson. In these, the children were introduced to a small teddy bear who apparently lived in a box on the experimenter's table. 'Naughty teddy' would decide to do random things, often messing the table up, to the great glee of the watching child. In copies of the Piagetian experiments, when the child had been shown the two sets and agreed that they were the same, 'naughty teddy' would jump out of his box and mess things up, spreading out the buttons or pouring the liquid into another container. Small children loved the game but, more importantly, when they were asked whether things were still the same, they knew they hadn't really changed.

These re-evaluations of the classic Piagetian evidence suggested not only that the theory itself needed re-evaluating, but also that the child's social knowledge is more sophisticated than people had believed. This idea paved the way for the general acceptance of Vygotsky's alternative approach; and it was further enhanced by a series of studies investigating the child's theory of mind, or TOM for short.

As we know, Piaget believed that children were unable to understand that other people might see things differently from themselves until they were roughly nine or ten, but later researchers found that this ability develops much earlier – usually at about three and a half years old. In a standard experiment, two children would see a doll or a sweet hidden in a particular place. One child would leave the room, and the experimenter would change the hiding place as the other child looked on. That child would then be asked where the absent child would look for the object. Three-year-old children would usually say the second hiding place, while four-year-olds would say the first, knowing that the other child had not seen the change.

The growing idea of the socially aware child was supported by the findings of two UK research projects, one directed by Jerome Bruner, who was now at Oxford, looking at different forms of UK childcare, and one from Cambridge headed by Judy Dunn, which investigated the family life of children at home. In the Oxford Pre-School Research Project, playgroups, nursery schools, child minders and day nurseries were compared in terms of how they fostered sociability, creativity and school preparation in small children. Overall, the research showed that having the opportunity to play with others resulted in children who were more socially skilled and emotionally balanced than those who had been cared for as individuals, or with only one or two others.

The Cambridge project was a set of ethological studies observing how young children interact with their siblings. Each researcher spent some time getting the family accustomed to their presence, so the children would act as naturally as possible. They recorded the games, squabbles and other interactions between two- and three-year-old children and their other family members. The study showed how small children are much more socially aware than research conducted outside the family in nurseries and playgroups suggested.

For example, they would tease their older siblings by deliberately provoking them by hiding or spoiling something the older sibling was fond of. They might tease their parent, for example by doing something they knew was forbidden, while looking at them and laughing. They showed an awareness of other people's feelings, trying to comfort their mothers if they were upset or distressed by cuddling close or bringing them a favourite toy – and sometimes doing the opposite with their siblings by doing things that they knew would upset or annoy them even further! As the children grew older, though, they were more likely to comfort than to tease. They had a keen awareness of rules, and what was or was not permitted, even though they might tease their carers by breaking those rules. It was evident that even small children's understanding of the social world was much more sophisticated than Piaget or earlier psychologists had thought.

CHAPTER 36

The Nature/Nurture Debate Continues
Types of Intelligence Testing and its Controversies

'I'm fed up with that rat training thing,' Jesse remarked. 'My rat is so stupid. It's taking so long to learn how to run these mazes.'

'Really?' her friend Judy responded. 'Snuffles – that's what I call mine – is a really fast learner. I think it's fun. I go to the lab two or three times a day for the practice.'

'I can't be bothered with that,' said Jesse. 'I just go once, to make sure I get my credit. But anyway, there's not much point doing any more. My rat is from that "maze-dull" strain that Professor Rosenthal told us about, so it was bound to take ages. I bet yours is a "maze-bright" one.'

'Well, yes,' Judy confirmed. 'He said they'd been specially bred for running mazes quickly. So that worked, didn't it?'

But despite what the students had been told, the two sets of rats were not actually any different. The rats had been carefully matched to be equal in maze-running ability. The difference in their perform-ance – which was very real – was all to do with how they were handled. Those students who believed that their rats were bright spent more time with them, handled them more, and treated them more gently, even giving them nicknames. But the students with the supposedly dull rats only did the minimal number of training sessions and said they hadn't liked their rats at all. The rats in the 'maze-bright' group learned far more quickly and ran the maze faster and more accurately than the other group, but it was the difference in handling that affected how the rats performed.

That experiment, reported by Robert Rosenthal and Kermit Fode in 1963, was the forerunner of a famous set of experiments in the later decades of the twentieth century which fuelled a growing debate about educational expectations. This was a time of massive social change, as older assumptions gave way to new ideas, colonies demanded their independence and people everywhere wanted the opportunity to a fair share in their country's fortunes. The civil rights movement in America focused attention on racial discrimination in the 1960s, the feminist movement of the 1970s embarked on a massive consciousness-raising programme to show women how to recognise everyday sexism in their own lives, and a new generation of consumers supported innovations in fashion and lifestyles.

As we've seen, psychology also changed with those times, as new areas opened up and older theories were widened by new research. But the change was gradual, and while newer areas were often accepted, in some areas of psychology challenges to older, more established ideas met with considerable resistance. That resistance often took the form of heated arguments, the strongest of which were the nature/nurture debates. These were essentially about whether a psychological ability was innate – that is, coming about through genetic changes at the right age – or learned through experience.

As our knowledge of genetics and the human genome has progressed, these debates have become largely irrelevant; as the Canadian psychologist D.O. Hebb pointed out, both environment and heredity are equally important for development. But from the 1970s to the early 1990s, they were a common theme in psychology. They weren't new: as we saw in Chapter 6, psychologists had taken opposing stances on child-rearing from the beginning of the century, with Gesell insisting that child development was genetically deter-mined and Watson insisting that it was all about conditioning – that is, learning. And it surfaced again, as we saw in Chapter 13, in the debate between Skinner and Chomsky about language. But the strong social move to open up educational opportunities meant that the nature/nurture debate on intelligence became particularly powerful in the later part of the twentieth century.

The problem, of course, comes with defining what intelligence actually is. We all use the word, but what do we really mean when we use it? That's one of the issues that brings us up short, over and over again. Is it a general ability that we have? We all know people who are intelligent in some ways but quite stupid in others. So, is it a collection of different abilities? If so, are they just mental abilities, or should we include physical ones? What about skilled craftsmen and craftswomen? Are they intelligent?

Charles Spearman, in the early years of the twentieth century, had insisted that there was an overriding factor, generally referred to as 'g', which was a single general ability that could be expressed in a single figure, the Intelligence Quotient, or IQ. The idea of g lay at the heart of the hereditarian argument, as it was used to support the view of intelligence as something that people had more or less of. That, in turn, was used as a rationale to justify the rank-ordering of people and groups in society – an idea that became popular as traditional values challenged the idea that people were born into their social class.

That wasn't an inevitable consequence of g, of course. Many academics disputed these ideas and used g as a simple expression of general ability, which could reflect changes in experience. Other theories attempting to define intelligence avoided the idea al-together. In 1955, J.P. Guilford argued that intelligence was actually a combination of different mental abilities and actions. He identi-fied between 120 and 150 different elements that made up an individual's overall intelligence. There were several other attempts to define intelligence, each of which led to a different approach to intelligence testing. This, together with other forms of testing, led to an exponential growth in the psychometric industry in the post-war decades. And the main attention focused on the use of intelligence tests in education, primarily for selection.

Rosenthal had speculated that if the students' rats had become brighter when expected to, then it was reasonable to assume the same would be true of children. Together with a colleague, Leonore Jacobsen, he went on to perform a similar study in schools. They gave a fairly standard intelligence test to pupils in an average city school and told teachers that this was a new test designed to predict late development in intelligence. Then they allowed the teachers to 'overhear' conversations in which they named certain children as being likely to show improvement in the classroom over the next year, although in fact these children were no different from their classmates in either their work or their test results. When they returned at the end of the year, the children they had named had shown considerable improvements in their academic work. Their test results were higher, and they were clearly more motivated. What had happened was that the teachers had higher expectations of their performance, so they had talked to these students more and were more likely to praise their achievements. The children had picked this up unconsciously and responded.

This study – inevitably criticised, but still widely circulated – added fuel to the idea that children from poorer backgrounds experience educational discrimination. It was argued, for example, that Black children in the US were consistently educationally disadvantaged, both in school and through the results of intelligence tests, and a number of compensatory educational projects were initiated, with only limited success.

But the old attitudes hadn't died out altogether, and a heated debate was sparked in 1966 by the physicist William Shockley. Shockley argued that the consistent group differences between Black and white people in the US didn't come from schooling: they were evidence of a genetic difference in IQ. The debate this produced was exacerbated by an educational psychologist, Arthur Jensen, who published an article supporting Shockley's ideas. Jensen argued that compensatory education schemes failed because of genetic differences in IQ between Black and white Americans.

Others jumped on the bandwagon, either to refute or to support these ideas.

It was the old idea about inherited intelligence resurfacing, and it had significant political implications. Research showed that these group differences were becoming less extreme in regions that were less discriminatory, which provided evidence for environmental factors and expectations as accounting for those findings. In some ways, the debate was exacerbated by the introduction of academic appraisal systems, which assessed academic merit according to the number of journal articles published and how often those articles were cited by others. Some academics secured their tenure by cynically exploiting these criteria – for example, by publishing an article supporting the 'genetic differences' claim and raising their citation count as other academics rushed into print to refute it.

Psychologists who supported the genetic theory, Arthur Jensen, Hans Eysenck and Richard Herrnstein, all insisted that intelligence was a fixed ability, measured accurately by IQ tests, and that its variability was almost entirely (80 per cent) inherited. The majority of other psychologists disagreed, pointing to evidence that (a) measured intelligence even in a single individual can increase as a result of experience; (b) that IQ tests are not accurate measures but suffer from cultural bias; and (c) that the heritability figure cited is arbitrary and not supported by genetic or social evidence. Geneticists themselves saw the whole nature/nurture debate as pretty silly: development comes from both, and to try to allocate percentages to one or the other was, in their view, just nonsense. And nonscience.

It also emerged that a lot of the evidence supporting the hereditarian point of view was dubious. In the early 1980s, the biologist Stephen Jay Gould published *The Mismeasure of Man*, in which he showed how several 'studies' of genetic influence, like the story of the Kallikaks (see Chapter 6), were demonstrably faked. Other challenges were also raised: the influential British educational psychologist and eugenicist Cyril Burt had published a number of twin studies that apparently gave convincing evidence for the hereditarian perspective, but close examination of his data showed unrealistically precise correlations in the numbers, while subsequent efforts to find both his research assistants and the original families were in vain and raised questions about whether they had even existed.

Although the old arguments still rumbled on, intelligence researchers towards the end of the twentieth century became more concerned with cultural variations and contextual issues in intelligence. Stephen Rose argued that the whole idea of trying to define intelligence is futile, because in real life it is an adverb, not a noun. We describe people as acting intelligently in particular situations, but that doesn't mean that there is really a separate thing called 'intelligence'. It's more of a way of going about dealing with problems than a thing in itself. Which might explain why trying to define intelligence has always led to so many problems.

Others, though, were less sceptical. Howard Gardner, for example, argued that what we see as intelligence was not a single thing, but a combination of seven different intelligences, each of which could exist in different degrees in people. We have 'linguistic intelligence' and 'mathematico-logical intelligence', he argued, which are the kinds of intelligence measured in conventional intelligence tests. But we also have 'musical intelligence', which is particularly highly developed in musicians but also possessed by others to some degree; 'bodily-kinaesthetic intelligence', which is particularly evident in sportspeople and dancers; and 'spatial intelligence', which is often particularly marked in designers and architects. Some people are really good at dealing with others, which is an example of 'interpersonal intelligence'; and we also have 'intrapersonal intelligence', which is all about how well we understand ourselves.

Robert Sternberg took a different view, arguing that the essence of intelligence is adaptability. So it was impossible to account for all intelligence using a single measure, since intelligence in the real world could be so variable. The intelligence you need to succeed in a mathematics course, for example, involves what he called 'componential intelligence' – intelligence that draws on intellectual skills like problem-solving and calculation. But the intelligence you need to deal with irate customers in a service department draws on what you have learned from your own experience, as well as your formal knowledge of regulations and procedures. Sternberg called this 'experiential intelligence'. And the intelligence you would need to interact effectively with people from other cultures would draw on your social and cultural sensitivity and skill: what Sternberg called 'contextual knowledge'. Western cultures, for example, prize quick thinking as part of intelligence, but in some Middle Eastern cultures that is seen as a sign of impulsivity and not giving the matter sufficient thought.

By the end of the twentieth century, the nature/nurture debates had more or less died out, at least in psychology, although they still tended to surface in the popular media. But a worldwide expansion in testing presented its own challenges, particularly with regard to achieving accurate translation, since different languages are rarely exactly equivalent, and cultural contexts affect how questions are interpreted. This ties in with the growing interest in indigenous psychologies, which we will come back to in Chapter 40.

CHAPTER 37

From Helplessness to Optimism
SELIGMAN AND THE ESTABLISHMENT
OF POSITIVE PSYCHOLOGY

'Daddy, why are you always so miserable?'

The eminent psychologist mumbled something.

'Well, if I can learn to stop whining, then you can learn not to be miserable all the time!'

That challenge from his seven-year-old daughter set Martin Seligman on a new track. He'd made a career in studying learning and how it works. As we saw in Chapter 34, he'd shown how animals could learn to be helpless, and how hard it could be to retrain them after that. He'd also studied 'one-trial learning', which is the way that we, and other animals, avoid foods that have made us sick in the past. Unlike other forms of learning, we only need one experience – one trial – to create a lifelong aversion, so it's seen as a special form of conditioning. Seligman often reminisced about having experienced it from being sick after having sauce Béarnaise. (The story goes that it earned him a lot of free meals, as people tried to encourage him to overcome the conditioning.) So it was a reasonable question to ask: why couldn't he learn to be more cheerful?

Seligman's work on learned helplessness had stimulated a lot of research into people's sense of control and agency. It had clarified both cognitive and behavioural processes in depression, which helped psychotherapists to develop ways of helping clients to overcome it, mainly using positive thinking techniques. Why, Seligman reasoned, didn't we take the same approach in mainstream psychology? Why did our studies of emotion, for example, always emphasise fear and anger, and not joy and happiness? Seligman was famous for learned helplessness. Now he wanted to be famous for learned optimism instead.

And he was in a good position to do it. Seligman had been elected president of the American Psychological Association during the year 2000, so he used his presidential address to promote a new direction for psychology. 'Positive psychology' would bring together existing psychological research into positive thinking and positive emotions, would show how people's attributional styles could make all the difference to their everyday life, as Seligman himself had discovered in responding to his daughter's challenge, and would generally help to make the world – or at least the psychological world – a better place.

Defined by some as the scientific study of what makes life worth living, the new approach attracted widespread publicity. Psychologists began to explore different aspects of the brighter side of being human. Positive psychology wasn't all new: it had its roots in the humanistic school of Maslow and Rogers (see Chapter 16), which had emphasised working towards happiness and improving people's psychological wellbeing. But it also brought together later research from many different areas of psychology.

The study of agency, for example, had developed considerably. Not only had laboratory research shown how important it was for people to feel in control, but Albert Bandura and his colleagues had opened up a new perspective: the concept of self-efficacy. This is about how capable, or efficacious, people feel about what they are trying to achieve. Carol Dweck had worked with Bandura in this area, and from her research developed Mindset theory: an approach to encouraging children to believe in their ability to learn, which gave a new direction for teaching and rapidly became popular in the educational world.

Another central concept promoted by Seligman was the idea of flourishing – that people shouldn't just have to cope with life but should enjoy it and really benefit positively from their everyday experience. Again, this wasn't a new idea, but fifty years on, psychologists were in a much better position to suggest how we could go about it, and Seligman knew from his own experience how possible it is to change your whole mental life around.

In the clinical world, attributional styles that are specific (as opposed to global), unstable and external had been identified as helpful to people in coping with problems, and this was one of the thinking styles that Seligman advocated in dealing with everyday living. It focused on making positive attributions instead of negative ones, so that sources of bad experiences are seen as temporary rather than stable, as only relevant to that particular situation rather than typical of everything, and as controllable rather than the person being a victim of external factors or events. So, for example, instead of Jim responding to his car breaking down on his way to an important event as being unlucky, or fate, or typical, he could see it as being because he didn't have his car serviced at the right time, and that meant that it wasn't likely to happen again, because he could do something about it.

Another aspect of learning to think positively has had many names, but one of them is the 'Pollyanna' approach. This is the idea of looking for good outcomes even when bad things happen – that is, ignoring the negatives as much as possible, and actively trying to find a bright side or potentially positive result. Although it might sound a bit unrealistic, it's a powerful technique, because it helps people to be more balanced in how they perceive events. The other side of it, which is much more common than it should be, is 'awfulising' – that is, seeing any negative or unpleasant events as a complete and unmitigated disaster.

Seligman's positive psychology drew on mainstream psychological research as well as psychotherapy. In the late 1970s, Michael Argyle at Oxford had opened up a new programme of research into emotions. Psychologists had always investigated fear, anger and stress, but there was relatively little study of positive emotions. Argyle and his team showed that these are more varied and wide-ranging than people (and psychologists) had assumed. In one study, they asked people to think about and describe twenty-four different situations that they had experienced as pleasant, like being outside and enjoying nature, having a long hot bath, spending time with friends, and being successful at work. They found that this exercise generated a range of positive emotions, which they categorised into four dimensions.

One of the four was absorption – how much attention or concentration is involved in the emotion. Some activities, like being involved in a creative hobby, are strong in this dimension, while others, like social experiences, are relatively light. The second was potency – the degree to which the person feels competent and capable. It ranged from being successful at sport or at work, which were strong in this dimension, to more passive experiences like listening to music or enjoying a hot bath. The third dimension was concerned with altruism or considering other people in one way or another. Commitment activities like church or charity work were strong in this dimension, while self-indulgent pleasures like getting a present or engaging in a personal hobby fell towards the other end of the spectrum. Their fourth dimension was whether the experience was personally meaningful, like enjoying nature or solving a challenging puzzle. More trivial experiences like watching a thrilling film or buying a personal treat came at the opposite end of the scale.

These dimensions were not intended to be exclusive: emotions are complex, and any single emotion might involve more than one dimension. Receiving an award that recognised valuable service you have done for the community might generate an emotion that combines a sense of potency and altruism, while the memory of a holiday with friends might generate emotions that were both personally meaningful and involve a sense of potency, but are light on absorption and altruism.

In his presidential address Seligman had mentioned Mihaly Csikszentmihalyi, the author of *Flow: The Psychology of Optimal Experience*. In this book, Csikszentmihalyi argued that the secret of happiness is being able to engage in 'flow': a state of concentration and being fully focused on what we are doing. Athletes refer to it as being 'in the zone'. Csikszentmihalyi had been a prisoner during the Second World War and had spent years among unhappy and distressed people, which led him to become curious about what makes a happy life. He became interested in psychology when attending a lecture by Jung and moved to America to explore it further. He interviewed artists, musicians and many others, and eventually came to the conclusion that people are at their most happy when they are being creative and in a state of flow.

Flow, as Csikszentmihalyi described it, has eight characteristics. The first is being fully concentrated on the particular task at hand. The second is having a clear sense of the purpose or goal of the activity, and also of immediate feedback implying that the goal is on the way to being achieved. That relates to the third characteristic, which is that the experience is intrinsically rewarding or satisfying for the person. Perhaps for that reason, Csikszentmihalyi's fourth characteristic is the way that flow generally reduces the sense of time, which might seem to slow down or to speed up, depending on the nature of the activity. But the experience itself – the fifth characteristic – is that the person finds what they are doing effortless: it comes easily and naturally.

The sixth characteristic of flow that Csikszentmihalyi identified is that it involves a balance between skill and challenge: while it might feel effortless, it is still exercising skills in new ways and responding to new demands. But there is a sense of control over the task, which is the seventh characteristic. But perhaps the most distinctive characteristic of flow that Csikszentmihalyi identified is the way that the person loses self-consciousness, merging their action and awareness into doing whatever the task is.

Seligman proposed three types of happy life as being suitable for further exploration by psychologists. One is the 'pleasant life', which is concerned with experiencing the positive emotions and expectations that form part of a healthy lifestyle. In this type of life, people are focused on what makes things enjoyable and stress-free, such as getting on with other people, doing the things that interest them, making a pleasant home, and so on.

The second type of happy life is what he called the 'good life'. This is a life that derives contentment and satisfaction from engaging in activities that are absorbing, involving concentration and flow. People who engage in sport, art and intellectual pursuits often describe their happiest experiences as being when they are 'in the zone' – that is, completely focused on what they are doing and feeling fulfilled and complete as they do it. For an athlete, that might be a sense of achieving peak performance; for an artist, being completely absorbed in producing an artwork; or for someone with an interest in, say, history, it might be discovering and finding out more about a new perspective on a particular set of events.

The third type of happy life that Seligman identified is what he called the 'meaningful life', in which a person derives feelings of wellbeing from their active engagement with others or society in general. Many people spend their lives helping others or working to make other people's lives better in some way. Those people, though often tired from their efforts, live their lives with a sense of purpose, and the knowledge that they are contributing to something larger than just their own lives, which can generate its own sense of contentment, if the person recognises what they are achieving.

As research continued, Seligman developed the PERMA model. This identified five elements that he believed contribute to overall wellbeing. PERMA stands for 'Positive' emotions, such as joy, happiness and contentment; 'Engagement', which is about flow and focus as we engage in things that we are interested in; 'Relationships' with other people, which are the source of most positive experiences; 'Meaning', which is all about feeling that one has some purpose to one's life; and 'Accomplishment', which is the search for mastery and achievement, whether through work, hobbies or interests. This model became widely accepted as a general approach to positive psychology and continues to be developed as researchers explore different aspects of it.

In bringing together and promoting positive psychology, Seligman made a major contribution to psychological thinking and opened up entirely new areas of research. Few psychologists in psychology's later history have been so influential.

Making Decisions

EVERYDAY JUDGEMENTS AND THE USE OF HEURISTICS
– KAHNEMAN'S SYSTEM 1 AND SYSTEM 2 THINKING

My Friend Cayla seemed to be the ideal doll for a young child. Launched in 2014, Cayla could talk, laugh and play games with her owner. She had a hidden camera, speaker and microphone, and she also had Bluetooth capability. All this meant that she could interact 'intelligently', responding to questions and talking with her owner as a real friend might.

But there was a problem. The doll's configuration allowed access to hackers, who could speak to the child and monitor what they were doing. This left the doll's owner wide open to attempts by predatory adults to 'befriend' the child for sexual purposes or even to engage in domestic spying. When this vulnerability eventually came to light, the doll was taken off the market and even banned in Germany. But that was some years later; for a long time My Friend Cayla was simply regarded as an interesting toy. Nobody suspected that she could be used for malicious intervention.

It was a clear example of 'functional fixedness': a bias in how we think that gives us a tendency just to focus on the main function of things, and not to recognise alternative ways they could be used. People saw the doll only as a toy, and so didn't notice that it could have a different function. Functional fixedness was first identified by the Gestalt psychologist Karl Duncker in the 1940s, but it wasn't until psychology really got to grips with the biases in our thinking that it became taken seriously.

It was Daniel Kahneman and Amos Tversky who brought to light how biases affect how we think. In 2011, Kahneman published *Thinking, Fast and Slow*, which brought together the findings of nearly half a century of research into cognition in the real world. In that book, and based on his research with Tversky, Kahneman proposed that we have two basic ways of thinking: System 1 and System 2. Most of our thinking is System 1, which is so automatic that we don't really notice it. We carry out everyday actions, respond to routine greetings ('I'm fine. How are you?') and make simple decisions without doing much conscious thinking at all. The brain has its routine ways of working, which lets us multitask: walking the dog while mulling over what we are going to have for dinner tonight, or recalling today's events while driving home.

Sometimes, though, what we are thinking about demands our full attention. You might be walking along with a friend, who for reasons of her own asks you to calculate 5+2, and you answer '7' without breaking stride. But if she asked you to calculate 27x17, the chances are you'd stop walking and stand still while you worked it out. That's System 2 thinking: it needs us to focus on what we are doing and shuts down the less important stuff while we are doing it.

System 2 thinking is systematic, careful, logical and much slower than System 1. It's when we really think things through. It can be rewarding if we manage to achieve a state of flow, but it can also be exhausting, because it uses up a lot of mental energy. That drains our physical energy too, which is why really concentrating on something for a long time may be satisfying but it also leaves us feeling physically tired. It's mental exercise, and exercise of any sort, whether mental or physical, is both tiring and stimulating.

System 1 thinking contains all our habits, well-learned skills and automatic routines. Most of the time, it's perfectly adequate. But at other times, it can be pretty flaky, and there are even times when it can lead us badly astray. That's because it takes shortcuts, known as 'heuristics', to get to the quickest answer. Working together, Tversky and Kahneman identified a number of different heuristics which usually work out OK, but sometimes lead us to overlook important information, or to make mistakes in our decisions or choices.

One of the first of these heuristics that Kahneman identified is known as 'satisficing'. It came to his attention when he was exploring how computers select the optimal option from a range of possibilities. He found that people, when faced with the same set of choices, would rarely choose the optimal ones. Instead of fully exploring all the options available to us, we settle on the first one we find that seems to do the trick, even if looking at everything more carefully would give us a better result.

As Kahneman and Tversky (or Tversky and Kahneman – they always alternated their names on their research papers) explored human decision-making, they identified several other heuristics of this kind. In each case, they were habitual cognitive shortcuts, which usually worked just fine in most situations but could produce significant biases when it came to making decisions. The 'availability heuristic', for example, is our tendency to choose the information that comes to mind most quickly, and not to bother putting additional mental effort into thinking of alternatives. It's a heuristic which has been used to great effect in advertising – and is the reason why advertisers are so keen to keep their brand name at the forefront of our minds!

Another example of unconscious bias in decision-making has to do with how the decision is presented to us. In one study, presenting a cancer treatment as likely to result in a third of sufferers being saved, or likely to result in two-thirds dying, produced very different results. When asked to choose a treatment, 72 per cent of the people asked chose the 'save' condition, but only 22 per cent chose the 'die' condition. In other words, the entire balance of the decision was changed by how the choice was framed.

Similarly, the 'anchoring heuristic' is when we choose our options by comparing them with something we already know. That gives us a kind of baseline for our judgements, and it's the reason why estate agents selling houses always begin with a highest-priced option. The first one becomes the standard, so the others seem cheaper by comparison.

That's similar to the 'representativeness heuristic', in which we base decisions on what we see as being typical – often our own experiences. But if we are making decisions that will affect other people, our own experiences are not usually a good place to start. If psychology tells us anything at all, it's that other people generally see things in a very different way from how we see them ourselves.

We're influenced by our emotions, too. The 'affect bias' is our tendency to make choices that make us feel good at the time. They can sometimes be right, but our emotional reactions to an idea can also mean that we reject it without really thinking it through. It's quite a strong bias, because we also have a powerful ingrained tendency right down at a neurological level to react strongly to anything we perceive as a threat, so we instantly reject options that appear to be threatening in some way.

We also tend to choose options that affirm our own beliefs. This is the 'confirmation bias': people tend to justify their decisions by ignoring contradictory information and looking for evidence that confirms their existing preferences. It's particularly common in expert decision-making, since experts often develop a 'feel' for a particular type of problem, based on their prior experience. That's not necessarily wrong, but it can be if they are considering a rare or unusual case. The confirmation bias connects with the process of cognitive dissonance, which we looked at in Chapter 24. It's uncomfortable to have ideas or cognitions that contradict one another, so we avoid them when we can.

It's not quite the same, but cognitive dissonance and affect are also involved in the 'entrapment bias' – also known as the 'sunk-cost bias'. This happens when we have already invested so much in one course of action that we become reluctant to change direction, even if it's obvious that we should. It seems like throwing away what we have already put in. The problem with entrapment is the way that it esca-lates our commitment, producing ever-increasing effort and wasting limited resources. Someone who has an old car, for example, may continue to pay for its repairs when it would be much more sensible to put that money into a newer model; company directors may decide to keep using expensive office equipment even though newer models would improve their profit margins; or a government that has already lost many of its troops in an unwise and futile war may become unwilling to end it because it would seem that those who have given their lives have done so for no good reason.

Quite a few of these heuristics and biases in human thinking were already familiar, but Tversky and Kahneman identified many more. Even before they got together, Kahneman had conducted research that compared human judgements with statistical or computing solutions, and had become interested in how different they could be. Teaming up with Tversky, who was already interested in decision-making, led to a stimulating and valuable partnership, and the Nobel Prize was well merited. Unfortunately, Tversky died before he could share it, but Kahneman has always shared the credit.

Their partnership was mainly concerned with cognitive processes. But social processes, too, affect how we make decisions. Many of the most important decisions affecting our lives are made by groups of people – committees, working parties, and so on. It's generally assumed that this is better than individual people making them, because more people can think about the problem, but that is only true sometimes, not always.

The decision-making exercise known as 'brainstorming' is based on that idea. That term is often misused just to mean a group of people sharing ideas, but brainstorming itself has two very different stages. In the first, people are invited to contribute any thoughts or ideas openly, but – and this is the important bit – there is no evaluation of those ideas. No matter how silly they may seem, all ideas are collected as if they were perfectly sensible. It's only in the second stage that each idea is considered and discussed, and the participants explore seriously what would be involved in each one. Separating the evaluation stage from the idea-generating stage allows people to be more creative: ideas that seem silly at first sometimes turn out to be useful, but people won't suggest them if they think they will attract ridicule or be instantly dismissed.

Brainstorming can allow groups to make better decisions, but unfortunately group decisions, particularly in long-term groups, are often worse than individual ones. The group's members become likely to suffer from 'groupthink' – a pattern of decision-making which at best restricts alternatives, and at worst results in catastrophic decisions. There have been many disastrous examples of groupthink. The US invasion of the Bay of Pigs and the Challenger disaster are the most famous examples, but there have been many more, like the failure of the world-leading camera firm Kodak, whose directors refused to acknowledge that digital cameras would take off (even though Kodak had invented the first one). The company collapsed as a result. Or, more significantly, the 2003 invasion of Iraq, which was based on the political belief that the country had weapons of mass destruction; this turned out to be untrue and a clear example of groupthink, and it created a humanitarian and economic disaster.

What these decisions have in common is that the group making them had an illusion of invulnerability, failing to recognise threats and believing that their knowledge of the situation was always correct. Groupthink is maintained through a number of strategies, including dismissing or ridiculing contradictory information and pressuring members of the group to conform and to self-censor what they might want to say.

The illusion of invulnerability isn't limited to group decision-making, either. Individual people sometimes make more risky decisions than they should. In 1975, Sam Peltzman showed how car drivers wearing the then-new seat belts tended to drive in a more careless fashion than they normally did. Since they thought there was less risk, they acted more recklessly. Now known as the Peltzman effect, it shows how we sometimes take too many risks if we think we are protected.

The way that human beings make decisions, then, is nothing like the way that computers do. We take mental shortcuts based on our own – quite extensive – knowledge of human life and social assumptions. When it comes to real-world problems, our decisions are not always logical, but they are not always wrong, either.

CHAPTER 39

Nodes, Networks and Neuroplasticity
THE CLASSIC TAXI DRIVER STUDY, RECOVERY FROM STROKE, NEURAL NETWORKS AND SOCIAL EMOTIONS

Being a London cabbie is no easy job. Dealing with traffic and dodging pedestrians is only part of it: London is a huge city which has grown up over centuries. Its street map is hardly straightforward, mixing tiny back roads with large thoroughfares, one-way streets and complex bus routes. And you can't become a licensed taxi driver in London unless you know them all. It's called 'the Knowledge', and all would-be London taxi drivers have to pass a gruelling test examining how familiar they are with all the city's streets and byways.

That puts quite a demand on your memory. So neuropsychologists Eleanor Maguire and Katherine Woollett wondered if it also made a lasting impact on the brain – particularly the area of the brain that stores spatial memory, the hippocampus. Brain scans of that area showed that London cabbies seemed to have enlarged hippocampi in comparison with other people, but that raises a chicken-and-egg question. Perhaps they only became taxi drivers because they already had the brain capacity to deal with it?

So the two researchers conducted another study, comparing people who were just beginning to learn the Knowledge with experienced taxi drivers. At the beginning of the study, the difference was clear: the experienced drivers had larger hippocampi than the novices. But by the end of their training, when they finally passed the test, the hippocampi of the novice drivers had also become bigger.

It wasn't just driving experience either: the researchers conducted yet another study comparing London bus drivers with London cabbies. They reasoned that the two groups would have similar stresses coming from dealing with traffic or wandering pedestrians, for example, but the bus drivers went on pre-established routes, while the taxi drivers might have to go anywhere in the city. And, sure enough, when they scanned the brains of the two groups, the hippocampi of the taxi drivers were significantly larger than those of the bus drivers.

It's become a classic study because of the way it shows us a vital finding about how the brain works. What it tells us is that the brain's functions aren't fixed: they respond to the demands we make of them. We know this too from people who suffer from aneurisms or strokes. These are interruptions of the blood supply to the brain, which can have complex results. They often produce partial paralysis because the neurones controlling that type of movement have died. But that paralysis doesn't have to be permanent. With enough determination, people can recover the lost functions. It's hard work with little reward at first, but with sustained effort the brain becomes retrained. New neural networks are formed which allow the right messages to get to the right areas, so the person gradually recovers.

This is neuroplasticity. It used to be thought that brain functions were set by the time we reached adulthood, and that, after that, brain cells just died, and didn't recover. Clinical experience with stroke recovery, and what we have learned from brain scanning, means that we now know that isn't the case. The adult brain is capable of relearning and rerouting its networks, and even growing new connections between nerve cells, right through our lives. But there's a cost. In the same way that a weak muscle needs to be exercised to grow stronger, so these new connections only develop if they are exercised too – and, in the case of someone who's experienced a stroke, that needs a high level of motivation and belief, because the effort and practice involved are such hard work.

Neuroplasticity is probably the most significant finding that has emerged from modern research into brain scanning. But being able to explore an active, living brain has transformed our knowledge in other ways too. We know now, for example, that we have mirror neurones right across the brain, which respond to other people's actions or emotions as if we ourselves were doing or experiencing them. And that's given us a very different understanding of how the brain works.

Scanning has changed our understanding of other aspects of the brain too. Language is special for human beings and, as we saw in Chapter 3, it was the first ability to be regarded as clearly localised in the brain. In 1861, Paul Broca identified an area that was concerned with producing speech, while Carl Wernicke, in 1874, identified another that was concerned with understanding it. In the following century, evidence from people with brain damage or tumours confirmed these findings, along with the brain lateralisation and the other functions that we looked at in Chapter 31.

But then came brain scanning, and that changed everything. Researchers could scan active brains instead of dissecting dead ones or taking general electroencephalograms (EEGs), so they could see exactly which parts of the brain were involved when people think, speak or listen. Scans showed how these functions didn't just happen in specific areas: they used neural pathways and networks, linking a number of different areas. One pathway, for example, begins with Wernicke's area, which receives information from the auditory cortex for spoken language, and from the visual cortex for reading or sign language. So far so good. But then it links with a bundle of nerve fibres that connect areas right across the brain: with Broca's area, which links it to the motor and premotor areas to control speaking, and also with other areas in the temporal lobes, the parietal lobes and the frontal lobes of the cerebrum. It's known as the primary language pathway – but really, it's a whole network of nerve fibres, all working together.

Neuropsychological research has revealed much more, like the way the brain spikes when we hear an ungrammatical sentence. That seems to be so fundamental that even young children are amused by Yoda in the Star Wars series, who uses language in an abnormal fashion. The network model is very different from our original idea that information simply passed from one 'decoding' area to the next one. But that's how the brain works: not as separate areas linked by single connections, but in networks, with many different areas working together. Listening to what someone is saying doesn't just involve Wernicke's area, as people thought in the twentieth century. It involves Broca's area and its connections and a lot of other areas as well – not to mention the way that we have mirror neurones, which reconstruct the brain activity that would happen if we ourselves were doing the talking. In fact, listening to someone lights up almost half of the left cerebral hemisphere and quite a lot of the right hemisphere as well.

That's told us some important things. For example, when we are listening to someone speak, we are usually looking at them and lip-reading. Language processing draws on both visual and auditory information, and we need both streams of information to make sense of what we are hearing. We can see that in the McGurk illusion, which happens if auditory and visual information contradict one another. If people hear the word 'baba' dubbed on to a video of someone saying 'gaga', they hear a totally different word: 'dada'. It's such a strong illusion that people still hear it even when they know it's happening. With eyes closed they hear 'baba'; with eyes open and no sound they see 'gaga', but even after doing that, if they see both together they hear 'dada'. It happens with other words too, but that's the clearest example. So, listening to speech isn't just about the sound: lip-reading is also part of ordinary conversation. It's no wonder that so many of us find it difficult to understand people when they are wearing face masks!

Like language, our senses have turned out to be networks rather than discrete areas. In Chapter 31, we saw how twentieth-century researchers identified various areas on the surface of the brain as the centres for different sensory experiences. They identified specific areas for all five major senses: sight, hearing, touch, smell and taste. Damage to those areas had been shown to produce problems with those senses – blindness, deafness, anosmia, and so on; and it was assumed that these were the places where the brain processed sensory information. But brain scanning showed that it isn't that simple: they too are simply part of whole networks linking different parts of the brain, all working together to produce our psychological experiences.

If we look at these networks, we find some interesting sidelights, such as the way that listening to rhythmical music also lights up those neurones involved with movement and balance. It's what makes us want to dance and is such a strong connection that dance happens in just about every human society. We could even call it part of what makes us human. Brain scans tell us a lot about how we listen to music too: trained musicians use different parts of their brains than the rest of us do, but we don't have the space to go into all those details here.

We've learned more about other specific areas of the brain as well. Scanning has shown us, for example, how a particular area of the brain – the paracingulate cortex – is directly involved with our intentions, even if those intentions don't actually translate themselves into action. That area also becomes active when we think about how our own behaviour connects with other people, and that in turn links with the theory of mind that we looked at in Chapter 34: the ability that children develop when they are about three and a half, which helps them to understand other people better.

The paracingulate cortex surrounds another area, the cingulate gyrus, which is just as important to our own sense of self. It becomes active if we are evaluating a risk or working out whether a course of action is likely to be rewarding or not. It also links with other parts of the brain when we feel emotion and has been shown to be particularly active in social emotions like shame, guilt or embarrassment, and in maternal love. That area also reacts to pain and, interestingly, it reacts in the same way to the pain of social exclusion, like being ostracised or lonely, as it does to physical pain.

All of which shows us how very intensely social human beings are. These areas are important for social experience, and they are tucked deep inside the brain, above the band of fibres where the two halves of the cerebrum meet. So they are very well protected and unlikely to become damaged by any superficial injuries.

Another set of personal functions is tucked right inside the folds of the cerebrum, where the lateral lobe of the brain folds underneath the frontal and parietal lobes. Those areas are all to do with personal memory: one of them allows us to recognise familiar faces. It's close to but not the same as the part of the brain we use to recognise celebrities or other people that we don't know personally. Another area is involved in identifying people who we are emotionally close to, like family or close friends – again, that's close to but not the same as the part we use to recognise other people we know. And, as we saw at the beginning of this chapter, part of our brain stores our memories of places. This is the hippocampus, which is connected with our other personal memory areas and, as we saw earlier in this chapter, is essential for storing new memories.

Both the paracingulate cortex and the cingulate gyrus are buried so deep inside the brain that we had no idea of their existence until brain scanning allowed researchers to look inside an active brain. Their locations show how important these functions are to our being human, as the brain's evolution has protected them from damage. Even our senses are more open to injury, being largely located on the brain's outer surface.

Brain scanning has really come into its own in the twenty-first century and, as we've seen, it's revolutionised our understanding of the brain and how it works. We now understand so much more about ourselves – how our use of language draws on our wider social and personal knowledge, using areas right across the brain; that physical movement in response to rhythmical music is hardwired into the brain's connections; and why a video call with strangers feels so very different from a video call with friends, to name but a few. That list continues to grow as neuropsychologists discover more about the brain's activity underlying our experience.

Above all we have learned that neuroplasticity isn't restricted to young children, as was previously thought, but can happen throughout our lives. We have always known that human beings as a species are characterised by adaptability – the way we can adapt to widely different demands and live in widely different environments, for example. Brain scanning has shown us just how deeply embedded that adaptability is, in all of us.

CHAPTER 40

A Methodological Revolution
Deconstructionism and Decolonisation, Challenges to Orthodox Research Methodology and WEIRD Sampling

Are you WEIRD? It's quite possible – indeed likely – that you are. And no, I'm not Google and I don't know anything about your personal habits. As a psychologist, I do know that everyone is different, and what one person sees as normal, someone else might see as weird. But that isn't what I meant. I meant WEIRD in capitals, as in people from Western, Educated, Industrial, Rich and Democratic societies.

Psychology, as we've seen, was largely developed in the Western world. But it made assertions that were believed to apply to all human beings, regardless of their culture or their different socio-economic circumstances. In part, this derived from the quest for a universal theory of psychology. In part, it originated from ignorance: an ongoing lack of awareness – or concern – about people living in parts of the world that were both physically and economically distant from the West. But mostly, it just derived from a somewhat arrogant assumption that the Western way of life was normal, civilised and natural to human beings. To people in other parts of the world, that assumption was weird in small letters, as well as in capitals. But it wasn't really until the end of the twentieth century that psychology began to acknowledge it, and that process is still ongoing.

The recognition of the limitations and cultural specificity of mainstream psychology has led to a growing interest in the decolonisation of the psychology curriculum. Decolonisation is a complex process, encompassing several different viewpoints. For some, it means rejecting conventional psychology as an artificial construction established by rich privileged elitists, and replacing it with indigenous psychologies developed within their own societies – as in the work exemplified by Frantz Fanon, which we explored in Chapter 30. For others, it means highlighting the often profound level of understanding underlying local practices, contrasting it with the application of insensitive Western assumptions.

As we saw in Chapter 21, as far back as the 1970s, Robin Horton showed how traditional medical practices in Africa were far more effective, given their culture and context, than Western imports. More recent examples of this cultural arrogance have happened as global corporations impose their practices on employees in very different cultures. Even within Western societies, there are cultural differences, as the Disney corporation experienced when they tried to impose American-style work contracts in Disneyland Paris and found that their prospective employees wouldn't accept them. It's not just psychology that needs clearer awareness of cultural differences!

For other psychologists, decolonisation means educating psychological practitioners in the way that Western assumptions have distorted psychological practice. Zenobia Nadirshaw has given many examples of how the failure to understand cultural practices has led to psychiatric misdiagnosis. For example, in many cultures it is entirely normal to talk to your ancestors, and simply reflects an awareness of the continuity of family life; but in the UK and America this practice is sometimes diagnosed as a symptom of schizophrenia. Similarly, young Black men often have a much more forcible way of expressing themselves than their white equivalents. It's a cultural difference, but it's often interpreted by white psychiatrists as emotional disturbance, with the result that young Black men are three times more likely to be prescribed sedatives or given electrical shock therapy. Recommendations from health professionals, too, are often insensitive to cultural requirements.

Decolonisation doesn't mean rejecting everything that psychology has to offer. Rather, it means reorganising the psychological curriculum to sensitise students and psychologists to the way that white male psychology has dominated research and theorising and highlighting alternative approaches. This connects with the movement known as 'critical psychology', which is about how psychology has traditionally ignored issues of social power, like institutional racism and discrimination, and acted to promote the interests of elite groups over those of minorities. Critical psychologists aim to make these biases apparent – for example, showing how psychological assessment has traditionally been biased against specific minorities.

Critical psychology's roots lie in Saussure's deconstructionist movement. Initially concerned with linguistics, it spread to social psychology in the growing interest in how language is used to perform social acts. Deconstructionism is all about decoding the hidden meanings of social interaction, and we saw in Chapter 28 how this was adopted by psychologists using discourse analysis. Critical psychology challenges the underlying assumptions and theories of mainstream psychology, showing how power and control issues often underpin its theories. It aims to highlight these assumptions and look for different ways of doing research and applying psychological understanding.

Research in psychology is all about acceptable ways of getting evidence. It's not acceptable, for example, to take what your neighbour did, or how a friend had this or that experience, as evidence. That's just anecdote and, if psychology tells us one thing, it's that anecdotes are an extremely unreliable way of gathering data. They're likely to have become exaggerated in the telling, and they are rarely typical of people in general. If we want to know how the human mind works, we need to be more systematic – and scientific – about it. But as we've seen throughout this book, what counts as scientific has changed over time, from Wundt's systematic approach to introspection to strict experimentation and experimental control, and finally, in the twenty-first century, to an increased acceptance of qualitative and interpretive research methodologies. That movement originated in the 1970s and is still continuing.

In 1977, Irwin Silverman published *The Human Subject in the Psychological Laboratory*, showing how the motivations, feelings and anticipations of the people who participate in psychological studies directly affect research outcomes. People weren't taken into account because the ideal model of psychological research was the classic (and somewhat mythical) physics experiment: inert subject matter being manipulated by the experimenter. That made psychological experiments increasingly artificial and divorced from everyday experience.

Human beings, of course are far from inert. Silverman showed how people anticipate what the experimenter expects of them, and how their own understanding of the experiment is much more influential than the experimenter's manipulations or instructions. Classic demonstrations of conditioning processes in students, for example, depended entirely on whether the students had caught on to what they were supposed to be doing. His book debunked classic assumptions and argued for an entirely different approach.

One version of that different approach was suggested in Peter Reason and John Rowan's 1981 book, *Human Inquiry: A Sourcebook of New Paradigm Research*. Their New Paradigm was also about recognising that psychology's subject matter is human beings, not automata, and showed how researchers can build respect for the people they are studying into their work. At the same time, there was increasing concern about the use of animals in research of all kinds, including psychology. Animal studies were a fundamental and often compulsory part of the psychology curriculum in the 1960s and early 1970s, but as social protests increased and ethical standards for research with animals were imposed, those student requirements died out, and psychological research emphasised ethological approaches to animal behaviour rather than experimental ones.

Ethical standards applied to research with human beings too. But it takes time for paradigms to shift and, despite relatively quick adjustments, like the use of the word 'participant' rather than 'subject', many found it hard to see how they could be implemented in conventional research practices. The answer, of course, was that they often couldn't. Ethical criteria prohibited deception and insisted on informed consent, but one of the basic tenets of the traditional experiment was that the 'subject' should be deceived about its purpose, in order to avoid excessive compliance, which might distort the results. In fact, the use of 'double-blind' controls, where neither the experimenter not the participants were aware of what was being investigated, had become the standard for 'good' research, and remains so in medical evaluations. Ultimately, though, it relies on deception. There was much soul-searching in psychological conferences and journals of the 1980s, as psychologists wrestled with these problems.

Then there was the importance of numbers. Right up to the end of the twentieth century, many psychologists viewed qualitative research with deep suspicion. Courses in research methods were entirely based on statistics, and qualitative methods, which often involve radical procedures like asking people about their experiences, were regarded as unscientific, wide open to researcher bias and self-fulfilling prophecies. PhD students who wanted to include qualitative data in their theses were warned off, and psychology journals automatically rejected submissions of research involving qualitative data as lacking scientific rigour.

In the 1990s, a group of psychologists aiming to challenge that prejudice came together, in what eventually became a section of the British Psychological Society devoted to qualitative methods in research. The result of that first meeting was a book, *Doing Qualitative Analysis in Psychology*, published in 1997, in which a number of psychologists gave examples of different ways of undertaking qualitative research and, moreover, showed how these methods are both rigorous and systematic, nothing like the woolly opinionising that the critics had assumed. Interest in qualitative approaches grew as a new journal, *Qualitative Analysis in Psychology*, was launched in 2005 and was further heightened by a seminal article in 2006 by Virginia Braun and Victoria Clarke, which provided would-be researchers with a clear guide to thematic analysis. It was a major paradigm change, helping psychology to become more relevant to everyday living.

Another major change in psychological research came about with the advent of everyday computing, which had major implications for statistical data analysis. A sample size of forty, for example, would be seen as very small nowadays, but that was considered to be a large sample in the 1960s, when statistical analysis had to be done by hand. Nowadays, it is not uncommon for an international research project to involve thousands of participants, and even relatively small projects may involve hundreds.

This brings its own problems, of course. One has to do with sampling. Social media allows participants to respond to open calls, but each of those people will have been self-selected. So the design of the study needs to allow for people trying to be too helpful and distorting the results that way. Global commercial organisations offer researchers large numbers of participants, paying each a tiny fee for participating. While this does open up the opportunity for a more representative and multicultural psychology, it has also raised questions about the ethical assumptions underlying many global research projects.

Another challenge, which may partly be the result of the change in data analysis, has to do with what has become known as the 'replication crisis'. Psychology, like many other sciences, uses the outcomes of past experiments to illustrate important shifts in our general understanding. But attempts to replicate the classic studies of the past have not always produced the same results, and the researchers concerned have interpreted that as calling into question the validity of the underlying concepts. (It's never bothered the subject of chemistry, of course, as school experiments fail to replicate classic studies, but that's a different argument. Or perhaps it isn't.)

As we've seen, psychological research was very different in the past: sample sizes were smaller, and social concerns in the 1960s and 1970s were entirely unlike today's, as were our basic assumptions about society, science and progress. Those studies became classics because they reflected – or challenged – the theories or assumptions of their time. But can any research claim to represent universal truths about human beings? Psychology, like other disciplines, reflects its social and political contexts, and our increasing political concerns about globalism are reflected in the growing research trend towards cultural specificity and relevance.

This brings us to the end of our journey through psychology's history. We've seen how psychology didn't have a single origin but has always involved different threads woven together into a loose, and often contentious, whole. There's no single school of psychology, and every psychologist brings their own understanding to the discipline. New areas are emerging all the time, and old ones either expand or die out.

At a global level, perhaps our main challenge as we look to the future is developing a psychology, or psychologies, which can reflect both human nature and the variability that cultures generate. In the past, psychology was distinctly imbalanced – not only focusing on WEIRD populations, but also ignoring diversity within those populations. But people everywhere are unique, and there is a whole range of areas, from psychiatric diagnosis to educational achievement, where imbalances need to be rectified. This new awareness makes for a more complex psychology – but whoever said people were simple? If we really want to understand ourselves, we have to come to terms with the fact that there are no easy answers. Throughout its history, as we have seen in this book, psychology has become ever richer, more relevant and more diverse. It is the multiplicity of approaches that gives psychology its strength. And that strength will only grow as we widen psychology to take into account the diversity of humankind.

Index